NLP in Business

A practical handbook for using NLP, easily and professionally

Peter Freeth

Published by

Communications In Action

2005

NLP in Business

A practical handbook for using NLP, easily and professionally

First Edition – October 2005   ISBN 0-954-57483-4
ISBN 978-0-954-57483-4

Communications In Action 2005

Published by:

Communications In Action   info@ciauk.com
49 Fishponds Road   www.ciauk.com
Kenilworth   0870 1620802
Warwickshire   +44 870 1620802
CV8 1EY
United Kingdom

Also available:

NLP – Skills for Learning – a practical handbook for increasing learning potential, written for anyone interested in learning with NLP.

Six Questions - a practical, creative problem solving guide with the powerful and unique Unsticker.

Change Magic - the evolutionary approach to change engineering and organisational problem solving.

Printed and bound by Antony Rowe Ltd, Eastbourne

Ingredients

NLP in Business

Every day, in every business around the world, NLP is being used. "Surely", you might say, "not that many people know about NLP?" and you're right. You're one of the relatively few people who have already taken steps to develop and enhance those most fundamental skills that we have all been given, but remember that everyone in the world has those same skills, so NLP applies to everyone.

NLP isn't something new. It's not something that was created in a dark cave on a mountainside somewhere. NLP is a study of real people achieving real and tangible results in their real lives. NLP is a way of sorting and organising our mental and behavioural skills, it doesn't add anything new. It simply allows us to understand and refine our existing skills so that we can achieve more, easily and consistently.

You may say, "If NLP's not new, what's the point of learning about it?" and it's the same reason as you might choose to go to a photography course, or a car maintenance course. Your car will run without regular maintenance, yet if you know some of the basics yourself, it will run more reliably and you'll be in a much better position to fix it in an emergency. Without photography classes, you can still pick up a camera and take photos, you just might not get the same results that a professional would get with their specialist knowledge of lighting and composition.

So, you can learn about NLP as a way of refining and enhancing the skills you already have - the skills for getting results in the world, for interacting with other people and for mastering your own limitless potential.

This has interesting implications for the people who say, "NLP doesn't work", because they're right. NLP does not sell or influence or lead. You do. NLP techniques do not help people to change – people do. The techniques those people use are nothing different to the intuitive talents used by people who are naturally skilful or effective. All that NLP is, at its heart, is a way of modelling and replicating those skills so that you can get the same results, more easily and more often.

NLP started life as a therapeutic toolkit, because the people who were first studied were therapists - professional communicators with a gift for helping others change - easily, quickly and permanently.

Many people confuse NLP with its techniques – including many NLP trainers I've seen. People who confuse NLP with its tools and techniques reduce NLP down to eye accessing and body language (which it isn't) and when they see NLP in action they say, "oh, that's just NLP". NLP is everything or nothing, depending on how you look at it, because NLP is the spirit of modelling excellence.

It's a bit like saying that art is just paintbrushes, or architecture is just bricks. The tools you will learn on a course, or read about in a book, are the results of NLP – they do not define NLP itself. A good NLP Practitioner will go on to model excellence in other people and create new tools in new situations. Someone who has not embraced this spirit of modelling excellence will use the tools in a prescriptive, inflexible way and – guess what? – sometimes they will work and sometimes they wont. People with the flexibility to model excellence and create new tools just keep on going until the problem is solved, and usually it doesn't look like they're doing anything at all.

Over the years, NLP training has developed significantly, yet much of it is still rooted in the therapeutic tools that make up the core content of Practitioner and Master Practitioner training. For this reason, NLP has been slow to establish itself as a credible professional toolkit. A few trainers in the UK are now offering business focussed courses and so organisations are quickly realising the benefits of investing in NLP training.

Aside from the obvious advantages of having staff who are more effective at managing themselves and their relationships with others, there is an important financial benefit which is often overlooked by those NLP trainers who do not have real business experience. In the past, employees would be trained in presenting, negotiating, time management and all of the other skills taught in traditional business training courses. NLP has the potential to replace all of these training courses, allowing individuals to focus on the key behaviours that ensure success.

Consider a typical presentation skills course. A delegate - at any skill level - will spend a lot of time learning what they already know. Then they'll spend some time proving they already know it to satisfy the trainer's evaluation criteria. Finally, they will learn some real presentation skills - according to the trainer's individual beliefs, attitude and experience. In short, the delegates will spend a small amount of time learning how to present like the trainer.

The difference with NLP is that everyone in your business - and every other business - already knows how to present. They can talk, and they can stand up. When they do both together in front of an audience, that's presenting. Everyone has the potential to be an amazing presenter, yet for many people something gets in the way - something unique to each person. NLP training gives people the opportunity to remove all of those barriers to exceptional performance, in all areas of their lives. Furthermore, NLP training gives people the NLP modelling toolkit that they can use to model and copy any skill from anyone.

Your company has a unique culture, with unique products, unique customers and unique people. Your sales process is unique and your branding is unique. The way you present to your customers is unique, and it's an integral part of your branding because it is an important means of communicating with your customers. Your potential customers will get a taste of what it's like to do business with you through the way you present to them.

So, what kind of presentation skills do you want people in your company to learn? The generic skills taught by a trainer, or the specific skills that are working in your company right now, defining your brand and winning business? You can model and replicate these skills, easily and quickly, using NLP.

NLP is definitely about the individual. It's not about categorising people, like psychometric approaches, and it's not about doing what's universally 'true'. It's not about giving body posture a universal 'meaning' - it's about responding to the person who is right in front of you.

Some people go into NLP training wanting to influence people or even use NLP on other people. Inevitably, these people fail to get anything of real value from the course because change must first come from within. The people who come to NLP training wanting to improve their lives and their relationships have already taken the first critical step - taking responsibility for change. These people already know that it is they who must adapt, not other people. Perhaps, in the past, they learned the hard way that you can't make other people do what you want. They learned that you can only do what you want, and if you need other people's help then you need to change what it is you want, or the action you are taking to get it.

For example, if your goal is to get a job promotion, and you put all your energy into achieving this, then you will mostly likely find it very hard going. If you're putting time and energy into getting someone else to change their mind then you are expending energy on something you have no control over. If you were to focus that energy on improving your own skills, developing yourself and positioning yourself for the right opportunity then you would be more successful and it would be much, much easier.

So, NLP is about you. It's not about what you can do to other people. If you try to learn about NLP with an attitude of 'I'm already good at this, I want to learn to do it to other people' then NLP training will just magnify that attitude so that it's even more apparent to other people.

If you are curious about yourself and other people, and if you are hoping to find new ways to get better results more consistently then you will definitely benefit greatly from learning about NLP.

NLP training has a tendency to magnify or amplify what you already are, or have the potential to be, and everyone already has the potential to be amazing.

The format of this book

Firstly, I feel it's important to let you know that about a third of the content of this book is taken from my previous book, NLP – Skills for Learning, which was written as a practical introduction to NLP for anyone involved in training or teaching. It proved to be a very popular and well liked book, which I thought deserved to appeal to a wider audience. I also had a lot of experience and material about the application of NLP in business which didn't fit into that book, and that's why I created this one. So if you have already read NLP – Skills for Learning, don't be surprised if you occasionally have a sense of déjà vu.

One of the key responsibilities of the NLP trainer is to provide a safe environment where, if you choose to take part, you will learn what's useful and important to you by exploring new ideas.

NLP training works best when it can work with all of your different learning abilities. You learn some things formally and other things informally. Sometimes you need structure, other times you need play. Sometimes you need logic, other times you need metaphor. Regardless of your learning style, you need a balance of information in order to create meaning that is useful to you. Therefore, this book has some structure and some exploration. It has some logic and lots of metaphor, or stories.

Sometimes you might find a particular approach seems more comfortable for you – take this as a sign that you are learning within your comfort zone. If an approach or idea seems new or confusing, take this as a sign that you are stretching your personal beliefs and boundaries, increasing both your flexibility and your ability to get the results you want.

Imagine a golfer who feels really good one day, is focussed on winning and is able to concentrate easily on his game. On a different day, he feels a bit tired, has a lot on his mind and finds it hard to focus on playing well. He's using the same golf clubs on both days, yet his performance is completely different. Therefore, just learning the tools of NLP will not enable you to get the most from them. That's why this book contains so many different approaches to helping you learn, understand and apply NLP in Business.

Some NLP training is highly experiential, almost to the extent where the trainers explain nothing and let you work out for yourself what you have learned. Other training is highly theoretical, where you first hear all about the theory and mechanics behind a technique before you get to play with it. Why do both extremes, and everything in between, exist? Clearly because the wide range of styles caters for a wide range of learning styles in the audience. Therefore, the first part of this book is designed for more experiential learning and the second part for more structured learning. Part three focuses in much more detail on some useful business applications. I hope that the combination will work well for you.

Above all, sit back, relax and enjoy the journey.

Part One

This section of the book is an exploration of both the techniques and the spirit of NLP – the attitude of curiosity, of wanting to know how things work.

This section is a journey through stories, ideas and threads that weave together throughout the following chapters. When you get to the end of this part of the book, you will have an understanding of a large number of NLP principles and techniques, and you will be already using many of them. You may or may not be fully aware of how you got to that point, yet sometimes learning works that way.

Like a novel, this part of the book makes the most sense when you read it through from start to end. When you have done that, and absorbed all the ideas that run forwards, backwards and sideways through it, you can turn to part two as more of a reference guide that you can dip in and out of to find the specific information you need.

Why is this part of the book so different to other NLP books you have seen? Because for the principles and attitudes of NLP, your brain works better that way. I hope you enjoy it!

Things to look out for

I've summarised some of the key points in this part of the book so that you can pick them out more easily.

The exclamation mark is there to draw your attention to really important points that may seem simple or obvious, yet by paying special attention to them you will learn more about yourself and other people and the results you get will improve dramatically.

So, if you see that symbol, just take a moment to think about the point as there may be relevance or importance in it that's easy to take for granted or overlook.

They say that the simplest things in life are the best, and in the case of these important points, it's true. Or is it that the best things in life are free?

Often, books give you a lot of information which is factually correct and informative, but which may not be related to your specific interests or needs.

A 'so what?' is a summary of a key point, specific to the application of the information. I hope to put the theory of NLP into practical terms that you can use every day to get better results.

First things first

What equipment do you have for gathering information about the world?

Obviously, I can't hear you, so I'll pretend you said, "Your five senses!!"

And I'll say, "well done!"….sort of. In that there are more than five. Here are some of the senses that you have - there may be more as we find out more about neurology and the way that your brain handles sensory information that is outside of our 'normal' conscious perception. Here are just a few of them…..

Now, this might appear to be obvious, and therefore trivial, but it is in fact the most important thing you will learn today.

Why? Because we must now accept that all of the rich memories, ideas, thoughts, pictures, sounds, poems, songs and desires that are in your head got there by coming in through your senses. They didn't appear mystically and they didn't arrive through intuition.

You might think that this is obvious, but it has an important meaning for our communication. The colour green, the sound of a car horn and the smell of lemon juice are easy to think of in terms of sensory inputs. What about honesty, professionalism and danger? What do these mean in sensory terms? What exactly does honesty sound like?

Almost everything that is in your head got there through your senses. Therefore, your senses are what you use to represent memories to yourself.

You see, hear, feel, taste and smell memories using the same processing systems that allow you to gather real time information from the outside world.

Almost everything? Yes, except for certain instinctive knowledge that you were born with, such as how to breathe, beat your heart or swallow milk. If you remember that far back then you'll know that it took you a while to learn how to regulate your body temperature and even longer to learn how to move, walk and speak.

Our senses are our only tool for interacting with the world, yet as we grow older we ignore sensory information more and more and replace it with 'experience' or what we 'know'. It will help you a great deal to gather more information if you try and forget what you think you already know. Intuition is one way that you notice subtle sensory information that gets missed in the fog of all the stuff you 'know' about.

Intuition is not mystical. It is the magic of your brain working far faster and more powerfully than you could ever think possible. It is the product of the amazing ability of your brain to gather and process both real time and stored information and produce something new and remarkable in the blink of an eye.

Of course, you may be unconsciously aware of sensory information that is outside of our normal awareness, so this may also play a part in what we call 'intuition'. For example, we have a sense of direction which, like in migrating birds, detects the Earth's magnetic field.

So, if you thought intuition was great, the natural function of your brain is even more amazing! But this isn't a book on Neurology. It's a book on the practical applications of this knowledge, so let's get back to those senses.

Over the years, you have taken in vast amounts of sensory data and attached linguistic labels to it. We don't fully understand this process, so as a consequence we can't tell computers how to copy it. We can teach a computer to understand that an object is both a table and wood, but if we smash the table up the computer struggles to understand that whilst it's still wood, it's not a table anymore.

You may have heard that you have a left brain and a right brain, or that you have a conscious and an unconscious brain, or that you have different thinking modes, or that you have an inner eye. All of this may or may not be true, depending on how you look at it. The coloured tint in your spectacles gives you a certain view of the world which may or may not be different to everyone else's.

You may be thinking, "I see the world clearly and objectively, so the fault must lie with other people". Well, the bad news is that there is no objectivity.

Have you ever lost your car keys, only to find them right in front of you? Have you ever pushed a door that was clearly marked "PULL"?

Can you see the dots changing from white to grey to black as you look around the picture?

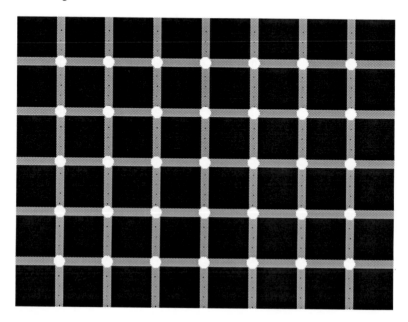

Are the horizontal lines curved or straight?

Have you ever heard someone say something totally different to what they actually said? Have you ever daydreamed? Have you ever dreamed at night?

Well, if you answered, "Yes!" to any of those, where did that voice come from? Was it the one in your head? Don't worry, we've all got one. Some of us have many, and they can come in very handy.

Here's the first useful tip for you, and I can guarantee it is a very useful thing to know about. In fact, if you ever feel nervous or if you ever worry, or if you ever tell yourself you should have known better, then this will be a very, very useful thing to know. Are you ready?

Did you know that you have total conscious control over that voice in your head?

Did you know that if it nags you or criticises you, you can change its tone of voice to be anything you want. If it sounded really soothing and supportive, would you be more inclined to listen to its advice?

If it sounded really excited and enthusiastic, how do you think you would feel? Try it out now.....In a really critical, harsh voice, say, "That was rubbish, you should have known better". Next, use a really kind and supportive voice to say, "Hey! That didn't work so well, what can you do differently next time". Pay attention to the difference in how you feel about those two voices.

 You can change the qualities of the voice inside your head. You can make it sound supportive, you can make it sound like a newsreader, you can make it sound like a cartoon character. Any of these will change your emotional state and allow you to benefit from the feedback from your internal commentator. In fact, you can change the qualities of any of your sensory systems to change the emotional content of memories.

Just so you're familiar with the NLP jargon, the voice inside your head is called your 'Internal Dialogue'. If you find that you criticise yourself when you get things wrong and that this makes you feel bad, just try this really simple exercise.

Next time you make a mistake and the voice says, "that was stupid" or, "that was a bad idea" say, in a genuinely curious way, "Thankyou! Now, how does that information help me?" You can try any variation on this, such as, "Thankyou! What do you suggest I do differently next time?" You will find that the results are quite different to when you just nag yourself. You can make up any form of words that are right for you as long as you follow the basic structure of 'acknowledge value' then 'redirect to a positive course of action'. You probably already apply this structure when other people offer you criticism - don't you? It just helps bypass the emotion of criticism and get to the real value - the feedback.

You may say, "But this doesn't apply to me" in which case you should pay twice as much attention. When you're in a business environment, some people will beat themselves up for making 'mistakes'. You'll know when they do this from listening to what they say, for example, "I told myself I should have known better" or, "I said to myself that this was wrong". When you hear this, you can helpfully intervene by helping them change their internal dialogue.

So, what we know now is that everything you know is represented to you using one or more of your senses. For example, you 'know' the colour of your front door by seeing a picture of it. We also know that your senses may not be giving you the full picture, the whole story or a real handle on the situation. This is a very useful thing for you to know as a professional communicator (and who isn't?)

So, the only way that you can gather information about the world is through your senses. As you get older and have more experiences, you filter your senses more and more and over time what you think you see, hear and feel about the world gets further away from reality. Often, this is a good thing and helps you to deal with the huge amount of sensory information that comes into your brain every moment of every day and night. Your biggest step forward as a professional communicator and learning enabler will be when you realise this and simply start paying more attention to what is outside than what is inside.

You will be totally amazed at the amount of information that is all around you if you take the trouble to pay attention. Instead of thinking that you know what other people are thinking or what their motives are - ask them! Instead of guessing, pay attention! Instead of knowing, forget and enjoy the experience of sampling the world through fresh eyes and ears.

On the radio today I heard an interviewee say, "There are no absolutes" and it made me smile. What, none at all? Not one? Not even one about there being no absolutes?

By listening to what people say, you will learn a great deal about the way that their internal world is organised. NLP training can teach you all the details of the Milton Model, the Meta Model, conversational postulates and unspecified nouns but the truth is that NLP came out of a set of beliefs from people who were gifted or talented communicators. They didn't stop what they were doing and say to themselves, "ooh...I should use a tag question next, shouldn't I?" You don't have to learn the way that this knowledge has been categorised and indexed, you only need to share their enthusiasm for learning more about other people.

When you went to school and learned about nouns and verbs, you didn't start speaking differently - you simply acquired a new labelling system for what you already knew about. You didn't start thinking, "I must remember to use a noun in this sentence". That labelling system only serves the purpose of letting two or more people share information using a common language.

All of the linguistic stuff in NLP is very powerful but you should regard it only as a framework to refine the way you already use language. You'll be amazed at the way you already influence people. Recently, I was watching a training session where the teacher (it was in a school) was running an exercise in which groups of students had to build a model roller coaster using card stuck to a hardboard panel. As she gave out the first panel she said to the first group, "Here's your board" upon which one of the students collapsed, comatose, onto his folded arms on the table. The teacher shouted, "Oi! Wake up, sit up straight, pay attention" and so on. Well, what did she expect? If she insists on going round hypnotising people then she has to accept the results she gets. Why?

Your brain uses context to derive the most likely meaning from similar sounding words. Whilst you extract the most contextually likely meaning at the conscious level, at the unconscious level you run through all possible meanings. If one of them is expressed as an instruction, there's a good chance you will act upon it, even at an unconscious level.

Having sat in a classroom all day, if someone said to you, "You're bored" then what meaning would you take from it?

In this example, the teacher needs to call her piece of hardboard a sheet, a base, a panel - just anything other than 'board'!

Just think about the impact of this for a moment. Every day, all over the world, there are groups of important people shaping our future by meeting in 'Board Rooms' Mind you, having sat through some bored meetings I think the name is very appropriate!

Taking it all in

The world we live in is a busy, busy place. In fact, the world has always been busy and there's more information available than we can consciously attend to. I don't mean information like news, TV etc. I mean sensory stimuli - things that you can see, hear, feel, taste and smell. Right now, you can see these words, you might also be reading to yourself using the voice in your head. You might also be aware of any background noise. Are you aware of the temperature of the air? How about the weight of your hands? How about that itch? Are you hungry? Thirsty? Tired?

You could think of your unconscious brain as your car's engine management computer and your conscious brain as your car's instrument panel. Normally, you don't need to know what's going on under the bonnet. If there's a problem, a warning light comes on. You don't need to know the status of every muscle in your body except for if there's a problem in which case you get a pain. Another useful analogy is that your unconscious brain is a dark room and your conscious attention is a torch.

The unconscious brain is, of course, the same brain as your conscious brain. The conscious bit is everything that you are aware of, and that will change from one second to another. You might be so engrossed in this book that you are unaware of any background noise until I call your attention to it. At least, I hope you're engrossed!

At any moment, you can attend to only a handful of thoughts. In NLP, these thoughts are called 'chunks' and refer to things like short term memory and activities. Try juggling and remembering a telephone number at the same time, and you'll start to understand the limitations of your conscious attention.

In a driving example, this would be like practising gear changes until you could change gear without thinking about it - then move onto the next element. I believe that a really good way to learn something like driving would be to run through specific behavioural sequences until they become one 'chunk' of information. For example, changing gear and working the clutch pedal at the same time is very difficult to start off with, although the motor movement in your arm and leg is not very complex. If that movement was already 'natural' when you first got into a car, putting together the individual movements and patterns would be a lot easier than trying to learn it all at the same time, under pressure. Driving simulators are a huge step forward as they remove the pressure.

This means that it's generally easier to learn tennis if you can already play squash, for example. Since many of the necessary motor programs are already there, you can concentrate on learning other aspects of the game. This has drawbacks too – I know people who have moved from squash to badminton and normally play well but under pressure revert to playing squash – hitting the shuttlecock very hard, sideways into the net..

Your ability to focus your attention is both a gift and a drawback, depending on the activity you're trying to master. If you are expecting people to remember something complex, they will simply be unable to process everything that is happening. For an experienced driver, the whole business of driving is mostly under unconscious control so an experienced driver can drive and hold a conversation at the same time. A learner driver needs to attend consciously to every individual component of operating a car, and there is simply too much going on. If the learner is also trying to attend to feelings of stress, hunger or thirst, the conscious brain will simply be overloaded and they will not learn anything at all. For an experienced driver, 'change gear' is one chunk. For a learner, it is about six.

You may have heard that words only make up part of communication. According to the social psychologists Mehrabian and Argyle, words only make up 7% of communication. Whether you agree with the figure or not, we can at least agree that words are not the only form of communication and that there are times when words are misleading.

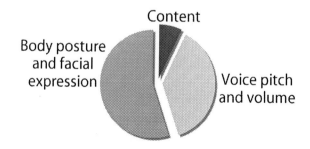

Do you know when someone is lying? How? Well, if you don't already know then I'll tell you. Your brain is analysing all forms of communication while consciously you are attending to the words. Your brain compares the content - the words - to facial expression, body posture, voice pitch, speech rate, volume, stability etc. and finds that the two don't match up. Your brain alerts you to this through a 'gut feeling' or an instinctive reaction - you can call it intuition if you want to. You might say something like, "Something he said didn't ring true" or, "I don't like the look of her" or even, "it was written all over his face".

When we take in information, we filter it to allow our conscious attention to focus on what seems relevant. The process of filtering works in three different ways, so that we delete, distort and generalise incoming information.

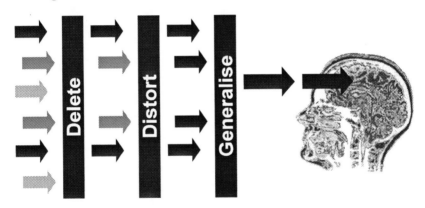

So, when communicating with a group of people, it's important to remember that they are all gathering information differently to each other and to you. They will only be attending to a small part of the information you give them. The more ways that you can deliver the same information, the more chance there is that they will find something of value to them, process it and remember it.

It always surprises me how many times I see people sit in meetings, trying to reach an important decision and saying, "Come on – we've got to make a decision before we go home tonight". Would you allow an estate agent or car salesman force you into making a decision you were not ready for? If the decision is that important, give people time to sleep on it and consider it fully. If it's not that important, what's the rush anyway?

People make bad decisions when they are not given the time they need to process all the information available. Even if you think the decision should be easy, you can accept that if people can make a decision, they will do.

Years and years ago, I gave my first big, formal presentation at a conference. I stood on a stage, behind a lectern and in the glare of a spotlight. There was a big screen behind me with someone working the projector when I pressed a button. I wanted it to go really well, so I wrote myself a script. The only problem was that halfway through the presentation I lost my place and read the same paragraph twice. Filled with dread, I finished my presentation just before a break.

Over coffee, a colleague of mine told me that the presentation had gone well to which I replied, "Oh no! It was terrible, I read the same paragraph twice and it was awful". My colleague said, "Oh, I thought you did that because it was a really important bit". In fact, one person in the audience who was getting a little sleepy after lunch even thought I was talking just to him to wake him up!

It just goes to show that even with the best planning in the world, people will infer any meaning they choose, regardless of what you do. The frame of reference that you create has a far bigger impact on this meaning than anything else you do. Because I was on stage, I took on the role of an expert who must plan methodically and have a reason for everything. People found meanings that fitted their frame of reference.

Of course, some people thought, "he just repeated that, he must be nervous" but the important thing is that nobody cared except for me. People have an interesting way of inferring meaning from everything you do, and it's usually much kinder than the meaning you attach.

While we're on the subject of public speaking I should tell you that, as a coach, a fear of public speaking is the single most common problem that comes up with professional people. Conversely, it's probably the most important skill in business today, for many different reasons. If you know someone who experiences this, you will often find that they are imagining that the audience is judging them, so you can see why my colleague's comment was so well timed, otherwise I might have carried on thinking that audiences actually pay attention when I'm presenting.

Later on this book, you'll find a technique called 'perceptual positions' which is absolutely perfect for a fear of public speaking that works in this way, and I have used it many times with an immediate and dramatic effect on the presenter's confidence and ability.

In a presentation or meeting, setting the frame of reference is the single most important step you can take, as people will search for meanings that are relevant within that frame. After this point, anything that you do, within reason, will reinforce your outcomes.

This goes much further than 'tell them what you're going to tell them'. If you start a meeting or presentation by setting the agenda, people will immediately run through it ahead of you, decide what they are going to pay attention to and then switch off. It's important that you make the agenda loose enough that the audience cannot decide by themselves what is important. An agenda is just a summary of what the presentation or meeting contains. As people gather information, they compress it down, make it less complicated and forget most of it.

By starting with an explicit agenda, you have already summarised your entire meeting or presentation onto one page and many people will stop listening at that point, or at least will decide which parts are relevant to them.

If you absolutely must use an agenda, then at least make it sound interesting. Tell people what they will be able to do, rather than what you will talk about.

If you don't agree break times in a meeting or presentation up front, people will not come back on time, will they? Well, some people will be late back whatever you do. I suggest you deal with this when you set the frame at the start of the session. Try something like, "We're going to take regular short breaks throughout the day and each time we take a break I will tell you the time that I will restart. If you're not back in the room at that time I will assume that, at that moment, you have something important that you need to do and that's OK with me. I would rather you take care of important matters when you need to so that when we are in this room together, we can all concentrate fully on what we are doing here."

So, bear in mind that people have a limited focus of attention. I read somewhere that young children can concentrate for about five minutes, and that this attention span gets longer as we get older. Personally, I don't think this ever changes. Instead, adults just devise ingenious strategies for appearing to pay attention when in fact they're thinking about something else.

So, you can get upset when people don't pay attention, or you can accept it as entirely normal and work with it, using it to your advantage to get better results

Plan your planning

I'm going to tell you what really effective communicators do to make their listeners sit up and pay attention. I'm going to tell you what they do to ensure their listeners respond as they are intended to. And you'll be surprised at how obvious it is.

Really effective communicators plan their communication.

That's it? Yes, but that doesn't mean that they sit down and write a script, it means they tell their audience what they are supposed to do with the communication. Here's are some examples:

- "I'm going to ask you a question"
- "In a moment, I want you to make a choice"
- "Here's something you need to decide on"

Before you say what you want to say, tell your audience what you want them to do. This is really just another way of directing people's attention, and it's very effective for managing the way people respond to what you say.

Here are a few more examples of this simple yet effective tool:

- "I'm going to ask you a question now that I want you to think very carefully about before you answer"
- "In a moment, I'm going to ask you to reach a decision"
- "Here's a really important point for you to consider"
- "This is what I want you to do"
- "Before you make a decision, I'm going to ask you a question"
- "Before you finish reading this book, I will ask you to think of at least three new ways you'll use all the great stuff you're learning."

If you tie this simple concept in with the goal setting exercises that you'll read about later on, you will quickly become a very powerful and congruent communicator, because the people you speak to will be able to understand easily and quickly what you want from them. It may be agreement, it may be an answer, or it may just be their attention. Whatever you want, you're more likely to get it if you tell people what it is!

In organisations, people often launch into transmission mode during meetings and then wonder why their colleagues pull their project updates apart. Sometimes, decisions go round in circles forever and never quite get made. We have come to learn what to expect from meetings, and if you are invited to a meeting then there may be an implicit expectation that you'll contribute. Meetings everywhere would be far more productive if people applied this simple principle. For example, saying, "Here is an update on my project, I don't need any advice or feedback at this stage, it's for your information only" tells people exactly what is expected of them. Conversely, presenting a huge volume of facts and figures and only then asking people to make a decision is simply asking for trouble. If you tell people up front what you expect, they will pay attention in the right places and be able to make a decision when you need them to, instead of saying they need more time to think.

So, this is what I'm asking you to do. Whenever you want a specific response from people, first tell them what you want them to do.

Logical levels

Perhaps you remember sets and Venn diagrams from school. Set theory is a way of categorising elements into groups to make logical calculations easier.

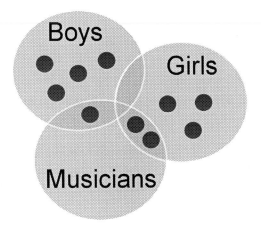

Here, you can see that two girls are musicians and three aren't. One boy is a musician and four aren't. Not surprisingly, there are no musicians that are both a girl and a boy and there are no musicians that are neither a girl nor a boy. This is a visual representation of a series of logical expressions which include:

- Boy AND Musician = 1
- Girl AND Musician = 2
- Girl OR Musician = 5
- Boy OR Girl = 10
- Boy AND Girl = 0

Which is easier for you to understand? If you just want a single piece of information, it might be easier to read it from a table or spreadsheet. If you want to see the whole situation, the big picture, then the diagram might be easier. Different methods of coding information are useful at different times and for different purposes. Human spoken language is one way of coding information, but it's not the only one.

Here's a way of visually coding hierarchies of information:

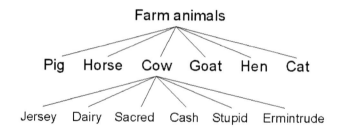

You can see that 'cow' falls into the category 'farm animals' and that 'Jersey' falls into the category 'cow'. I'm afraid I'm not an expert on cows so some of them may not be farm animals in the strictest sense.

As you might expect, someone used this logical approach to categorise language too. Whenever we make statements about ourselves, our beliefs, our values, our rules and our needs we use language that falls neatly into levels of abstraction.

With language that relates to ourselves, the categories are:

Identity	Me, who I am
Beliefs	What is true about the world, my values, my rules
Capabilities	What I can do, everything that I know about
Behaviour	What I am doing right now
Environment	Where I am, the people around me, the world I am in

Here's another example, using the language of 'limiting beliefs'. Limiting beliefs are things that will hold you back and prevent you from succeeding, and the only thing that makes them true is that you believe they're true.

Identity	I'm not a manager
Beliefs	I could never be a really good manager
Capabilities	I can't manage
Behaviour	I don't manage
Environment	I'm not managing these people

If we turn the above examples into positive statements, we get:

Identity	I'm a manager
Beliefs	I could be a really good manager
Capabilities	I can manage
Behaviour	I manage
Environment	I manage these people

Remember, positive doesn't mean good, it just means something that exists or is not negated.

 When you want to communicate effectively with someone, especially in a facilitation or conflict situation, you will get better results by using your knowledge of logical levels. If someone says, "I can't do this" then you can choose to stay at the same level (What *can* you do?) or you can move up a level (I know you will be able to do it) or down a level (What are you doing now?)

By identifying the logical level in language, you are able to determine how a person is structuring their thinking.

Simply, moving up one level from where a person is now will tend to open up their thinking, make them more creative and allow them to think 'laterally'. Moving down one level will tend to force them into detail or action and will tend to restrict their thoughts and ideas. Moving more than one level will tend to confuse people, which may or may not be intentional for you.

Here's a recent example from a NLP Practitioner course. On the subject of goals, one delegate said that her goal is 'to be able to paint'. Notice how this differs from 'I want to paint' or 'I want to paint people'. She is asking for the skill, the capability - she may not actually do any painting. Of course, we can say that she already can paint, it just doesn't turn out how she'd like it to. You can use this structure to understand and clarify the problem, so that you're working at the most appropriate level to effect change.

When people talk about problems and in particular when they talk about things they can't do, you can use your knowledge of logical levels to either constrain their thinking within the problem or open their mind up to generate new ideas. Remember, if you address the stated problem directly you are saying, "Yes, I agree that you have this problem". In fact, that's so important I think we'll have a box:

If you address the stated problem directly you are acknowledging and accepting the problem as real. Always move to a more useful position first before looking back to the problem if you need to. Many problems will disappear immediately as a result of directing your thoughts to the desired outcome. Any lingering problems are much easier to handle from a position of knowing the problem can be solved.

For example, if someone says, "I want to be able to paint" and you respond with, "How have you tried to learn?" then you are non-verbally saying, "You're right. You can't paint". A more useful response might be, "So when you paint now, how does it look?" Oddly enough, this person had a particular problem with visualisation, so it's no wonder that she couldn't see her internal pictures clearly enough to transfer them onto paper. By the way, that's effectively what creative drawing is. You imagine a picture on the paper, and then you draw round it with a pencil.

If you choose to remain at the same level, you will constrain your thoughts within the problem. You will probably not generate any new ideas at this level, as the problem itself sets the boundaries for the solution. However, you may want this to happen, so it may not be a bad thing.

If you move up a level, you are able to think about other examples of this problem, and you will have better access to similar experiences to draw from. You will have better access to your skills by moving to a higher level than the problem.

If you move down a level, you will move from thinking to doing, you will increase the chances of taking action. You will start to motivate other people to take action.

Here are some examples of questions you can use to clarify problem statements:

"I'm not a xyz"	"What *are* you, then?"
"I'm not a xyz"	"What does that *mean* for you?"
"I'm no good at this"	"What *are* you good at?"
"I'm no good at this"	"What sort of person *would* be?"
"I'm no good at this"	"What *else* can you do?"
"I can't learn this"	"What makes you think that?"
"I can't learn this"	"What *are* you learning?"
"I can't learn this"	"What *can* you learn?"
"I'm not doing that"	"What *can* you do?"
"I'm not doing that"	"What *will* you do?"
"I'm not doing that"	"Where *could* you do?"
"I'm not doing that here"	"Where *could* you do it?"
"I'm not doing that here"	"What *will* you do here?"

It's no coincidence that every response to these examples is a question. Remember, the person speaking these phrases is operating from an incomplete map of the world. They do not have an internal representation of the world that is complete - and neither do you! Your job is not to give the complete map to them, as you are only giving them your map and that is only useful to you. Your job is to help them recover the missing pieces of their own map. Consider how the likely answers to those questions above differ to what would happen if you asked, "why not?"

You will not help people by giving them your internal map, as it is only useful to you. Your job is to help them enrich their own map, and the way to do that is to ask them questions about the missing pieces.

Since you have no way to know how someone else structures their experience of the world, you have no way of knowing what parts are missing from their map. What may seem like missing information may in fact be a different way of organising that information to you. You may have experienced talking to someone who 'just won't be told' and now you know why!

In any case, our critical filters protect us from information that may be harmful, so if we really want to give someone some useful feedback, we have to structure it in a way that it bypasses those critical filters.

The logical levels concept can also be used as a very effective diagnostic tool to locate a problem and solve it more effectively.

Using the logical levels format, we can guide someone through a thought process which allows us to explore a problem in a structured way that automatically creates alignment between the levels, leading to a high degree of congruence which means that the person's natural motivation and energy is transferred more efficiently to the goal or outcome.

Think of a situation that you would like to explore or resolve. You can write the levels on pieces of paper and arrange them in a 'ladder' on the floor, or you could just think through the steps. Here they are:

Environment: Think only about the environment of this situation – the physical environment, the people in it, the layout, the colours and so on. Think about (or talk about) all aspects of the environment.

Behaviour: Think only about what you currently do in this situation. The important thing is to think only about what YOU currently DO. Ignore what anyone else is doing or what you're not doing at this stage.

Capability: Think about what is possible, what you could do. Make this as broad and creative as you can – you could fly to the moon, you could do a dance, you could do many, many things that you are not doing or that you would think are inappropriate or that wouldn't work. It doesn't matter what you think will work or not, think only about what is possible.

Belief: What is true in this situation? What do you believe about yourself and the other people involved? What is important to you?

Identity: Who are you in this situation? What is your role? What kind of person are you? Complete the sentence, "I am…."

Now step off the top of the 'ladder' and look back through all the levels, remembering anything that is on your mind or that you have noticed. Step back down through the levels, collecting up all the experiences and insight you have gained. When you reach the bottom, step off again and absorb whatever you have learned that will help you in this situation.

Another way to use this tool is to map the levels onto the levels of an organisation. This is a concept which is a cornerstone of the Change Magic toolkit, which you can read more about in the Change Magic book. It would be unfair to give you a hint of that and not tell you more, but then life is often unfair. Only joking! Here is one way you can map an organisation onto a logical levels structure:

Identity	Brand image, CEO or board
Beliefs	Values, brand ethics, 'culture'
Capability	People skills, range of products or services
Behaviour	Customer service, procedures, sales, advertising
Environment	Office environment, customers, marketplace

So, how does this constitute a diagnostic tool? Well we can begin by writing the names of the levels on pieces of paper and arranging them on the floor. Step onto Identity and imagine you are operating only at the level of your company's brand image or, if you have an iconic CEO then that person. Some companies have a strong personality who embodies the brand, for example Richard Branson for Virgin or Mickey Mouse for Disney.

Imagine what the company's brand identity is, how it impacts on people, what it means, where it came from, where it is going and so on. Then ask, as you step onto the Beliefs level, what culture or values align with this brand image. The 'culture' is simply a set of behavioural rules for an organisation and that is also what beliefs are. Imagine what kind of ethical rules fit within the brand identity you explored. Then step onto Capability, thinking about what skills you need and what products and services would fit with those values and that brand image. Step onto Behaviour, thinking about what people will actually do in order to deliver those products or services. Finally step onto Environment and imagine where those people would do that, and which customers and suppliers they would work with.

By stepping through in this way, you will create a model of an organisation where activity is very well aligned throughout the levels. Now ask yourself if the real organisation is as well aligned.

For example, think about a food retailer who says they will start selling cars. Does capability align with beliefs? Think about an IT company with poor customer service. Does behaviour align with capability? Think about a company with a high tech, slick identity, operating out of a garden shed on an industrial estate. Does environment align with behaviour?

Contrast this with organisations that take care to create the right environment, which shapes the right behaviour to create the right capabilities that determine the right culture to create a compelling and coherent brand image.

A client of mine once shared a secret for business success that he had learned at University and that he had built a global recruitment consultancy business on. He said that the three elements of a business were People, Place and Program.

Which one would you start with?

Would you start with the right team of experienced, talented people?

He says that if you start with the people, they will eventually want to take the business in a different direction. You will become too reliant on individuals, and when they go, the business will go with them.

Would you start with the right program of activity? The program is simply what you do, so would you start with the right business plan?

He says that if you start with what you do, you will become sucked into working in the business and will find it difficult to work on the business. If you focus on the program first, you will become trapped in activity rather than thinking about your purpose.

Would you start with the right place, building a physical working environment that echoes your dreams?

He says that if you build the right place, it will attract the right people, and those people will create the right program.

I think it's a fascinating idea. At first, I thought program should come first, but I must admit that the more I think about it, the more I understand the role that the environment plays, and the need to separate the physical business from the people within it – no matter how important those people seem to be. I have seen many successful businesses fail when the founding partners or directors disagree over strategy or execution and go their separate ways.

I think it's also a very interesting model that relates very well to Logical Levels, which we'll leave in peace for now, as they will pop up again later on.

Maps

Language represents a tiny part of the experience that every person has in their head. Language does not convey experience – it summarises it.

In NLP, there is a 'presupposition' or guiding belief that says, "the map is not the territory". It simply means that your understanding of the world is a representation of it – it is not complete and therefore not true. I often hear people say they are worried about presenting to a more senior audience because they can't have anything new to say. I tell them that their job is not to convey new information but a new perspective. The information can be as old as the hills, it is your unique interpretation of that information which is important.

When someone makes a statement like, "I can't do this", you can ask yourself, "What must their experience be, in order for this statement to be true?"

 Often, people do or say things that don't make sense to you. Every behaviour makes complete sense for the person concerned. Your job is not to judge based on your map, it is to ask yourself, "what must this person believe, think or need for this behaviour to be the best choice available?"

To understand someone, you must enter their world, not stand on the edge of your own and pass judgement.

By doing this, you are gaining a glimpse into their internal world. You must not be tempted to fill in the gaps you perceive in their experience. You can help them recover lost information themselves, not give it to them on a plate, because if you simply give them your map, you will be at the mercy of their critical mental filters.

You can't get a cat out of a tree by standing on the ground, yelling at it. You have to climb into the tree and push the cat out.

Giving someone a piece of your map – 'a piece of your mind' - is pointless as your map is incomplete too. In fact, they have bits that you don't so think of this situation as an opportunity to exchange ideas, not to transmit them.

It's very useful to realise that the more people you talk to about an event or experience, the more accurate your representation of it becomes - if you are willing to accept their version of events as true too.

The interesting thing about truth is that people often think it's mutually exclusive. Can you be right AND other people can be right too? About the same thing? Of course, being a reasonable person, you knew this already.

The more interpretations of the world that you build into your map of the world, the more complete and useful it will become. This won't happen if you continually judge other people's maps as being wrong because they're different to yours. After all, two different maps can't both be right can they?

Think of a street map of London and a tube map of London. Which is right? If one is right, the other must be wrong! Of course not, and by using both you get twice the useful information. Think of maps of experience in the same way and you'll find things much easier.

When someone is saying that they can't or won't do something, there are two amazingly simple yet effective questions that you can ask to change forever the way that they think about their problem. These questions are very powerful, so you must promise to use them wisely.

These two magical questions are, **"what stops you?"** and, **"what would happen if you did?"**

No, you didn't miss anything. That's all there is to it.

Remember that you tend to get what you focus on. By asking people about their problem, you are focussing their attention squarely on the problem itself. The more they look at it, the bigger it gets. Throw in some well meaning counselling or empathy and the problem will soon be big enough to be insurmountable.

"Tell me about it"..."Oh dear"... "Why?"... "Why not?"... These words just embed the problem deeper.

The first question – what stops you? - focuses attention on the barrier that stands in front of the solution. The question puts the person back in control of the problem and separates them from it. When people talk about problems, they are often referring to things that happened in the past as if they are happening through the present and future. By asking, "what stops you", you are freezing the problem in time and preventing it from affecting the future which is, of course, unwritten.

A sneaky variation on this is, "how do you stop yourself?"

The second question focuses attention on the future after the problem has been solved. Asking, "what would happen if you did" forces the person to create an internal experience of the future in which he or she has solved the problem. In order to answer the question, the person must create this new future representation. In order to create that representation, a very important change must happen inside the person's head. Their world now contains the possibility that there is a solution to the problem. If they can imagine it, then it can exist.

When someone says, "I can't do that" and you ask, "what stops you?" they will tell you what barriers exist in their perception of the world. You can now work on these barriers directly and remove them, move them aside or lower them – whatever metaphor works for the person in question. You don't even have to work on the barrier itself in most cases, so you don't have to spend time 'solving' the problem. You can just ask them to move it aside for a moment and, if they still need it, they can move it back again afterwards. Since the person imposes these barriers, the person can move them too. If you listen to their language and watch the way they gesture when they talk, you'll see them describe the barrier and tell you where it is. You can either move it yourself, or you can get them to move it. If you just go right ahead and work on the assumption that they can do whatever they're having difficulty with, you'll find that the barrier disappears by itself in most cases.

You might be thinking that there are often business problems that are real barriers – not imaginary. I would say that if it's possible for anyone, anywhere in the world to overcome these real barriers then they cannot stop you. If they stop you from taking action then it is not the barrier but the perception of the barrier that stops you – and that is in your head. For example, your sales people might say, "we can't sell this product because the pricing is wrong". Do you believe them? If you work in marketing, you probably don't. You might even think, "you haven't even tried to sell it". Businesses talk about 'barriers to entry' for a new market. If your competitors are already there, then there are no barriers. We have explored and can thrive in every climate on the Earth, on every continent. We can walk on the moon, send satellites into orbit, explore the oceans and fly across the world whilst watching films and making telephone calls. Can you honestly tell me that there are barriers in your business?

Instead of saying that you can't do certain things, choose not to. Take control over the things you have not done in your life and in your business. Whilst you can do anything that you choose to, you are unlikely to do everything that can be done, so accept the responsibility of choice.

NLP training is very much about creating choice. Many people think of choice as freedom – it is a responsibility too.

When someone says, "I can't do this" and you ask, "What would happen if you did?" they have to create an internal representation of themselves having done whatever they can't do. The possibility now exists that this thing can be done by them, given time and resources. The barrier is now gone!

In contrast, if you respond with, "why not?" then you accept their model of the world and the limitation that exists within it. You are effectively saying, "Yes, I agree that you can't do this. Now justify yourself". In return, they will do just that – they will give you a list of very plausible reasons that support their limiting belief. In fact, every time you ask, "why not?" they will convince themselves, and you, a little more.

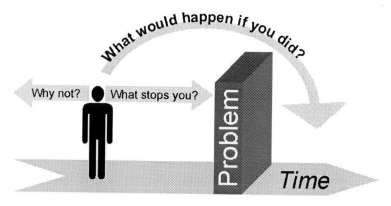

This process of recovering lost information is very relevant to Logical Levels too. If, when you are explaining something, you jump levels, you are demanding that your audience makes a leap of logic to fill in the missing levels. A nice, smooth progression through levels guides the listener's brain on a journey. They will pay more attention to you because they are not 'inside' creating missing information and they will find information easier to absorb and learn.

When you are proposing a business idea, this approach works very well because, by linking ideas together smoothly, you create familiarity which leads to agreement.

When explaining a new idea or concept, the name that you give this idea is expressed as an Identity level statement. A smooth progression through levels would be something like this:

- The name of the concept
- What it is good for
- What it can do
- An example of how you might use it
- When and where you would use it

If you are the kind of person who likes to build knowledge up rather than start with abstract theories and work down, then this might suit you better:

- A situation you might find yourself in
- What you would normally do in that situation
- All the things that you could do in that situation
- What is true to say about that situation
- A name for the concept or idea

Of course, in order to fully communicate with your audience, you would use both to appeal to different learning styles. Here's an example.

NLP is a personal development toolkit that can be applied to personal change, problem solving and a great many other situations. In business, you might use NLP to communicate effectively with your customers during a presentation where you want them to remember important information easily.

If you're in a situation where you want to explain the features of a product, you might start by running through a list of customer needs or applications, then assemble those applications into a set of capabilities. Then you might position those capabilities against other products in order to understand the market situation, and then finally you would focus on one product name that you want to impress upon the customer.

Hopefully, you noticed that the two last paragraphs were an example of this idea. In the first half, the Identity level label was 'NLP' and in the second half it was 'your product'.

In order for a person's natural language to shift from one level to another - from 'I know how to drive' to 'I'm a good driver', for example - specific internal processes take place. We have names for most of these processes, for example, if someone shifts from talking about what she can do to what she is doing then we might call that either motivation, or making a decision, depending on the context. If someone shifts from talking about what they are doing to what they can do, then they have moved from conscious competence to unconscious competence - a process that we might call mastering a skill.

You can hear these shifts in language patterns as you take people through a change process. They are a very important indicator to you that people are rearranging their internal thought processes to integrate what you are helping them to learn. They are adding new information to their maps of the world.

Of course, not only your audience's language can shift during a change experience - yours can too. You can intentionally shift language patterns at specific points in time to effect change in your audience.

You can think of motivation as being the mental process that takes place when a person naturally moves from thinking at the Capability level to thinking at the Behaviour level. Therefore, by changing the structure of your language you can directly influence people to take action.

By listening to how people talk, you can understand how they think. The reverse is also true, so people will switch thinking modes depending on how you talk.

When you listen to people talking about skills, tasks, learning and abilities you will hear a number of interesting language structures that give you a great deal of useful information about what they have learned.

When you hear, "I can" or, "I can't" you know that the person is talking about capabilities. When you hear, "I do" or, "I don't" you know that they are talking about behaviour. The two are fundamentally different and must not be confused or generalised to the same meaning.

Language is a key component of state, and this works in two important ways. Firstly, your vocabulary will change depending on your state, so this offers an insight into your state and internal thought processes. Secondly, hearing that vocabulary will tend to lead you into the corresponding state.

Choosing your words carefully will help you lead the people around you into more resourceful states.

As you start to hear the way that language reveals the structure of experience, you will hear many different ways that people organise their internal resources. The more you listen, the more amazed you'll be at the differences between our maps of the world, and the better you'll be at communicating effectively with other people.

Of course, there is another way to get a cat out of a tree. Just put some cat food on the ground and wait...

Paying attention

Although this isn't strictly anything to do with NLP (in that you wouldn't see it in a course manual) it actually demonstrates one of the key principles that underpin NLP. Without understanding this, people who complete NLP courses just go around doing NLP to people instead of really absorbing and integrating it. Maybe you've met people like that in the past - I have, and they certainly put me off NLP!

Many years ago, I had a proper job as a telecoms engineer. I remember when I was an apprentice, young and impetuous and with a talent for problem solving. I really could understand complex systems very easily, although sometimes I started taking the thing apart before stopping to find out what was actually wrong with it. I really believe that my formal training in systemic problem solving was a real asset to the work that I do now. Anyway, one day I went to a factory in the West Midlands with the local engineer to fix a telephone. I went straight to the telephone, picked it up and started taking the back off with my screwdriver. The engineer stopped me and suggested I just pick up the handset and listen instead of diving straight in. What I heard wasn't dial tone, but the kind of sound you'd hear if a button were pressed down. Just by stopping and listening, I heard everything I needed to know to solve the problem.

A few years later I went to a big tyre factory in Stoke on Trent to carry out a software upgrade on a piece of equipment. I waited until everyone had gone home, and then set to work. The upgrade should have taken less than an hour but half way through the equipment developed a fault. I spent a few hours trying to fix it, and then drove back to Telford to pick up a spare, and then back to Stoke. I finally gave up at about one o'clock in the morning. The next morning, I met my manager on site and immediately set to work on the equipment again. He stopped me and suggested that I just stand in front of the equipment rack and watch. I didn't see anything helpful, so he suggested I pay attention to the lights on the front.

These things have lights just like the ones on your car's dashboard, telling you what the status of the system is. This piece of equipment had two circuit boards which were physically identical apart from the position of a switch that told the system that either Telex terminals or

Telex lines were attached. On the back of the equipment, terminals or lines would be physically plugged in. In this case, there were 7 terminals and 2 lines, so on the terminal card there were 7 lights and on the line card, 2 lights.

So, as I watched, I began to notice that the system was telling me it had 7 lines and 2 terminals attached. Remember that switch? All I had done was take the two cards out then put them back in the wrong slots. That was it, and all I had to do was watch. On the other hand, I got 8 hours overtime, so it's not all bad news.

On a NLP Practitioner course recently, someone was trying to do an exercise called the 'fast phobia cure' with her partner, who said he was afraid of cockroaches. She couldn't get the technique to work, so I asked him what he was afraid of. What he told me was that he lived in Spain for a while and one day he saw a cockroach in his kitchen that ran out from behind a chopping board. The cockroach surprised him, then sat, looking at him in an evil way. Now, as you know, cockroaches don't look evil. In fact, neither do people - words like 'evil' or 'happy' tell you that the person is adding some information on top of what they directly saw, heard or felt - they're adding some of their own experience. Now, if you really pay attention to what this person was saying, you can hear that he's not afraid of what the cockroach actually did - he's afraid of what he imagined it might do. When we asked him to run through the actual experience, he wasn't scared at all. When we asked him to run through what he imagined might happen, the cockroach flew up into his face and attacked him. Who in their right minds wouldn't be afraid of that?

Here's another example - someone asked me to help him overcome his fear of public speaking. Now, you might jump to the conclusion that he was afraid of public speaking, so here's his original request for help, exactly as he said it.

"I would like to be able to accept an invitation to present as easily as you did".

So, what does that tell you he's afraid of? Public speaking? No! He loves that bit! In fact, he's afraid of accepting. So, what happens between accepting and presenting? He worries. He's afraid of worrying. When he gets to do the presentation, he loves it - he gets a buzz out of it. Then he says to himself, "I wish I could remember the feeling of the buzz for next time", so that was exactly what I had him do.

In problem solving, people will tell you the exact nature of the problem, and give you the solution, within the first sentence or so, as long as you pay attention to what's really there instead of inserting your own experience or expectations.

Another important thing to bear in mind is context, in that there is another presupposition in NLP that essentially says that all behaviour is fine, it's the context that makes it useful or not. Let's take a behaviour like fear of snakes. In a typical office environment, that's not a useful behavioural response. In a jungle, it's very useful. If I ever go walking in the jungle, I would be sure to take someone with me who is terrified of snakes. So, you can begin to accept and appreciate all behaviour, whether it gets the desired result or not. The problem then shifts considerably from the person's behaviour to their ability to judge the appropriate time for that behaviour. For example, it's often difficult to get someone to accept that their behaviour in the office is wrong. If they thought it was wrong, they wouldn't do it. Instead, you can recognise that there is some situation where the behaviour is just fine. All we need to do is help the person develop a better way to choose their behaviour.

In fact, people who are belligerent, awkward, pushy, arrogant or manipulative can become the most effective people in your organisation, when helped to develop an effective behavioural choice mechanism. Why? Because they have a greater range of responses than people who feel compelled to be nice, kind and considerate to everyone. Consider two people who, 80% of the time, respond in the same way to your customers. What happens when they meet a customer who is rude and demanding, and who represents bad business for you? The person who has to be nice gives into the customer, whilst the person who has the capacity to be tough back will end up in a better position – either the customer will get a fair deal, or they will walk away. Both are better for you than winning business at a financial loss just because the customer bullies the salesperson.

I had a colleague, many years ago, who became more and more arrogant in internal meetings, getting into technical arguments with colleagues and behaving in a generally unprofessional way. The situation was getting very bad, but no-one told him about it. An influential sales manager wanted to have him fired, so I took him aside one evening and told him all about it. He said something like, "I know you're right, I need to change" and I said, "No you don't. Please don't ever change, because what you do is wonderful when you're up against a competitor or arrogant customer. You just need to recognise the right time and place".

So, you won't find that in any NLP book that's based only on the visible techniques of NLP. A book like this, that lets you soak up the attitude and approach of NLP is full of stories that help you to learn what's really important.

Remember - if you don't have the mindset right, the techniques will never work. If you have the right mindset, the techniques will come naturally. It's easy to write down techniques, it's not so easy to help people learn an attitude. For this, we need a highly advanced, highly efficient and highly overlooked form of communication - the story.

Time for a story

Time is subjective. We don't have a primary sense of time, as we do with sight or sound, so we perceive the passage of time indirectly through our other senses. This means that every person thinks of time differently. We all have a shared hallucination of the passage of time that is indicated by clocks, but two people in the same room at the same time, looking at the clock and seeing the same time will have different perceptions of time flying or dragging, depending on their focus of attention.

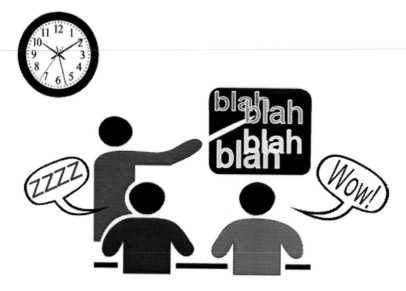

Someone who is totally focussed and enthralled will think that time has flown. Someone who is thinking of other things will be clock watching and will perceive time passing at a crawl.

What makes the difference? Well, partly it's to do with the way that your ability to absorb information is controlled by a part of your brain called the Reticular Activating System. This information is of no use to you unless you have your electrodes handy. What is more useful is to know that you tend to get more of what you focus on. Focussing on boredom will therefore make you more bored. There's certainly a connection between being bored and being boring, as proven by the Pet Shop Boys. I don't mean that they're boring, I'm just reminding you that they sang about it. You may think they're boring which is entirely up to you.

You can use a number of methods to direct someone's attention, and the first we'll talk about is engaging whatever is being focussed on and using it to draw in the listener. A very powerful way to engage attention is with stories. Stories encourage the brain to create internal representations, which, surprisingly enough, are what memories and facts and figures are.

Later on, you'll learn about the brain being an analogue computer. Don't learn about it now, just forget I mentioned it. Go on, really try to forget it.

Are you starting to get the idea of how to focus attention? Anyway, since the brain is an analogue computer it cannot directly represent anything that doesn't exist. This includes anything which is somewhere else, any time other than now and involving any person other than you. Why do you think you identify with characters in films or songs? Because they're YOU!

So, if you tell a story about someone who lived a long time ago in a faraway land who was really, really excited at the thought of being able to learn really easily then your brain can only make sense of the information by transporting you to that land and time and into the mind of that person.

I knew someone once who was very inquisitive and always wanted to know how things worked. As the years went by, this person stopped wondering how things worked and turned his attention to how people worked. You know what it's like, to watch someone and wonder what goes on between their ears. Sometimes, you watch someone and wonder if anything at all goes on between their ears! Anyway, one day this person found herself sitting and reading a book that answered all the questions that he had had and giving her insight into all those curious things that went on in the world. Now, it doesn't always matter too much what the exact detail of the book was. I forget anyway. Time's like that - things that you're really certain about one day become a bit fuzzy the day after. Soon you can't quite remember what you were certain about all those years ago and once again your mind becomes open to new ideas because certainty is a sign that your mind has pulled down the shutters and that's the last thing you wanted, wasn't it?

Stories are a very powerful way of communicating directly with each person in a large audience. Why? Well, in order to make sense of a story, the listener identifies with the story, searching for relevance and connecting their own experience with that of the characters in the story. Therefore, your story will connect with the unique experience in each listener's mind, creating a totally new story that involves the listener at a very personal and relevant level. If you tell a story to 30 people, you'll end up with 31 stories.

Stories are one form of communication that bypass our natural critical filters. These filters protect us from other people's commands that might otherwise pull us off track. When someone gives you a direct command, you can normally choose to follow it or not, depending on your beliefs about the person and the situation.

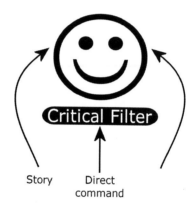

Stories   Direct
                 command

Stories bypass this reasoning process for a very simple reason. Stories aren't true, and they're not about you anyway, so there's no need to think about them.

As you can see from the diagram above, there is another communication format that bypasses the listener's critical filter. Can you guess what it is?

Everyone loves a story. You can call it an anecdote, gossip, a tale, a rumour, a case study, a report or anything else you like that makes it acceptable, respectable or true. Some people have a problem with the word story because it implies that the information is made up or untrue. Sometimes this is the case and sometimes it isn't and that's not relevant to the structure of the story or its effect on the listener.

If you believe in truth then consider this - how do you know that the news is true? You can read two newspaper accounts of the same event and read two totally different stories because of different political affiliations. You already know that the truth can be bent, but how far will it bend before it becomes a lie? That is entirely subjective and depends on your point of view. If you're a Star Wars fan you'll recall that Obi Wan Kenobi told Luke Skywalker that his father was dead. When Luke found out that his father was very much alive and living as Darth Vader, he thought that Obi Wan had lied to him. It turned out that Obi Wan had used the term 'dead' metaphorically, which made it all right. Language is such a collection of metaphor and distortion that it's hard enough to be precise, let alone true.

So, if you want stories to be true, use true stories. If you don't mind either way then let your imagination run riot. Years ago when I was a service engineer (yes, I had a proper job once) I used to visit a large international bank where there was a big room full of people sending and receiving Telex messages. This was the first job for many people joining the bank from school and at the end of the room, behind a desk, sat the supervisor. Breaks were strictly policed and at lunchtime the whole room closed down. I remember on a few occasions walking in to that room at lunchtime. Do you think the room was empty, all these young bankers down the pub or enjoying a frolic in the park? (The room had no windows!) Well, every day, all the young Telex operators would bring their chairs down to the end of the room and sit and listen to stories. Every day, the supervisor would tell stories about how life used to be in the bank, about the people wjo had been and gone and about her own journey through the ranks. Every day, the audience would sit in a hushed and reverent silence until lunchtime was over and they would shuffle back to their terminals.

Now, if you had told them that they weren't allowed to leave the room at lunchtime, what would have happened?

Time can easily be distorted and used to suspend perception of 'real' time - whatever that is.

Here's a really simple way of moving people, internally, back to another time. Start off talking about past events using past tense for your verbs. The easy way to do this is just to imagine that 'now' is the present moment and that you are looking back to the past. Your language will naturally reflect this.

When you notice your audience doing things like staring into the distance or to one side, shift your verb tense to the present. Again, you just imagine that you have stepped back in time and that 'now' is in fact 'back then'. Here's an example.

Do you remember your first day at school? What was it like? Do you remember the sights, sounds, maybe you remember the taste or smell of school dinners? Perhaps you can imagine what the layout of the school was like for you back then, the rooms, the hall, the playground. I don't know if you can imagine it really clearly but as you look around you and just soak up the sounds, what is the first thing that you notice? Do you see a teacher? Does everything seem bigger? Do you hear those sounds of children playing outside? Do you remember the summer of your exams? Can you hear the calls of the children outside in the sunshine as you sit in the examination room? Maybe the smell of the freshly cut playing field wafts in through a window? Maybe particular people spring to mind? Friends? Teachers? Dinner ladies? Well, you can enjoy it for as long as you like before you return to the present time.

After you have read through that paragraph, go back through and notice the verb tenses. Notice how they shift from past to present just before half way. Imagine how different a History lesson would be if you were really there. The great thing about this is that everyone listening gets drawn in to their own personal version of the story.

Did you know that Roman soldiers used to drink vinegar when they were marching? I don't know if that's the same kind of vinegar that they have at the chip shop, or if it's something like my Dad's home made wine that just used to taste like vinegar but you can imagine how you feel on a really hot, dry day when you've been running around or walking a long way and you can imagine sitting down under a shady tree with your Roman friends and taking a long, refreshing drink of….lovely warm vinegar…. Maybe not.

Anyway, the point is that our perception of 'the time' and of the flow of time is subjective, changes from one moment to the next and can be influenced by the simple use of language. Language is a digital system used to encode analogue information, so, just like in your CD player at home, the end result is not exactly what you started with but it's usually close enough. Yes, all audio recording systems lose information. The telephone network carries only a tiny part of the frequency range that we use in human speech. We can cope with this loss because we are able to rebuild the lost information based on our experience. The richness of experience that is lost in the translation from thought to speech is far greater and, unfortunately, when we rebuild the lost information, the end result is never what was intended, and I use the word 'never' with caution.

A digital system like language can represent things that aren't here and now but your analogue brain can only process this information within a framework of 'here, now, me'. This also means that instructions starting with the word, "Don't..." often get the opposite result to what you intend. More on this later. Don't think about it just yet.

Some words are stories in themselves in that they represent a complex collection of memories - sounds, images, feelings, tastes and smells. In order for your brain to process any language, words are converted into basic sensory representations. In fact, every word is a metaphor in that the word itself is not the object or idea described, it is only a label for it.

> Every word in every language is a metaphor. A word is not the thing it describes; it is only a label for it. To process any word, your brain converts it into a basic sensory representation. Therefore, all language has the same effect as telling a story, to a degree.

So you can't eat the word apple, but you know what an apple is. How about rich, dark, moist chocolate fudge cake on a white china plate, with warm chocolate fudge oozing out of it, topped off with a big dollop of cheese? Your words have more emotional impact when the listener can engage their internal senses and become fully associated with what you are describing - as if it is really happening to them.

By the way, I used the word cheese rather than cream to demonstrate how some people use this as an influence tool, leading your mind in one direction and then surprising you. It's the basis of something called a pattern interrupt, used extensively by stage hypnotists to create a state in which you are more receptive to suggestion.

It's important to realise that people choose words because they represent the internal sensory experience that's going on. If you're running a meeting or workshop and you're summarising comments on a whiteboard, you may be tempted to translate, summarise or rephrase in order to write the comments down. You should only do this if your intention is to confuse and frustrate the audience, demonstrating to them that you are paying no attention to their ideas.

Think of the most indulgent and delicious pudding or dessert you every had in your life. Describe it to me. Now let me write on the whiteboard 'cake'. Does that do it justice?

Asking people to give you synonyms for words that you suspect to be vague is a good way to uncover the experience represented by the word. For example, if you ask people for a synonym for 'professionalism' you will get answers ranging from 'looks smart' through 'honest' and on to 'confident' and 'expert'.

For years, presentation and business communication courses taught that in order to demonstrate understanding, we have to paraphrase and restate. NO! This demonstrates that you understand your version, not that you understand the other person. If you really want to demonstrate understanding, repeat back the key words verbatim.

Paraphrasing demonstrates that you are representing someone else's memories by converting them into your own.

Repeating someone's own words demonstrates that you are respecting their thoughts and memories.

Choose which outcome you want before deciding whether to rephrase or repeat.

Some words are far richer than others. A word like 'apple' means something different to everyone, in that everyone will think of a different apple. However, when we see an apple, we all use the same label for it so whilst it's still a generalisation, it's vague enough to be OK. When a course delegate describes an apple and you write 'apple' on the whiteboard, everyone will know what you mean, even though everyone will translate the word into a different internal sensory representation (i.e. a different apple).

If someone in a workshop describes a situation where people sometimes arrive in the office late, you might write the word 'unprofessional' on the whiteboard. Maybe you've done something like this in the past, and experienced first hand the disagreement and confusion that it leads to. When people are disagreeing in this situation, they are not arguing over the word, they are arguing over their internal representations. If you try to condense every suggestion and find a single, unifying word, you will be standing at the whiteboard all day, unless you summarise every suggestion and write only the words 'important things' on the whiteboard.

There's a simple reason for this complex problem. People are arguing because they are talking about completely different memories and experiences to that originally described. Everyone has an experience of people being late for work. Some people get really upset about it whilst others don't even care. Even though they are talking 'in general', they are describing specific events in their personal history. They are telling you about their beliefs and values. You will never, ever reach an agreement because everyone is talking about a different experience through different perceptual filters.

If you have to, write 30 different words for 'being late' on the whiteboard until you have successfully captured each individual memory. You may even stand back in amazement, never before having realised that people could see things so differently. The people involved may be amazed too, and may even start to develop a respect for each other's beliefs and language. You will only achieve this if you respect the words that people use.

If your intention is to create a single, common representation then I still don't advise you use the bulldozer of paraphrasing as you are only using synonyms that make sense to you. There are far better ways of gaining collective agreement, and here are three of them.

Go up

Take all of the different suggestions and find the level at which they unify. Take 'arriving late at the office' and ask, "what is that an example of" or, "what is important about that". Sooner or later you will end up with a collective agreement that 'respecting the value of your colleagues' is important, even though being early or late is down to individual preference. You may well find that 'professionalism' is important to everyone, but the difference is the process by which you arrived at that word.

Instead of saying 'Punctuality equals professionalism' you are saying 'Punctuality is an example of professionalism' which is very different. If you go back to the chapter on logical levels, the first example here is like saying, "a pig is a cow" whereas the second example is more like, "pigs and cows both live on farms". One respects people's maps of the world, the other doesn't. You decide which to use.

Start again

If you can't agree on a representation, make up a new one. For example, what is the best state to be in to deliver a presentation? You may get lots of different replies including 'relaxed', 'objective' 'confident' and 'knowledgeable' in which case you could make up a new state called ROCK, which allows each person to integrate their own beliefs with some new ideas that they've picked up.

Use brute force

What if two people disagree over ideas that are exact opposites? Well, with all of these things I suggest you cheat. This is a special form of cheating that appears to everyone else to be highly skilful but which you know is really easy. Let's say one person says you should be confident and the other says you should be nervous. The word 'should' tells you that they are comparing what is being suggested to their internal set of rules and values. You 'should' be confident because their rules say so.

Again, you can handle this in many different ways, and here are two suggestions.

First, you can say, "I can see that you both strongly agree with each other that your state of mental preparation is very important", so you force them into an agreement. In fact, they are agreeing with other if you look at the situation from a certain level. If I say red and you say blue, we both agree that colour is important and we both care intensely about making the right choice. We're just arguing over detail.

Second, you can say, "Would it be most useful to be confidently nervous or nervously confident?" Not possible, but useful. You know that it's possible, and asking which is most useful creates a new state that encompasses the most positive aspects of the two original states. Even the most opposite views can be squashed together in this way because in order to make sense of the new suggestion, the brain must move up to a higher logical level where it is possible for the two states to co-exist.

What may look or sound like disagreement is in fact an agreement over necessity and a disagreement over detail.

Stories are a very powerful means of communication and you'll be surprised at how much factual, specific information can be conveyed more meaningfully and memorably by using a story. You've probably heard mnemonic stories for remembering sequences of data or components of a business process and these are certainly very useful as they engage more parts of the listener's brain than mere repetition of the list.

The idea is that the learner goes for a walk in a park, or a shopping trip, or a day at the seaside, and along the journey sees things that link back to the sequence to be remembered. They key to using this successfully is to create a natural flow from one element to the next.

Our brains can recall huge amounts of information, but many people find sequencing that information difficult. Therefore, any format that can create a structured sequence around 'raw' data can only be a useful thing.

I should finally add that every story in this book is absolutely and entirely true. Only the places, times and people involved may have changed during the editing process.

Critical filters

I just wanted to tell you a little bit more about those critical filters that I mentioned:

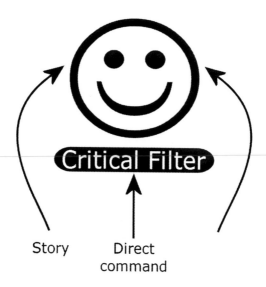

Imagine that a presentation or meeting goes badly and a colleague says to you, "It was great, really!" and you answer, "Yes, I suppose so". On the inside, you know that the meeting really did go badly.

When you have a problem, how do you respond to helpful friends who give you advice in the form, "I'll tell you what you need to do…"?

This direct form of communication simply bounces harmlessly off your critical filter so there's no chance of it pulling you off course. Your expectations, state and goals program the filter so that you only hear what you want to hear. When you are convinced your idea is brilliant, you might not hear criticism, and when you are convinced things are going badly, no-one can convince you otherwise.

In the last chapter, I asked if you could guess what other form of communication bypasses the filter. Did you work it out?

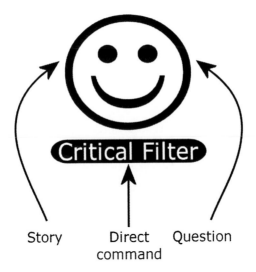

Story   Direct   Question
command

Stories bypass the critical filter because they're not true and they're not about you, so there's no need to worry.

Questions bypass the critical filter because they instantly put the listener into a receptive state. Don't take my word for this; try it for yourself.

Next time you are in a meeting and you want to ask a question, say this:

"Let me ask you a question"

And before you carry on, notice what happens. You will be amazed to see many people stop what they're doing and look up, giving you their full attention.

Of course, questions don't only request information – they can carry a hidden payload of information too. Questions are therefore amongst the most powerful influence tools that you have at your disposal.

Memories are made of this...

You know how one little thing reminds you of a whole series of memories? Maybe a smell brings an entire holiday back, or a certain colour or sound reminds you of something special? In NLP jargon, these triggers are called Anchors.

Anchoring is a perfectly natural process that is part of your brain's memory storage system. By connecting sensory experiences with simple reference markers, an entire memory can be brought to life with one simple stimulus, like a certain smell takes you back to that holiday, or a certain piece of music brings to mind a vivid memory of someone special.

How can you use this natural process to your own advantage? Here are a few ideas.

Preparing yourself for an important presentation, reprogramming phobias, as an accelerated learning tool, as a tool for focussing the attention of a group, for influencing behaviour, for relaxing yourself or other people, for getting yourself out of bed on Monday morning, for getting yourself to sleep on Monday night or just for making yourself feel great about dealing with life's distractions.

Advertisers know how this process works and they use it to connect a particular emotional state with their brand name and logo. If you watch commercials on TV, you'll notice that some of them seem to bear no relation to the product they're advertising. You'll see a series of images that have certain connotations, like security, happiness, love and desire and at the end of the advert you just see a brand name. You should pay attention to the music, as it's just as important as the images. One group of adverts that spring to mind are those for the Peugeot 406. The images were of great heroic acts, saving lives and being generally manly, whilst being caring and understated. The music was M People's 'Search for the hero'. There's no need to say what Peugeot wants its customers to think of themselves.

So, how does anchoring work? Well, you basically get yourself into a heightened emotional state – any one will do – and then see, hear or feel some unique, simple sensory stimulus such as a word, sound, image or touch. You could visualise a colour, hear a word, speak a word or squeeze your hand in a certain way – all of these work well as anchors and work best when used together.

There's a picture in the NLP Practitioner course manuals that looks like this:

This is slightly misleading as it only relates to states that increase in intensity, and it tells you to anchor when the state 'peaks'.

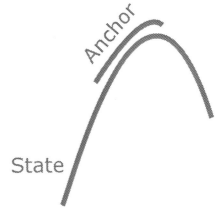

Unfortunately you have no way of knowing when the state will peak!. To wait for the peak implicitly means that you have missed it!

If you're driving to the brow of a hill, the only way you know you have really reached the top is when you start going down again.

The more effective way to think about anchoring is to anchor a state change or transition. Your computer (or any device in your house with electronic control) uses a clock to synchronise the processor with the other parts of the system – memory, disc drives and so on. The entire system is synchronised to the clock pulse's transition, like this:

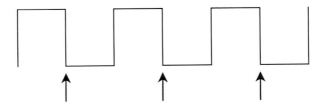

It's exactly the same with anchoring, The key to making anchoring work is to set the anchor at the moment of a state transition. Many people try to anchor a relaxed state which, from your normal rest state, looks something like this:

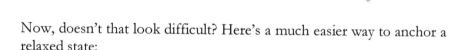

Now, doesn't that look difficult? Here's a much easier way to anchor a relaxed state:

So, to anchor a relaxed state, it's much easier to first go to a more energetic state and then come down to a relaxed state, simply because there is a more significant change for your brain to associate with the anchor.

You'll usually see anchors demonstrated as a touch. This isn't because only touch anchors work – it's because they're easier to demonstrate during a training course so that the audience can see what's happening.

You might even wonder what the use of anchoring is – especially if the only way you have ever seen it demonstrated is with a touch.

If we think back to states for a moment, you can imagine that certain states are very important for certain activities. You get the most out of a party when you feel in a party mood, and you perform best in a sport when you feel energetic and focussed. Similarly, in business, good negotiators, presenters, leaders and sales people are able to perform at their best when they are able to access the right state.

A typical example is a sales person sitting down to make their regular sales calls. They often have a routine that they go through in order to mentally prepare. Good presenters also have a routine that they perform to access the right state for their presentation.

So, is it likely that accessing a particular state is only important for some business activities, but not all of them? It's surprising how much time I spend coaching clients into the right state for important business activities. Just in the past week, I have used this process to get business people into the most useful state for:

- A presentation as part of an interview for a Director's job
- Another interview for a Director's job
- A disciplinary meeting
- A meeting with a difficult customer
- Solving a problem

Could those five people have performed in any state? Did their state really make that much difference? Many people say, "it doesn't matter how you feel, you have to put that to one side and get on with the job". I always find that people who say that find life much harder than they need to!

The person who had to present during a job interview would probably get the job anyway, but he would get the job on the board's terms instead of his own because of their expectations of him.

The second person had been interviewed for a previous job where the recruitment panel had told her that there was nothing to choose between her and the other candidate in experience, qualifications or ability. They gave the job to the other candidate because she seemed nervous during the interview and so they doubted her performance under pressure.

The disciplinary meeting went well with the person in question accessing a balanced, philosophical, sensible state. Her original state was quite distraught, looking for people to blame. The outcome would have been quite different because people will always defend themselves when attacked. If this person had gone in, looking to blame the people who had made the complaint, the manager who she met with would have defended them. As it turned out, she took no sides and said that she wanted to find out how to solve the problem and move on. The manager reflected this philosophical view and said that the blame was equally on them for handling the situation badly. Imagine what would have happened if she had said, "You have to take half the blame for this!"

What you can infer from these examples is that, when you are under no pressure and you are operating well within your capabilities in a situation where the outcome is fairly certain, thinking about your state first will probably not make a big difference. If you buy a cup of coffee in a bad mood, you get the same cup of coffee as if you were in a good mood. Or do you? I met a NLP trainer who used to practice rapport with the lady in the fish and chip shop to see how many more chips she would give him!

When you're in a situation where the outcome is important and uncertain, and you want to make sure you perform at your best, it is vital to access the most resourceful state. Anchoring is simply one of the quickest and easiest ways to access a particular state.

Anchoring has always been a difficult process to describe in a book as your attention is on the book instead of your own state, so I've tried something different here. Have a go and see what you think.

Read through this following piece of text, only turning the page at the end when you have finished reading. As you reach the end of the text, pay attention to any feelings you have and then turn over the page.

It's probably a good idea to have the page ready to turn before you start reading so that you can catch the relaxed state while it lasts.

Imagine yourself lying in a warm meadow. You feel the warmth of the sun's rays on your skin and in your hair. A cool breeze whispers past the hairs on your skin like someone gently breathing your name.

You hear sounds, very quiet and distant and as you lie there with your eyes closed, you can just make out the distant music of birdsong. You realise that the birdsong is all around you, moving left and right, up and down. You open your eyes and see swallows darting through the crystal blue sky. Realising how bright and clear the Sun is, you take a deep breath, let your eyes gently close again and your attention drifts back to those sounds. You can hear the wind moving calmly through the trees and the sigh reminds you of the voice of someone special.

With the breeze drifting so lightly across the meadow, you reach out and feel how cool the grass is. The touch of the grass is so soothing on your hands that you press your palms into the grass and feel your fingers stretching right out as far as they can stretch.

As you hold your hands up to your face to shield your eyes from the brilliant Sun, you notice the smell of the grass on your hands and it reminds you of long summer evenings at home when the smell of fresh cut grass lingered in the air. Letting your mind wander through these wonderful memories for a while, your attention is slowly drawn back to the meadow as you realise that this is the most relaxed you have ever been in your life.

What do you think of that?

Now, you can wake yourself up and think about something else, maybe what you had for breakfast or what you'll do tonight. What colour is your favourite hat? Does a rainbow have red on the inside or the outside?

An important step in establishing an anchor is to break the anchored state and then return to it, so imagine yourself feeling really calm and tranquil and quickly look back at the star.

Now that the anchor is beginning to set, you can think of the last time you really laughed and the last film you saw.

Now, look back at the star again and notice what happens to your feelings of relaxation.

Having said that relaxation can be a difficult state to anchor, it's usually a safe one. Here's another way to anchor relaxation which is actually a way to directly control how energetic you feel.

Begin by imagining a big dial. It's marked from zero up to ten and you can imagine reaching out and turning it. Just play with it for a moment to get a sense of how it feels to turn the dial, and how far you turn it to go from zero to ten.

Next, pay attention to how you feel right now. Are you quite relaxed? Wherever you are now, consider this a '5' on a scale of zero to ten. Imagine seeing the dial set at 5 and pay attention to how relaxed you feel right now. Recall a specific time when you felt quite excited or 'fired up' and as you remember what you saw, heard and felt, and as you become aware of feeling more excited or energetic, imagine turning the dial up to 6.

Recall a specific time when you felt really calm, tranquil or 'chilled out' and as you find yourself settling into that memory, turn the dial down to 4. Enjoy that for a moment and then return the dial to 5.

Continue to do this, allowing yourself to feel even more energetic, perhaps even 'buzzing' as you turn the dial to 7, and even more relaxed and comfortable as you turn the dial down to 3. As you recall a time when you were really excited and energetic, perhaps even buzzing, turn the dial to 8. Now turn the dial back to 5 and remind yourself that your wonderful brain has now learned what this dial does. Turn the dial all the way up to 10 and feel the tingling, buzzing energy. Turn the dial all the way down to 0 and feel that energy drain from you as you settle into a very comfortable, almost serene state. Continue to practice this until you can wind your state up and down at will.

Can you imagine all the times you could use this? Wind the dial up to 10 to deliver a presentation, wind it down to 3 when you want to sit back and enjoy something, or all the way down to 0 when it's bedtime.

Once again, anchoring is a natural state and so the other useful thing you can do with anchors is to use the ones that people already have.

People naturally emphasise the things they say. They point in a certain direction whenever they talk about the future. They use a certain voice tone to indicate uncertainty. They touch you whenever they laugh. Words, voice tone, facial expressions and gestures are all an integral part of a person's state, and can be used both to understand and to influence those states.

Is confusion a useful state to anchor?

You may be thinking, "Oh no! This is manipulative" in which case don't do it. Just carry on doing this the way you already naturally do.

As you may already know, a lot of NLP is used in the area of influence and persuasion. This doesn't mean that NLP is inherently persuasive, it just means that in the course of developing NLP, some very influential and persuasive people were modelled. This issue always comes up on NLP training courses, so here's my view.

You can be quite certain that people had the ability to be manipulative, influential and persuasive long before NLP came along. You shouldn't give NLP more credit than it deserves!

From black to white

Let's just go back to confusion for a moment and mention one other point that is critical in using NLP to help people change. Let's say that a colleague or customer has a very fixed opinion about something that you disagree with. How do you change their mind? Do you present the logical sides of the argument, reasoning that your opinion is the right one? Do you exert emotional influence? Do you argue? I'm sure you can think of colleagues who use those methods – and more. Which techniques are the most effective?

It's a trick question, of course. No one method is effective all the time if we are thinking at the level of content. It's like those sales courses that you'll see advertised that promise to teach you the seven guaranteed ways to get past a gatekeeper. Those seven ways only work as long as gatekeepers only have six ways to say, "no". Guess what? When the gatekeepers learn eight ways to say, "no", you have to go on another training course.

Let's think instead about the structure of the situation, not the content. It doesn't matter that you say, "black" and your colleague says, "white". What you both have in common is a state of certainty. Let's look at what we want to achieve in terms of content:

And now in terms of structure:

So, whilst we think we want to change someone's mind, in fact we're not introducing any change at all in the person's state. That is a big drawback. It doesn't matter whether we're changing black to white, yes to no or hire to fire. If we don't first bring about a state change, there will be no change in the person's position, and anything that you do to argue with or persuade them will only push them further into their state of certainty.

Now, if you want to bring about a state change in yourself or someone else, it's useful to bear in mind that smooth, progressive state changes are much easier to make. You are unlikely to get a customer to change from a state of doubt to a state of total passion for your product in one step, so what would be a reasonable step on from certainty? How about doubt? Then uncertainty? Then confusion?

Now you can see where confusion fits in – it's a very useful transition state to move someone from just about any current state to any desired state. Confusion is relatively easy to elicit as well – if you already have rapport, you only need to be confused yourself and the other person will often follow you!

Let's take another look at the structure of opinion change:

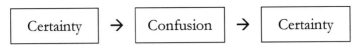

People generally do not like being confused as it can feel uncomfortable. When people are confused, they will tend to move towards whatever makes them feel comfortable and certain again. It doesn't have to make sense logically, it only has to be compelling.

If we add our content back in to the equation, we get:

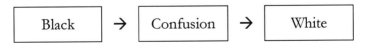

A simple process for this could be:

1. Never, ever disagree!

2. Gain rapport

3. Elicit confusion

4. Act as if the other person already agrees with you

I was recently running a NLP course for the trainers of an insurance company and they asked me to demonstrate this process, so their manager volunteered and offered the belief that black is black, so my goal was to have him believe that black is white. I ran through the basic process outlined above and, as I was entering the confusion phase, he crossed his arms and began to indicate some resistance.

This is an interesting point in itself – you might take resistance as a sign of disagreement but you have to ask yourself the question, "resistance to what?" If someone is resistant, they are already imagining the thing they are trying to resist!

At this point I paced his resistance and suggested it was a perfectly natural prelude to belief change!

Shortly afterwards, he said, "Well, I suppose I can imagine how it would be possible for someone to believe that black is white" and then it was all over! His colleagues were very excited by this and were talking about it for a few minutes, after which he said, in a completely certain and direct tone, "Well for a moment there I felt a bit confused but I still know that black is white" and he didn't even realised he had said it until his colleagues cried out in amazement!

And that, believe it or not, is all there is to it, as long as the target opinion is genuinely useful for the other person. As Dale Carnegie said, "If you are wrong, admit it quickly and emphatically". I would just add that if you are right, don't be afraid to share it with the world.

Making an Impact

Really **impactful** communication takes place when you are delivering the same message with all of your communication systems - your words, your voice, your eyes, your hands, your breathing, your body posture, your movement and every thought that you have.

You can spend a lot of time trying to remember all of these different activities, or you can do it the easy way - and you know how much I like the easy way!

The easy way to be 'congruent' is to start by **believing what you are saying**. If your conscious and unconscious minds agree, you will send the same message through all of your communication systems. You don't have to remember all that body language stuff you read about years ago. It will all happen naturally and thereby be far more convincing.

If you've ever stood there, speaking to a group and not really wanting to be there, do you think it's enough to just say the words? No! They can tell! Audiences, like dogs, can smell fear.

Many people have written excellent books on how to focus your thoughts and clear your mind in order to be totally congruent. I won't rewrite them here, but I will give you a few handy tips that you can use right away.

What do you want?

It's very important that you are very, very clear about what it is that **you** want. In order to set your brain up to automatically achieve your goals for you, your goals must conform to certain rules.

It's just like making sure that a computer program conforms to the syntax of the programming language. If it doesn't, it might still run but the results may be unexpected.

Here are the rules for 'Well Formed Outcomes'. Your goals must be:

Positive - Something you want, rather than something you don't want.

Under your control - It is no use having a goal such as 'to get a new job' because that is probably not entirely under your control. A better goal would be 'pick up the phone and call ten recruitment agencies today'.

Real - It is not enough to say that you aim 'to successfully complete' something. What does successful completion look, sound and feel like? Lets say your aim is to write a proposal for a customer. How will you know when it's finished? Will you see it, sitting printed and bound on your desk? Will you read it, noticing the words? Will you pick it up and feel its weight, or flick through the pages? Everything that you 'know' is a sensory experience, stored in your memory. To easily achieve a goal, you must have a specific and direct sensory test for it.

Ecological - You must not lose anything as a result of achieving this goal, otherwise you will sabotage your own attempts. This often happens when people try to give up smoking.

When you have adapted your goal to meet these criteria, you can test it using this simple set of four questions, which check the goal logically (as in real logic, not just common sense). Ask yourself each question and wait until you get an answer. You can write your answers down if it helps.

If I achieve this, what will I gain?

If I achieve this, what will I lose?

If I don't achieve this, what will I gain?

If I don't achieve this, what will I lose?

And finally, pay really close attention to any feelings that you get as you ask yourself this last question:

If I were offered this right now, would I take it?

If there is anything that you haven't considered, or if any part of you would object to this goal, you will get a definite reaction to that question.

Have a dream

When are you at your most confident? Is it when you try something new, or when you do something you know you can do easily?

First, remember four or five specific times when you used skills or abilities that you value highly and that you want to have easy access to.

Allow yourself to daydream into those memories. See everything that you saw, hear everything that you heard and feel everything that you felt - both touch and emotions. Take some time to remember the whole event in as much detail as you can.

Now run the whole event again from a different point of view. If you were talking to someone, watch the event from over their shoulder. Notice how you look, your facial expressions, notice your tone of voice. Watch the event again from other points in the room. Make a mental note of anything new you learn whilst running through these memories.

Next, do the same exercise again but this time daydream into the future. Think about how the room will look, the people, the sound of your voice. See things both as yourself and also from the audience's chair. Notice how confident you look and sound. Take as long as you need to fully imagine the whole experience. See the audience nodding and smiling.

Repeat this a couple of times so that it becomes very easy to imagine. Run through this new 'memory' whenever you get a quiet moment. Imagine everything going well. If anything gets in your way, you are able to easily overcome it.

Splash in the puddle

First, pick the emotional state you want - certainty, confidence, passion, etc. Then, stand about 2 feet in front of an imaginary puddle on the floor.

Notice how the puddle is made of a pure colour - pick any colour you like that makes sense for the emotional state that is in the puddle. Watch the puddle for just a moment and then, only when you're ready, jump in! - make as big a splash as you like! See the colour splash up and feel the emotional state take over. See the colour dripping from you as the emotion flows through your body.

If you want to be a little more reserved, just step into the puddle. An alternative is to place the puddle outside a door or on a stage, so that as you walk towards your destination you walk straight through the puddle, seeing the colour splash up as you step into it.

The puddle splash uses existing colour associations as anchors. You can do the same thing with a word, a favourite piece of music or an item of clothing, creating different coloured puddles or other anchors for different occasions.

Motivation

Opinion seems to be divided over whether the carrot or the stick is best for motivation and some people think 'both' is right. It's worth us just applying what we know so far to this important subject.

Motivation is a process that translates thought into action, so the first thing to ask is, "what exactly do you want people to do?" You can use various language structures that naturally generate motivation which you can read about elsewhere in this book, including logical levels, moving in time and Well Formed Outcomes. When you choose to generate a feeling of motivation you must be certain that what people do as a result is what you intend, therefore it is most important to start with clear goals.

One of the ways in which personalities can differ and thereby be categorised is the natural direction of motivation. Motivation is always a strong, compelling, positive force. In some people it is generated towards goals and desires and in others it is generated away from things to be avoided. Some people like tidiness, others like avoiding mess. Some people like security, others like to avoid insecurity. In both cases, the motivation is positive. It doesn't involve fear or threat, it just heads in a different direction.

This is very important when you structure your language. If your preference is naturally 'towards' then you are likely to say things like, "Do this because the end result will be really great". This will be fairly meaningless to all the 'away from' people who like to hear things like, "Do this because it will save you work later".

It's very useful to pay attention to what people say when they're listing reasons for decisions or actions. If you tune the direction of your language to theirs, you will simply tell them what they want to hear and reassure them that there is a purpose in what you are asking of them.

When you choose to use either the carrot or the stick, you are choosing between pleasure and pain, desire and fear. By using the stick, you are often threatening to deprive someone of something that they want, or threatening a course of action that they will find unpleasant. "Do this or else…" is a stick command. "If you do this then…" is a carrot command.

As usual, I'm going to leave it to you to decide which, if either, is appropriate for your situation. Neither is right or wrong - it all depends on how you choose which to use. One thing that you should bear in mind is the effect that the carrot and stick have on the brain and in particular the focus of attention. Remember that humans cannot think of doing nothing, they must think of doing something, even if it doesn't seem like much.

When we generalise our own thoughts into language, ambiguous, analogue alternatives tend to take on a binary quality. When you say, "don't drop the glass," you usually mean, "hold the glass tight". In a digital, binary system this holds true. In an analogue system like the human brain, the opposite of, "don't drop the glass" can be, "hold the glass tight", "yesterday" or "a turnip". There are no opposites in an analogue system, only an infinite number of alternatives. An interior designer will tell you that the opposite of red is green, but that's only because they have a frame of reference for colour matching. What is the opposite of a zebra? What is the opposite of Tuesday? With no digital frame of reference, opposites and negatives have no meaning.

The effect of this binary generalisation is that we tend to think of motivation as being linear. We tend to think that people have limited choices because our own choices are limited by what we are currently thinking about. In fact, other people's choices are rarely as limited as our own because they don't share the thoughts that generated our choices!

We tend to think of carrot or stick motivation like this:

In that the person can be motivated to go either one way or the other. This is misleading and leads to expectations that people will do what you want them to when motivated correctly. This is not the case.

We think in this linear way because our own thoughts are constrained by our own goals and worries. When we apply a carrot or stick, we expect people to move as if they have the same map of the situation as we do. They don't – unless you share that map with them.

Because of the analogue nature of thought, the bizarre way that your focus of attention is pulled from one idea to another from one moment to the next and the fact that, regardless of what you want, other people have needs too, the way that stick motivation works is actually more like this:

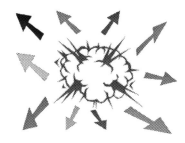

You provide the impetus, the compelling event, the driving force. You light the blue touch paper and retire.

If you're not careful, you will set people off in all directions and they will do some very strange things indeed to avoid what you are threatening them with.

In many companies, I have seen sales people given huge targets and threats of losing their jobs if they don't perform well. Some of them panic and immediately rush off to call customers. Some start ringing recruitment agencies. Some give up all hope and go home. Some go to the pub to drown their sorrows. Some laugh. Some cry. Only a small minority actually do what was intended.

Conversely, this is the effect of carrot motivation:

The carrot gives people a direction and draws them towards your desired outcome.

You already know about how to set goals, use positive language and direct people's attention, so this really shouldn't come as a surprise.

Which of those two is more useful to you? Don't answer now - decide when you need to make the choice, based on the situation that you are in and the information you have then.

Think back to what you learned about logical levels and apply this to motivation. Very often, you'll hear people tell each other to be more positive, or more professional, or more open. This information is absolutely useless because these words mean totally different things to different people.

Imagine a scenario where a manager tells a group of people to be more professional. Some people will dress smarter, some will tidy their desks, some will charge more for their services, some will go on a training course to become experts, some will go to law school and some will start speaking to customers in a more condescending way. Only a few of them will actually do what was intended.

When you want to change people's behaviour, use language at the behaviour level. Tell them what to do, not what to be.

For the people who are motivated towards outcomes, you need to tell them what will happen if they do what you ask. For the people who are motivated away from problems, you need to tell them what they will avoid if they do what you ask. To make sure you cover everyone, use both:

"By using this method, you'll reach the goal more quickly and avoid some common mistakes"

"When you use what you've just learned about motivation, you'll be able to motivate people more easily and avoid resistance more often, creating a more effective and less stressful learning environment."

Finally, it's worth bearing in mind that if your requests for action are reasonable, and people can see benefits for themselves, people generally don't need much encouragement to take action.

Remember - there's one easy way to get people to do what you want - TELL THEM WHAT YOU WANT!

Now it makes sense...

Unless your business involves cookery, wine tasting or perfume mixing, the chances are that your staff and customers will be mostly gathering information using three of their many senses:

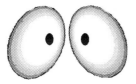 

Although we could also say that language is a special, additional sense.

Any one person will be preferring one of these, the whole group will be a mixture and any one person will change from time to time. So, how can you structure your presentation, proposal, letter, email or training course to supply the maximum information to your audience, given that you have a natural preference too?

The answer is that you must structure your communication to appeal to all three of these sensory systems. You must also pay attention to times that the audience shifts from one system to another. You will find that you can influence this shift, and use it to communicate more powerfully. Here's how.

Firstly, how do you know which sensory system a person is using? Remember that the brain is gathering information using all of your senses, the preferred sense is the one that you are currently attending to consciously. Right now, you could be seeing the words, hearing them in your head or deciding how you feel about them as we all have the ability to translate between senses.

As you might expect, NLP has special words for these three senses. They are Visual, Auditory and Kinaesthetic. In fact, NLP has a special phrase for the word 'sense'. It is 'representational system' and it is meant to indicate that our senses are not reality, they only represent reality.

 Our senses are not reality, they only represent reality. Therefore, they may or may not represent the same version of external events as other people's senses. None of us can claim to have a full version of external events, as there is just too much information to handle consciously.

The internal processing of the brain is available to you externally as a set of 'symptoms'. Here are the ones that we know about today - you may find some new ones:

Language

As you will know, a proper grammatical language structure contains lots of words that don't add anything to the meaning. In other words, meaning not need grammar. It is these non-essential words that we're interested in. How many ways do you hear people say, "I understand"? Do these sound familiar?

I get it	I can grasp that
I see	That sounds good
I hear you	I'm with you
That's crystal clear	I dig
That's clear as a bell	Looks great

When you hear these, you probably translate them all into a confirmation of understanding, rather than paying attention to the particular words used. Well, start paying attention! Here are those phrases again, with their associated sensory system:

I get it	Feel
I see	See
I hear you	Hear
That's crystal clear	See
That's clear as a bell	Hear
I can grasp that	Feel
That sounds good	Hear
I'm with you	Feel
I dig	Feel
Looks great	See

When you next watch the news on TV, or listen to it on the radio, pay attention to the unscripted interviews. Listen out for people using these words and their language will come alive with a new depth and meaning. Once you have had some practice at this, start matching their language up with the physiological symptoms described below. Of course, you can try this with real people too, it's just that people on TV don't seem to mind as much when you stare at them.

All of this is useful, not in categorising people, but in communicating with them more effectively. You may have heard people labelled as 'visual' as if they are only able to understand pictures. In fact, everyone uses all of their senses. Imagine listening to a presentation in a language that you can speak, but not fluently. You translate in your head as much as you can, but after a while you can't help letting your mind wander as you get tired. The same thing happens even when you communicate using the same language, so we are talking about a degree of refinement here which will add to and enhance your existing skills.

Here's a bigger list of words that will help you discover a person's preferred sensory system. Preferred doesn't necessarily mean 'always use', think of it as meaning 'using right now'. I'll use the NLP headings for this list.

Visual	See	Vision	Sharp
	Picture	Outlook	Background
	Look	Bright	Shine
	Watch	Clear	Reflect
	Perspective	Focus	Eye catching
Auditory	Listen	Quiet	Whistle
	Hear	Amplify	Whine
	Sound	Tell	Roar
	Noise	Resonate	Silent
	Loud	Hum	Tone
Kinaesthetic	Feel	Push	Down
	Touch	Embrace	Ache
	Grab	Warm	Gut reaction
	Hold	Cold	Queasy
	Contact	Sinking	Shaky

Physiology

To a highly visual thinker, kinaesthetic thinkers appear to be slow and boring. The kinaesthetic thinker might feel that the visual thinker is too flighty, never settling on a particular idea or topic or conversation and talking too fast to pay much attention to.

Visual thinkers see a constant movie in their heads, so their language has to keep up. Strongly visual thinkers hardly ever finish a sentence, as the generation of words just can't keep pace with the images they're trying to describe. They breathe high and fast to keep up with their fast pace of speech, and their hand gestures show you what they are talking about. To make upward eye accessing more comfortable, they look up and lean back a lot, often supporting the backs of their heads with their hands when they are thinking.

Auditory thinkers hear a constant, harmonious flow of words and sounds. They tend to breathe regularly from the centre of their chest and their gestures add impact and emphasis to their words, much like the conductor of an orchestra. They talk smoothly and freely and you can often hear a musical quality to their speech, marking out sentences and phrases. Auditory thinkers tend to sit upright and when thinking will often tilt their heads to one side.

Kinaesthetic thinkers base their language on their feelings, so they constantly check their internal feelings and sensations to verify what they are saying. Feelings move much more slowly than words or pictures, so a kinaesthetic thinker will tend to pause a lot and speak without making much eye contact. They tend to breathe slowly and deeply from their stomachs, and their rate of speech is much slower than the other two sensory thinking modes. Their hands will often be still, or they will touch themselves to stay 'in touch' with their feelings. Kinaesthetic thinkers tend to lean forwards when thinking as this makes their downward eye accessing more comfortable.

During the course of a conversation, you will move freely between these different modes, although you will tend to prefer one as a 'default' mode.

You'll find that, when you're deeply in rapport with someone, your physical posture and breathing will be closely matched. Consequently, you will both be thinking in the same sensory mode. Next time you're in a social environment like a pub, watch out for people who are this deeply in rapport. The first thing you'll notice is the similarity of their posture, but this is not the most important thing to pay attention to. Instead, notice the pace and rhythm of their movements. Notice how they are both using the same type and range of gestures, so that they are either both pointing to the same picture, both conducting the same orchestra or both checking the same kinds of feelings. Essentially, they have entered a shared world - a bubble, within which they seem to have an almost telepathic connection.

Just watching this process in some detail will give you everything you need to know about the role your senses play in creating a shared reality for you and your colleagues or customers.

There are a number of elements in physiology, so we'll cover each one separately, looking at the 'symptoms' that relate to each sensory system.

	Posture	Breathing	Hand gestures
See	Leaning back, head tilted up, hands often behind head	High in chest, fast and shallow	Moving quickly, drawing the object or events being described. Pointing to specific locations in space.
Hear	Sitting upright, head tilted to side	Middle of chest, regular and moderate	Moving smoothly, 'conducting' or demonstrating the rhythm of speech or punctuation.
Feel	Sitting forwards, head titled down or down to right	Low in stomach, deep and slow	Relatively still, often in lap or clasped together.

Eye movement

Seeing

Hearing

Feeling

Listening
to voice in
head

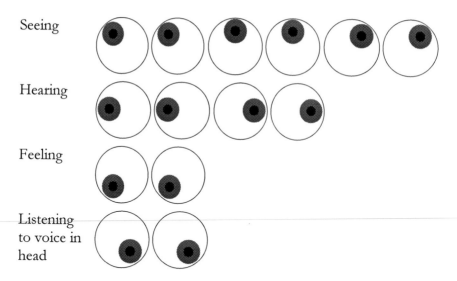

In general, movement to the left infers the recall of an existing memory whilst movement to the right infers the construction of a new experience. This doesn't apply to everyone, and it certainly doesn't mean that someone is lying, just because they're making new pictures in their head. With some people, the left to right accessing is exactly reversed so, once again, it's important to pay attention to the person in front of you, not the generalisation.

If I ask you to recall some visual detail of a memory, such as the colour of a colleague's shirt, you may not remember it right away. You might recall the overall scene, then 'try out' a number of different colours until you feel you've got the right one. This would, for many people, involve a lot of eye accessing up to the right – but you wouldn't be lying. It's only important to pay attention to the person in front of you and to follow what they uniquely do.

If you want to test this out, find yourself a willing subject and sit down, face to face somewhere quiet. You can ask them these questions, or make up your own more relevant questions. The important thing about this exercise is that they don't have to answer you, they only have to process the question. You should memorise each question and then look the person right in the eye as you ask it. If you read from the page, you will miss the eye accessing as it will happen as soon as the person understands the question - which is long before you have finished reading it.

- What colour is your bedroom?
- Where is the bed in relation to the window?
- What would your bedroom look like if it were pink? (i.e. not the current colour)
- When you pull back the curtains, what sound do they make?
- What sound would they make if you pulled them back faster?
- What sound would they make if you pulled them back slower?
- What do they feel like?
- How easily do the curtains move?
- What can you feel with your toes?
- How do you feel when you hear chalk used on a blackboard?
- How does your favourite person's voice make you feel?
- Say to yourself inside your head, "Mary had a little lamb"
- Say to yourself inside your head, using the voice of Donald Duck, "Mary had a little lamb"
- What's the thing you enjoy doing most?

You will probably notice your subject's eyes moving about rather than going to one place and staying there. This is an example of something known as a 'pattern'. For example, if you asked the question, "How easily do the curtains move?", your subject may look up to the left, then up to the right, then down to the right before answering. This indicated them trying to remember seeing their curtains move, then making up a picture of their curtains, then finally checking the image against the feelings in their muscles. You can check your interpretation with them after they answer the question.

As you might suspect, all of these are related to each other. If someone is making pictures in their head, their eyes move up so to get comfortable they lean back. In order to keep pace with the rapidly moving pictures in their head, they have to talk fast and this is supported by rapid, shallow breathing which comes from the upper ribcage. If someone is concentrating on feelings, they look down and to really concentrate hard they lean forwards. Feelings change much more slowly than pictures, so their breathing becomes deep and slow to quieten any movement in their bodies, allowing them to really focus on their feelings.

You may have already noticed that I seem to say the same thing in a number of ways. This helps to make communication loud, clear and easy to grasp. In other words, it helps you see what I mean, hear what I'm saying and get the hang of it.

Are you getting the picture yet? Does it ring a bell? Do you get it?

What's most important is that you pay attention to the other person's state and that you notice when their state shifts. If you spend all your time trying to work out people's eye accessing, you're missing the point of paying more attention to other people.

My advice on this whole chapter is to simply be aware that people do not speak the same language as you do, even though it sounds the same. Language conveys experience and other people's experiences are not the same as yours. Pay attention to the differences and use them to become a more effective, more empathic communicator.

Whatever you do, don't

Before we start, don't think of a pink elephant, don't notice that itch and whatever you do, don't make a mistake.

As you already know, our brains are analogue computers. In practice, this means that, like Roman numerals, we cannot represent zero. We can only represent the absence of something within a framework of the thing that is missing.

Here is an empty box.

What was in it?

Here is another empty box.

What was in it?

So, hopefully you get the idea.

Computers work digitally, so computers can quite happily cope with 'not zero', which is most definitely the number one. Analogue computers struggle to understand 'not zero' as it essentially means 'anything at all except zero' – for example one, two, a hundred, a tomato, a goldfish or an itch. Are you starting to understand the problem with the word don't? Well, don't worry about it too much if you're not.

Have you ever said something like that? Don't worry, don't try too hard or maybe even, "don't do that".

There are two fundamental problems with the word don't. The first is that our brains cannot make sense of the language without first representing that thing that the word 'don't' applies to. In order to decode the language, "don't drop the glass" your brain first has to have a representation of what dropping the glass is like in order to know what not dropping it means. That thought alone leads to tiny, involuntary relaxation of the muscles in your hand as you make a picture of the glass dropping. The result? You drop the glass.

The second problem is that telling someone what you don't want them to do gives them absolutely no useful information about what you do want them to do. Ask a decorator to paint your bedroom 'not blue' if you want to test this out. At best, you will create confusion. At worst, you'll get a punch on the nose.

Of course, your objective may be to create confusion, in which case don't think about applying any of the information in this chapter.

Whilst our brains are analogue computers, they do operate within rules of context. If you tell someone, "don't use a red pen" then they will create a list of alternative behaviours constrained by the context of the language. They will guess that you either mean use a green/blue/black pen or that you mean use a red pencil/crayon. If you say, "don't do that" then they will search for a meaning based on 'what am I doing right now?'

If you ask someone to stop an annoying habit by saying, "don't do that" then they will have no context on which to base alternative behaviour. The habit is unconscious – that's what makes it a habit – so they have no awareness of what they are doing.

If you catch yourself saying, "don't", quickly backtrack inside your head to figure out how you have decided on this course of action. Usually, you will have made a picture, sound, voice or feeling inside your head of how things may turn out for the worst. Go back to that worry state and pick a more useful, specific outcome. Now follow up your 'don't' command with a 'do' command.

Worry is simply a process of imaging something that you don't want to happen, which of course makes it more likely to happen.

Imagine what you don't want	>	Respond as if it's happening now

When you find yourself influencing other people with your worries, take a moment to ask yourself, "what specifically do I imagine is going to happen?" and then change the picture to something more useful.

| Imagine what you do want | > | Respond as if it's happening now |

For example, let's say you're worried about a particular project going badly, so you help the people involved in it to do a good job by reminding them, "don't forget to check the pricing" or, "don't put that there" or even, "make sure we don't lose this deal". It's far more useful to say, "check the pricing", "put that there instead" or even, "what else do we need to do to win this deal?"

Now, once you get the hang of telling people what you want you can start being more creative with your use of the word 'don't'. For example, if you tell someone, "don't forget", you can imagine the result you might get. You could have some fun with this, and it's an interesting way to experiment with motivating people, but don't start thinking about all the ways you'll use what you've learned just yet.

End of part one

Well, that was a journey through the country roads of NLP. We talked about the importance of state, clear outcomes, different forms of communication and time.

Woven through part one were the beliefs and attitudes that will help you to apply NLP techniques most easily.

Remember – if you focus on the techniques only, they will work some of the time. If you get the beliefs and attitude right first, the techniques will come naturally and they will work every time.

I find that with NLP, and also with coaching, people often think that the first thing they need is the techniques so that they know how to coach properly.

Being able to read a recipe book and follow the recipes to the letter doesn't mean you can hold a dinner party. To do that, you have to think systemically, first creating the right atmosphere for your guests and only then serving them dishes that complement each other and arrive in the right order.

The first step I always take in developing coaches is to get them to a place where they realise that the tools and techniques are not important. Only then are they ready to learn the tools and techniques.

Part Two

This part is a more structured exploration of the components of NLP as you'll see them during a typical NLP Practitioner training course.

Some of the techniques and principles in this part of the book have already been covered in part one in a less structured way. This part of the book is designed to help you understand some of the workings of the techniques and the thinking behind the principles, for those of you with more enquiring minds.

Unlike part one, this is more like a reference manual for NLP. You can dip in and out of this section when you know what you are looking for, to find what you need. This style is more appropriate when you understand a subject and know what you want to know.

The components of NLP

If you go to a NLP training course, you'll find it organised into segments of content, with a number of exercises and techniques in each segment. It seemed sensible to organise this part of the book in the same way, so that you can easily relate it to NLP training that you've done, or may do in the future.

The content of NLP training breaks down into a number of areas. Some people talk about the "four pillars" of NLP and other people include content from other disciplines.

For our purposes, the components of NLP are:

- State
- Outcomes
- Rapport
- Questions (Meta Model)
- Hypnosis (Milton Model)
- Time

We'll take a closer look at each one in the next few chapters. I have also included a chapter on modelling, as that is the basis of all of the NLP techniques. By learning the principles of NLP modelling, you can easily learn new tools and techniques for yourself simply by modelling people around you who are exceptional at achieving their outcomes.

State

You tend to perform well when you feel like it. No surprise there.

'State' means your present physical and mental condition, so you might be tired, happy, curious, careful or fascinated - all of these are states. Your state is partly influenced by your thoughts and partly influenced by what's going on around you in the outside world. You'll realise by now that this really means that your state is wholly influenced by your thoughts!

So, is there a way that you can choose the day you're going to have?

Oh yes!

The two key ways to quickly influence your state are through your physiology and your focus of attention.

First, we'll talk about physiology as it's really simple, really powerful and really easy to ignore. If you are alert and have plenty of water and oxygen, you will feel energetic and perform well. If you are lacking in any basic physiological needs such as sleep and light, you will perform below your best.

Getting the right physiology for an activity is the first thing you can do to improve your performance. In a warm, cramped room with no natural light, you'll be lucky to keep your customers or colleagues awake, let alone in a productive state.

In a room with lots of fresh air, light and water, it's much easier to keep people in an attentive state. There is absolutely no good reason for making life hard for yourself, so get the environment right first before you think about anything else.

People have all kinds of methods and routines for controlling or maintaining states. Perhaps you have a routine for getting ready for work, or for going out on a Friday night. Perhaps you have a lucky charm or item of clothing that helps you get into a certain state. Perhaps you can just think of a state and you're there. The reality is that everyone has total control over their state, yet most of the time we just go with the flow, letting external events and people cheer us up or put us down.

Here's an exercise you can try with a friend that influences their state through their physiology:

Ask your partner to name three states that they would ke to explore.

Have your partner come up with a single word tha describes each belief - usually a state adjective such as proud, relaxed r alert.

As you walk together, coach your partner to find the ace, breathing, posture and full physiology of the first belief. Having ully settled into the first belief, have them now adopt the second on Continue with the third until they have tried on all three.

Finally, have them try on aspects of all three to cre te a new state. Find out how that feels for them.

State is an important starting point in NLP because, in a way, state is everything. Your state defines the meaning you make of the world, the choices you make, the risks you take and the language you use. The differences in your behaviour between a great day and an awful day may be tiny, yet they add up over time creating a state that builds throughout the day, reinforcing itself.

When you wake up, knowing it's going to be a bad day, you program your sensory filters to notice things that go wrong. Anything that goes well is set aside as an accident or coincidence. When you plan for bad things to happen, they often do.

When you wake up, knowing it's going to be a great day, you notice everything that goes well for you. Anything that doesn't go your way is set aside as just a temporary setback. When everything seems to be going your way, it probably is.

You might say that you can't predict or control what happens to you, and you might be right in saying that. What you can control is your response to what happens. Here's an example.

A salesman leaves a message for a customer to call him. After two hours, the customer hasn't called back. The salesman knows that the customer always returns calls promptly, therefore something must be wrong - the customer must be avoiding the salesman. Self doubt starts to creep in and the salesman's state changes to reflect his negative mood. When the customer finally calls (he had lost his mobile) the salesman's voice tone reveals his state and the customer thinks something is wrong. The customer's state changes accordingly, confirming that salesman's suspicion and they descend in a spiral of emotional states.

The only thing that the salesman can say for certain about this situation is that he has not spoken to the customer since leaving a message. The salesman's response presumes that he has read the customer's mind; the customer has heard the message and has made a conscious decision to not call back. None of this is true, so it's just as acceptable for the salesman to imagine the customer going to the dentist, or just taking a quiet afternoon out to make an important decision. Neither this nor the pessimistic version is 'true' in an absolute sense, so which is the more useful to believe?

Let's say the customer has gone away to decide whether to buy the salesman's product or not, and currently the customer is undecided. When the customer calls back for more information, the salesman's state could be the deciding factor. You may think that no customer would make a decision so lightly but in fact everyone does exactly this - we all buy from people we like to do business with. A friendly voice on the end of the telephone could be all the customer needs to decide. Conversely, a negative or pessimistic voice could swing the decision the other way by making the customer more aware of their doubts.

You've probably read adverts for instant, cure all influence techniques that will guarantee sales. The reality is that people succeed in any area of life by consistently being one tiny step ahead. A salesman who is consistently positive, helpful and persistent will succeed a little more than a colleague who lets his state reflect his worries. Those small changes are iterative over time and they build on and reinforce each other. Success is about doing the basics well, consistently - not about having the latest and greatest guaranteed technique. Oddly enough, NLP is about doing the basics well, even though many people try to sell it as a cure-all.

Your state is the filter through which you experience the world, and it's the mechanism by which the people in that world experience you.

Anchoring

Your state is the basis for everything you do, so in NLP there are many techniques for managing your, and other people's state. Possibly the most well known is anchoring, which is the process by which Pavlov famously got his dogs excited at the sound of a bell ringing. Of course, we don't like to think of ourselves as being as easily influenced as animals so we don't like the term 'conditioned response' yet it's exactly the same principle, and advertisers know this too well.

When you see an advert that seems to bear no relation to the product, you can be certain that the music and imagery is designed to invoke a specific emotional response which you will then associate with the product or brand which is shown at the end of the advert.

Anchoring in NLP is demonstrated earlier in this book, and it's an integral part of the exercises taught on a NLP course. In order to understand anchoring, we first have to understand a couple of concepts relating to our emotional state. Firstly, our memories are an important resource in accessing states, and secondly, we respond most strongly to changes in state rather than the state itself. If a state does not move or change, it ebbs away.

Typically, anchoring is taught by using a memory of a time when you felt a particular emotional state. Often, on a NLP course, people will pick 'relaxed' and will then have trouble anchoring the state, and there is an important reason why; imagine yourself sitting down during a training course. From there to 'relaxed' is not a big change, and anchoring works by associating an event with a state change. In this example, your brain is picking up too much background noise for the state change to really stand out.

Here's a picture of the state transition from 'rest' to 'relaxed':

Now, what if we anchor a state such as 'excited'?

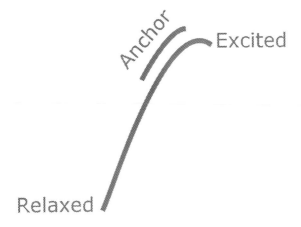

Much easier!

So, in my experience, most NLP trainers don't understand this principle, therefore they don't explain it and the people on the courses then have unimpressive results with anchoring. Anchoring can have an extremely profound and immediate effect, when you follow the basic principles. Of course, it's obvious that if you use any tool properly, you'll get the best result.

So, let's go back to first principles with anchoring. What makes an emotional response? In particular, when you recall a memory, how do you know how to feel? Think of something that makes you feel warm and fuzzy, now think of something that makes you feel that sinking feeling. How do you know the difference?

You might say, "Well it's a happy memory, so of course it makes me feel good" but it's not that simple. When you think of a happy memory, where is the picture? How big is it? How bright is it?

Here's the interesting thing: for many people, happy memories are big, bright and colourful. Unhappy memories are small and dark. Why is that interesting? Think of the implications. It turns out that the emotional label on a memory is not directly related to the content of the memory – it's related to the structure of it. By structure I mean the qualities of the visual, auditory and kinaesthetic components of the memory.

In NLP, your senses are called either representational systems or modalities, so these qualities of your senses are called submodalities. Here are some of them:

Visual:

- Motion/still
- Colour/black and white
- Bright/dim
- Focused/unfocused
- Associated/dissociated
- One image/many images

Auditory:

- One point/all around
- Loud/soft
- Fast/slow
- High/low pitch
- Clear/muffled

Kinaesthetic

- Location in body
- Breathing rate
- Temperature
- Weight
- Intensity
- Movement

Olfactory/Gustatory

- Bitter
- Sweet
- Acrid
- Sharp
- Acidic
- Pungent

You can try this at home: ask someone to remember a time when they experienced a particular emotional state – anything will do, but strong states are easier to work with. Go through each of the submodalities listed above and find out how your partner structures the memory. Now, have them pick a very different state and go through the submodalities again, noticing which ones have changed.

Let's say for example that 'joy' had a picture above eye level, at about arms length, bright and colourful, whilst 'sadness' had a picture down on the floor, over to the left, dark and colourless.

What if we take the picture of sadness, move it, turn up the brightness and colour, would it become joy? If you are specific enough about the submodalities, then often the answer is 'yes'.

Handy, isn't it? Think of something in the future that you feel bad about – some work you have to do, for example. The work isn't what makes you feel bad, because you know you have to do it and that you will be relieved when it's finished. If you check out the submodalities, can you change your response, so that you actually feel more motivated? Yes you can, very easily. In fact, it's easier to change responses because the events haven't happened yet.

Let's move onto anchoring, and once again here is something you can try out with a friend:

Ask your partner where they would be happy ha ing an anchor applied - to their arm, hand, shoulder?

Ask your partner what state he/she would like to exp rience. Imagine being in that state yourself to lead your partner in.

Ask your partner to remember a time when he/she wa in such a state.

Ask your partner about the submodalities of the me 1ory, and when you notice them go strongly into state, apply the anch)r – touch their hand, squeeze their arm, have them say a trigger word tc.

Break state, then have your partner imagine experi ncing the state strongly as you apply the anchor once more.

Break state, then test the anchor.

A break state is a very important part of the process, because you need to reset your partner's state, ready to set the anchor again. To break state, either ask them about something in the room – the colour of the carpet, for example, or ask them to remember something that's hard to remember such as which side their hot tap is on at home.

The more times you set an anchor, the better it will work and the longer it will last. Remember, you want to leave your friend's brain in no doubt about what to do when you fire the anchor. To test, just reproduce the anchor and find out if the memory or state comes back.

Language is a powerful anchor, and you can easily recall a state if you have anchored it with a word. A friend of mine is a professional squash player, and her current anchor is "Get off my court!!"

You've now learned a number of ways you can influence your state, and all of these techniques fall into two broad categories; focus of attention and physiology.

In reality, both work to influence our state and also as elements of our state. You know that if you smile while on the telephone, your voice tone changes. You also know that when you feel miserable, other people can see it because you sit and move differently.

To get people to move in their minds – for example, in a learning or negotiation context – it's important to get them to move in their bodies. If a meeting is proving to be hard going, suggest you all get some fresh air and a drink. Get people moving and their minds will move with you.

Many high level, professional negotiators tell me that they rarely make any progress when sat around a table. The time when the negotiation really moves forwards is when they take a break, go for a walk and end up chatting at the coffee machine.

If you look at the chapter 'From black to white' you'll find a lot more detail on how a change in state is the foundation of a change in belief – and what is an opinion or negotiating position but a belief?

Do not underestimate the importance of physiology, because your mind and body are part of the same system so getting someone moving on the outside is often the easiest way to get them moving on the inside.

Finally, the simplest way to recall a specific state is to think of a time when you felt that way. If you want to be confident, remember a specific time when you felt confident. In order to process the memory, you feel the confidence not in the past but right now.

Swish

Sometimes, people will act in a certain way through a habit or other unconscious process. No matter how hard they try, they always wind up acting or responding in the same way because by the time they realise they're doing it, it's already too late.

Anchoring was the process of connecting together a simple sensory input with a complex physiological output. We can also reverse the process of anchoring to break existing associations.

The technique for this is called a Swish

This can be used to change almost any habitual pattern of behaviour e.g. smoking, habits, phobias etc. Here is a visual version that you can try out.

Identify context:

Ask your partner what he/she wants to change

Identify current state picture:

Identify what your partner sees just before the behaviour that they want to change. You need to track down the precise moment that the 'program' runs, so that the person has choice over the response. For example, if you want to swish a fear of mice, don't picture standing on a chair. Hold your hand up in front of the person's face and ask them to put the picture there.

Create outcome picture:

Now create a picture after the desired change. Make the picture more exciting and desirable. Hold your hand down and over to one side and ask your partner to place the outcome image there.

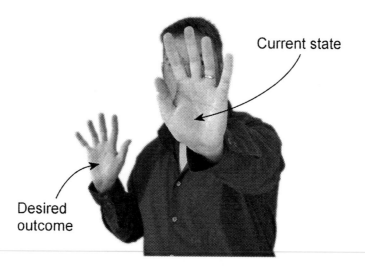

Current state

Desired
outcome

Swish:

See the first picture clear and bright in the palm of your hand.

Put a small image of the outcome picture in the bottom corner

Quickly grow the outcome picture to replace the first picture as the first picture shrinks away over the horizon. As the images swap over, make a 'whoosh' or 'swish' sound.

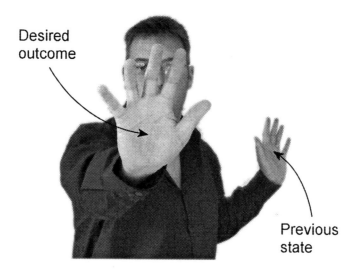

Desired
outcome

Previous
state

Repeat three times.

Test:

Try to think of the way you used to react to the situation. What is different?

You might feel a little self conscious, waving your arms at people and making 'whoosh' noises, but remember that everything is there for a reason.

In practising the swish, you will learn how to change habitual behaviours. There is a sequence of events here that happens very quickly because your brain only learns things quickly. Slow learning does not work, because it gives you time to think and thinking is not always helpful!

Helpful friends and colleagues often try to help by getting you to talk about the problem which usually makes it worse, because you get more of what you focus on. From a NLP point of view, the problem is already in the past and the swish pushes it even further behind you, focusing you on the present and future. A traditional counselling and therapeutic concept is that if you understand why you have the problem, you will be closer to solving it. The NLP concept is that understanding why you have the problem is of no use in solving it because the problem is not happening in the past – it is happening now. You feel your fear of public speaking now, not in the past when you recall a presentation that went badly for you.

Therefore, in order to solve the problem, we need only to understand how it is operating now – the sequence of mental steps that operate now to lead you from the first thought to the emotional response that is the hallmark of the problem. In fact, we could say that the problem is not public speaking, or cold calling, or spiders – the problem is that you feel bad when you think about those things.

By finding the choice point in the process, you are finding the point at which it is easiest to introduce change.

This is a similar approach to stress management. There's no point trying to manage stress once you are stressed, as it's too late and trying to manage your stress (or anger) just makes you more stressed. Instead we need to focus on what happens before you get stressed so that you can go off in a different direction altogether.

It makes a lot of sense when you think about it. There's no point looking at the map for directions to London when you're already in Edinburgh. It's easier to plan your route before you go in the direction you don't want to go in.

The second important part of the swish is the outcome. You cannot replace something with nothing. You cannot just take a thought out of your head. It's like trying to stop thinking about an annoying piece of music. You cannot turn it off, you can only replace it. This is because your brain is an analogue computer, so it cannot represent nothings or negatives. Therefore the swish does not take away the unwanted thought – it replaces it with a better one.

There are lots of ways you can do the swish without the amateur dramatics. You can swish with a piece of paper, by writing down aspects of the problem and then, when the person is really focussed on the paper (their state is anchored to it) just screw it up, throw it away and start again on a blank sheet with what the person really wants.

The simple process to remember for adapting the swish technique to any situation is:

- Find the point at which the person has choice
- Stop them
- Focus their attention on what they do want

Remember – state is not just the trivial matter of how you feel – it is the mental, physical and perceptual foundation for everything you do, and it will greatly affect the results that you get.

Outcomes

The secret to getting what you want is knowing what you want.

Of course, that's obvious, yet you'd be surprised how many people don't have a clear idea of what they want. When you have a very clear set of outcomes, every action and thought reinforces those outcomes and takes you a step closer to achieving them.

When you don't have clear outcomes, your thoughts and actions tend to be more random, so you have to think consciously about what you do, and you have to waste time correcting actions that take you in the wrong direction.

Frequently, people have a very clear idea of what they don't want, and they only know when things are going wrong for them. They tend to bounce from one wrong course of action to the next, never settling on a clear direction.

In business, we think we set clear goals all the time, yet mostly these goals are not phrased in language your brain understands, so they're actually quite useless.

A goal like "To complete this project by September 1st" sounds very specific, but it really doesn't mean much to your brain. For a start, everyone involved will have a different definition of 'complete'. Although we use dates and times as fixed, absolute markers, your brain treats them as very elastic concepts because we all have a different way of coding and representing time. In particular, the concept of 'now' is different for each of us. There's more on this in the chapter on Time, so for our current purpose I'll just say that 'now' is a flexible period of time that contains everything that's on your mind; both things you're currently attending to and things that you're thinking about that stop you from doing what you ought to be doing.

In order to process a goal like "To complete this project by September 1st", your brain has to create a representation of a completed project (different for everyone) and to imagine it as if that were happening right now (different for everyone) so when September 1st comes round, people disagree over the status of the project for two main reasons. Firstly, definitions of 'completion' differ from one person to the next. Secondly, and more importantly, in the time coming up to September 1st, people differ in their sense of urgency. You can imagine how disagreements can arise so easily.

Just to remind you of what constitutes a 'Well Formed Outcome':

Positively stated:	What you do want instead of what you don't want
Under your control:	You don't need anybody else; achieving the goal is solely down to you
Real:	You can see, hear, feel and perhaps taste or smell the outcome
Ecological:	You don't lose anything, or gain anything undesirable as a result of achieving the outcome

You might think to yourself, "Surely I don't have to go through that checklist for every goal" and you're right. A goal doesn't have to be well formed, it's just that if it is well formed you are more likely to get what you want. What are the implications of a goal not satisfying those criteria?

Positively stated:	You'll move away from what you don't want, but you may not get quite what you do want.
Under your control:	You can't put 100% of your energy into achieving the goal, so it will seem more difficult or frustrating to achieve.
Real:	You'll get something, but it won't be exactly what you want.
Ecological:	You may get what you want but at some point an unplanned side effect will pop up, or you may lose something that you didn't expect to.

So if what you want is some chocolate, and you don't have a clear representation of the outcome, it probably doesn't matter what kind of chocolate bar you get. If you want a new job or a new car, then you can't afford to be so vague. You can determine how well formed a goal needs to be, based on how important it is to you.

Of course, since it takes only seconds to create a Well Formed Outcome, why should you go through life not getting exactly what you want more easily?

People often ask how Well Formed Outcomes relates to goal setting tools like SMART. The way people generally apply SMART is to very superficial goals that are not well formed, such as "complete a project or "present to the board".

SMART is usually applied to the activity rather than the outcome. The other big problem with SMART is that a goal is meant to be Achievable and Realistic. From a NLP point of view, if you can imagine something it is achievable, and it's not up to me to decide if your goal is realistic. In Well Formed Outcomes, the ecology check automatically tests that the goal is achievable and realistic, because if it isn't, you know you wont achieve it and you will convey that information during the ecology check.

The one useful idea in SMART is that a goal is time bound. There is no time limit for a NLP Well Formed Outcome because a Well Formed Outcome will generate instant action, therefore it doesn't matter when the goal has to be achieved, as the act of planning it will lead to the action required to complete it.

I find that in practice it's useful to have an idea of time, as it is often helpful in creating a sense of urgency which is vital in an effective prioritisation process. If you don't know which outcomes are more important or urgent, you can't prioritise your resources effectively.

If you do want to use SMART or any other goal setting process, my advice would be to use Well Formed Outcomes to check the goal being set before applying SMART criteria to it.

Earlier on I mentioned our perceptual filters that reduce the sensory complexity of the world. Now that you know about state and outcomes, I'll just tell you a little more about those filters.

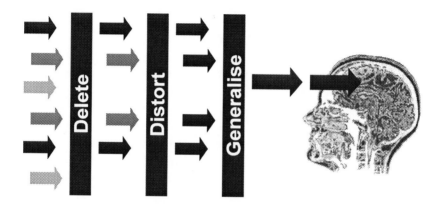

How do those filters know what to filter in and what to filter out? Simply, you program them. Mostly, you program them unconsciously so that you are more aware of opportunities to satisfy your current interests and needs.

Your beliefs are an essential component of your filters. What you know to be true about the world tends to influence the world – or at least it seems that way. You see and hear things that are true for you, and only when a situation conflicts with your beliefs do you become aware of them.

Your beliefs allow you to delete what is contrary to them and to distort and generalise the world so that it conforms to your beliefs. For example, if you believe other people to be intelligent and considerate, you will interpret their behaviour and respond differently than if you believe other people are generally stupid and selfish. Therefore, your beliefs mould your behaviour by colouring your perceptions.

Another important component of these filters is your state. Depending on your state, you will perceive the world differently. When you are feeling overly critical of yourself, a colleague's praise sounds like sarcasm. When you feel good about yourself, a colleague's sarcasm is shrugged off and you might even feel sorry for them. Your state influences how you interpret the world and the actions of people around you, so when you feel like doing something, you notice more opportunities to do it.

Finally, you program your perceptual filters with Well Formed Outcomes. When you have an outcome, you notice more opportunities to achieve it.

This is essentially why Well Formed Outcomes is so universally powerful – because it is a means of programming your natural, internal resources. External tools such as SMART require you to keep checking your progress against external criteria, whereas Well Formed Outcomes programs the goal into your unconscious, so that you don't have to think about achieving it – you just find yourself moving towards the goal, easily and naturally.

The downside of Well Formed Outcomes in an organisational context is that you may be asked to achieve goals that are in conflict with your own needs or values. You can either choose to live in conflict or you can choose to take a different course of action, based on what is in your own best long term interests.

Outcomes are key to life and are not just a NLP concept. We are goal directed animals, and we act in pursuit of goals, both large and small. All that NLP offers is a way to access those natural resources so that you can achieve goals that lead you to the life you want.

This could be one reason why, when you realise what you want and admit to it, chance seems to act in your favour, coincidences bring you new contacts and new opportunities and your efforts seem to have a greater influence on the world and other people.

As Louis Pasteur said, "Chance favours the prepared mind".

Rapport

You probably remember 'body language' from the 1970s, where a certain posture had a specific meaning for everyone. To get round the problem inherent in generalising the behaviour of individuals, the idea of 'clusters' was introduced. If you lean back in your chair and put your hands behind your head, you're arrogant. If you wiggle your toe then that's a cluster, so the original meaning may be different. Or not. It's the same with Tarot cards, where a card has a certain meaning, unless the client looks doubtful in which case the card was upside down and the card means the opposite.

Anyway, rapport isn't something you do - it's more like a measure of the quality of a relationship. It may be a long term relationship or it may be a simple transaction.

You could think of rapport as being that thing you have with people you like, when you're on the same wavelength, see eye to eye and feel a real connection with them.

You can think of rapport as being a conduit for effective communication. Without it, it's very difficult to engage the processes of agreement and compliance. In other words, people are more likely to do what you want if they like you. Having said that, and assuming that you're a naturally likeable and gregarious person, there are still many things that people do to stifle natural rapport.

The most common is the placing of barriers between people. A lectern blocks the audience's view of a presenter and restricts the flow of non-verbal information - a key component in establishing rapport. Without rapport, the audience loses interest, the speaker gets nervous and the relationship descends in a spiral of infectious states.

A desk blocks your view of an interviewer, so you feel nervous in the interview. A partition in an office blocks your view of your colleagues, so you don't communicate as well as in an open office.

The first and most important thing is to be in rapport with yourself. Self doubt and confusion lead to incongruence that other people will pick up on instantly. They may not recognise it consciously but they will still find it hard to accept what you say. When you're in an incongruent state, you're more likely to generate confusion and doubt in other people. You may choose to do this, in which case incongruence is a very useful tool.

In general, in most situations, it is more useful to have rapport than not. You can practice all the body language stuff, matching and mirroring body posture and echoing voice tone, but how do you do that with a group of people?

The simplest answer is don't bother. If you are congruent and friendly, you will find that a group or audience gradually gets into rapport with you. You'll know the experience of getting the audience 'on your side' and you may also notice the moment when that happens. What you can start to notice is what exactly you do that makes that change happen. When the audience's state shifts, what did you do that made it shift?

Rapport is a very good indicator of group compliance and you will find that when you raise subjects in a meeting which are contentious or engage opinion, the audience splits into smaller groups. Pay attention to who shifts first and who follows them and you will learn everything you need to know about the hierarchical power structure of the group.

Most of the time, we get into and out of rapport with people unconsciously, so our beliefs and thoughts are revealed non-verbally, regardless of our efforts to hide our true feelings. Regardless of what people say, they will show you who and what they agree and disagree with.

If there's one simple thing you can learn about rapport, it's that you can choose the people you want to get into rapport with. If you feel that a salesman is being a bit too persuasive, or that someone secretly disagrees with you, even though they say differently, then it's worth having a quick check of your state to see what's going on.

"Body language", as devised by Allan Pease in the 1970s possibly came from a Freudian era where psychologists thought that people's behaviour could be neatly packaged and explained with clear cause and effect, and where everything had its own meaning. For example, if you put your hands behind your head, you're being arrogant. I think that the idea of body language is helpful in that it gets people to think of their physical state as a means of communication, but it's not helpful to think of specific gestures as having specific meanings. I think Pease's basic premise here is fine, but he falls into the trap of having to assign meaning to each action, rather than thinking of an action or posture as being one component of overall communication. This ties in with Mehrabian and Argyle's work where you could think of 'body language' as being part of the 93% of unconscious communication, rather than being a language in itself.

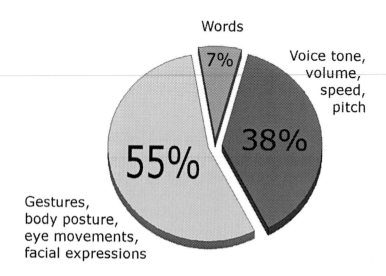

Therefore, we all understand non-verbal communication, but we are consciously aware of its meaning to different levels. At one end of the spectrum, some people need a slap in the face to pick up on unspoken information, whilst people at the other end of the spectrum are now said to have a high EQ, or Emotional Intelligence quotient. Whilst you may or may not believe in EI, there's no doubt it has helped revive interest in good old fashioned people skills.

You've probably heard about sales training courses where people are taught to 'match' or 'mirror' the way that their customers stand or sit in order to get into rapport. There are certainly some interesting things you can learn from doing this, but personally I don't recommend you actually do this in real life.

Personally, I think it's a bit contrived to adjust your 'body language' to get into rapport with people. If you get on with someone, you'll be in rapport with them. If you're not in rapport, there's probably a reason for that and you should pay attention to what it is.

If you think of rapport as a barometer of a relationship, rather than something separate to it, then you'll probably get better results.

It's worth having a play with rapport, and paying particular attention to the way that it influences communication. If you're out shopping and you see someone selling something like double glazing or credit cards, stop and watch - from a safe distance! Watch how the level of rapport influences the conversation and shows you how good a job the sales person is doing. In particular, watch the intricate dance that ensues when a sales person is trying to match the body posture of a customer who doesn't want to be matched.

For you to be interested in NLP, you may already think of yourself as a 'people watcher'. Well, don't just watch, watch and learn! Notice patterns, sequences and connections in relationships and - most importantly - put what you've learned into practice.

There is another very important aspect of Mehrabian and Argyle's work which we might overlook. As animals, we cannot consciously process the huge amount of sensory information that is available to us, so we rely on short cuts to help us reach conclusions and make decisions. Robert Cialdini offers an excellent description of these short cuts in 'Influence: Science and Practice'.

When our words match the non verbal components of our communication, our communication is said to be 'congruent' and when one of the components does not match the others, our communication is said to be 'incongruent'.

The problem that congruence presents is that it is a short cut for determining honesty.

When the words match the sounds and pictures, we tend to accept what is being said as true, or at least believable.

This means that if someone lies to you and they absolutely believe what they are saying then you won't be able to detect the lie. Of course, if they really believe what they are saying then they are telling the truth – from their point of view.

So, it seems that most of the time, people interpret congruence and incongruence as follows:

Congruence	Incongruence
Honest	Dishonest
Believable	Unbelievable
Credible	Lacking knowledge
Confident	Evasive
Knowledgeable	Uncertain

So the mental short cut is "congruent=good, incongruent=bad"

Unfortunately, some people have intentions that may conflict with our own, and their congruence can fool us into making decisions that may not work in our favour. Used car salesmen and politicians are two common examples.

At other times, we have good intentions but different reasons for incongruence. When people give presentations, we often see incongruence as a result of nervousness, so the audience will tend to interpret the incongruence based on their expectations or beliefs about the presenter or the subject – which might mean that they think the presenter is nervous, or it might mean that they think the presenter is not telling the truth.

It is useful to think of congruence as a state of harmony between conscious and unconscious communication. When we detect incongruence, what we can be aware of is a misalignment of conscious and unconscious intention.

For example:

- A salesperson presenting about a product that he does not fully understand

- A manager having to reprimand a member of staff over something he believes is actually OK

- Someone agreeing to a course of action that she does not believe is right

- Someone committing to a goal that he does not think he can really achieve

So a useful response to incongruence is to explore the unconscious intention that it represents.

You will recall that we filter our sensory information:

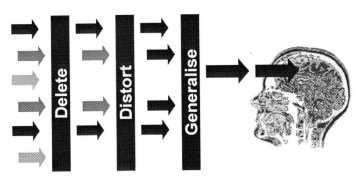

In some situations, we distort sensory information to turn incongruence into congruence, because that is what we expect. For example, when a sales manager asks a salesman if he is going to hit his target, and the sales man says, "yyyyesssss....I'll try", the sales manager might hear "Yes!" because that is what he needs to hear.

So in order to make the world meet our expectations, we sometimes distort sensory information in order to create the congruence or incongruence that verifies our expectations. As if things weren't complicated enough already!

So the moral of the story is to be aware of mental short cuts and look beyond the superficial level of communication to find the answers you need.

Language

Language is central to NLP – it's the L! Neuro-Linguistic Programming is a study of the brain's organisation of language and behaviour, so language is part of our behaviour and it also influences or even guides our behaviour.

Our entire mental map of the world is based on linguistic labels. From the moment we learn to talk, we want to know what things are called. When we learn a foreign language, we start by asking, "what is French for...?" Words are labels that represent our rich sensory experiences.

Our ability to encode the world using our linguistic labelling system is central to our society, our culture and our working lives. Language is the means by which we are able to communicate knowledge, enabling us to share information, solve problems and explore our surroundings. We can cure a disease and transfer that information to a doctor on the other side of the world, instantly. An explorer on the moon can describe what it's like for the viewers back home. You can tell the people you are close to how you feel about them.

We can include visual communication such as icons, graphical user interfaces and even semaphore in this too, as these are extensions or representations of linguistic labels or coding mechanisms.

In NLP, there are broadly two models of language – the Meta Model and the Milton Model.

Virginia Satir used to ask her clients very specific questions that forced them to accept or explore unconscious thoughts and beliefs. For example, when a wife would say that her husband didn't love her because he always worked late, Virginia would ask, "how do you know that working late means he doesn't love you?" Of course, from our distant perspective, we know it doesn't. You have probably had many experiences of basing a whole series of responses or behaviours on a single belief that later turned out to be misleading.

From people like Virginia Satir and Gregory Bateson, the Meta Model was created. Simply, we construct sentences which are grammatically correct yet which delete, distort or generalise information. For example, if I tell you that you shouldn't eat chocolate, it's bad for you,

you might believe me. If I tell you that you shouldn't trust young men then you might believe me too.

Are those beliefs useful? Is it more useful that you also know how I know that, so that you can decide for yourself? Parents infect their children with beliefs every day – some are useful, some are not. The Meta Model therefore allows you to explore and unpick beliefs, assumptions and rules that have simply dropped off the edge of your conscious attention and become accepted as facts.

Milton Erickson was a Hypnotherapist in Arizona. He can perhaps be credited as the person who made hypnotherapy acceptable in western medicine, using it in a wide range of situations and helping patients that other therapists had declared 'incurable'. Erickson was even able to help Cancer sufferers relieve their pain, simply by telling them stories. Milton Erickson suffered from polio in his early life and found himself able to spend many long hours paying attention to the effect that words had on people.

Milton Erickson's language was the opposite of the Meta Model – it was full of deletions, distortions and generalisations, designed to influence the listener in a certain way.

If you listen to any statement or speech prepared by a politician, you will hear a lot of Milton language. For example:

"People will understand that the solutions to these kinds of problems are to be found not in the past but in the future, and everyone will appreciate what a difficult task this can be. You can also be absolutely certain that the government you have now is in a far better position than any other to tackle these problems and to resolve them in a way that is economical, effective and respectful to the local community."

Does that sound familiar? Perhaps you remember hearing that before, about asylum seekers, or racial problems, or local policing policy? Actually, I just made it up.

Milton language is a vague framework within which the listener can place their own meaning. If someone tells you that you will be richer if you make a certain decision, you may or may not agree depending on whether money is important to you or not. If they say that you will enjoy even more of the things that are so important to you, you can only make sense of the sentence if you insert something of importance to you. The sentence, whilst sounding vague when we analyse it in this way, actually becomes totally unique and personal to each listener.

In this way, politicians, business leaders and storytellers can communicate directly with every listener or reader in a very personal way.

Let's explore these two language models in more detail.

Meta Model

The Meta Model is based on the basic rules of grammar. These are not specific to NLP, you'll find them in everything from books on transformational grammar to school books.

The Meta Model recovers information lost through our filtering process. We don't just filter sensory information coming in, we also filter information going out in the form of language. When working with a client, I'm not interested in what they say, what I'm more interested in is how they have converted their experiences and perceptions into language, as that gives me an understanding of how they perceive the world differently than I do. By understanding their mental map, I can work with them to change it more effectively.

Each of the following categories is a specific form of deletion, distortion or generalisation. Of course, real language contains all of those, so the Meta Model as covered in Practitioner training is a good way to train yourself to recognise the potential for missing information. You can then choose either to use the Meta Model to recover that information, or to do nothing. Possibly the worst aspect of the Meta Model is that people can use it excessively which is not helpful either to Practitioner or client.

Unspecified Nouns

Example: "I want a new job"

Response: "What new job?"

This is classed as a simple deletion, leaving out what the speaker wants to change. You might think that your natural inclination is to ask "What change?" anyway, yet in practice, people just accept the statement by inserting their own meaning.

For example, a wife might say, "I fancy a change" and the husband thinks it means a new hairstyle whereas the wife means a divorce. An extreme example? Perhaps, unless you can think of a situation like this in your own experience.

We process language and derive meaning within a frame of reference. For example, what is the opposite of black? What is the opposite of red? With no frame of reference it's harder to answer the question.

When a conversation is taking place within a particular context, or when you have a high degree of rapport, vague communication is processed as if it is specific. For example, my wife often asks me to pass her "the thing" as if I know what she is thinking. Often, I do – but not always – because sometimes our frames of reference are different.

Here are some more examples for you to practice with.

- I need it now
- Talk to the customer
- Get the problem fixed
- We need this done today
- Get me a sandwich
- I need a new car
- I read it in a magazine

Unspecified Verbs

Example: "She ignored me"

Response: "How exactly did she ignore you?"

As with the nouns, this is a simple deletion. We often accept that something has happened yet fail to find out how it happened. Conversely, we often have a problem with how things are done rather than what people do. "I don't mind being made redundant, it's the way they told me that upsets me".

As with the unspecified noun, we accept the validity of the action by interpreting the language within our own frame of reference. We need to check the action or behaviour in order to understand the speaker's frame of reference and recover the meaning that they intended.

Here are some more examples.

- He did it
- I calmed the customer down
- I've taken the heat out of the situation
- I've seen the writing on the wall
- He's running the department badly
- This company is going places
- I told him, now he should do it properly

Nominalisation

Example: "I want recognition"

Response: "How do you want to be recognised?"

A nominalisation is a verb that has been turned into a noun, indicating a 'stopped' mental process. Imagine yourself at a meeting, making a decision. Now imagine yourself meeting with people, deciding about something. Different? My guess is that in the first example, you imagined a still image whereas in the second example, you imagined a moving image.

When people are 'stuck' you will hear them using many nominalisations. One of the most useful things you can do to help them is to ask questions where the nominalisation is turned back into an active verb.

At other times, it's useful to turn a verb into a nominalisation in order to stop a mental process. If someone is talking about something that is emotionally distressing, stopping their verbs can stop them from having a strong emotional response. Another context for this would be to turn someone from an active deciding process into a stopped decision state – once they have reached the decision you want!

- We made a decision
- I have a bad feeling
- There's no relationship
- Our customers have no patience
- He makes a bad impression
- We need better management
- I want more direction
- Your work needs more attention
- We had a great meeting

Lack of Referential Index

This deletion misses out the source of the information. Without it, we could start to believe everything that other people tell us!

By testing the course of the information, we can start to distinguish beliefs that have been formed by personal experience from those that we learn second hand from other people.

Example: "They don't rate me"

Response: "Who says they don't rate you?"

- The writing's on the wall
- They should know better
- People make mistakes
- Those products are expensive
- This happens every day
- We shouldn't do that
- You must turn your mobile off in the office

Simple Deletion

Example: "I'm unhappy"

Response: "Unhappy about what?"

An even simpler deletion than the unspecified noun or verb, the simple deletion is also known as a 'sentence fragment' and is unusual in the Meta Model in that it's not grammatically correct. With the other examples, the fact that the grammar is complete and correct tends to make the listener accept what is said automatically. At least the simple deletion alerts most people to its presence by providing insufficient information to the listener.

We tend to process simple deletions by filling in whatever is necessary to complete the grammatical structure. When you are strongly in rapport with someone, you can almost finish each other's sentences. We finish each other's sentences anyway, and with simple deletions that means we sometimes insert meaning which was not intended by the speaker.

- You can't
- We can manage
- I know
- I just can't start
- It's perfect
- It's all wrong
- I don't want to

Comparative Deletions

Example: "Our new product is more effective"

Response: "More effective than what?"

Response: "More effective than when?"

With a comparative deletion, the speaker is creating a statement based on an implicit comparison criteria. The criteria itself is implied, and so the listener learns the 'rule' by absorbing the language. Often, the object of the comparison is missing too, so the listener learns to equate 'better' with 'best'.

Challenging comparative deletions is useful, not because it's important what is 'best' but because we can learn a great deal about the speaker's perceptions and criteria.

- This is far more efficient
- Everything is better now
- She's much brighter
- This is more like it
- She's more fun
- Blue is better
- He's more tolerant

Complex equivalence

Example: "He's silent.....He doesn't like what I've done"

Response: "How do know that him being silent means that he doesn't like what you've done?"

This is a very interesting generalisation. The speaker takes two complex, unrelated concepts and holds them as equivalent. The, if one is true then the other must logically become true. If I equate my personal worth with promotion, and I miss out on a promotion then I feel worthless. If I equate love with being listened to and someone doesn't appear to be listening to me then they don't love me.

The complex equivalence and the cause and effect are the basis of how we generalise rules about the physical world and are vital for our survival. In the case of the complex equivalence, rules such as "red sky at night, shepherd's delight" would have been critical to our survival as a species. The same rule generating program now creates rules such as "Boss's door is closed, he is in a bad mood" which may not be useful.

- A good relationship means never having to say sorry
- If I stay in this job I have to work harder
- You can't have a well paid job that is enjoyable too
- You can't trust sales people
- Marketing is an easy job
- If you want success you have to give up your home life
- If I do that I'll get into trouble

Lost performance

This is quite similar to the lack of referential index. In this case, what we need to recover is the person doing the thing in question – the person performing the action.

We often take the response or behaviour of one person and generalise it to apply to all people. You'll hear sales people say, "Customers don't like this product" when what they really mean is, "I couldn't sell this product to one customer".

Once again, some universal rules are useful. If one person can be successful, anyone can, so a belief such as "people can be successful" could be useful, whereas a belief such as "people always fail" might have less desirable results.

Example: "Things never get done here"

Response: "Who doesn't do things?"

- People make mistakes
- They should have seen it coming
- They're always doing that
- This report needs finishing
- A meeting was held
- Mistakes have been made
- Nobody is pulling their weight
- Customers won't buy this
- Sales people are pushy

Mind reading

Example: "You don't rate me"

Response: "How do know that I don't rate you?"

Response: "What leads you to believe that?"

Response: "What makes you think that?"

I know what you're thinking…you never mind read. With a mind read, we act as if we know what someone else is thinking. Of course, you may be right so the point is that you do not know for certain and it may not be useful to respond as if you do.

With a mind read, you might do something, or not do something, because you know how someone would react. You may know that person very well, but the only way to know what they are thinking is to ask them.

- I know you don't believe me
- He doesn't want to help me
- You just don't care
- My boss thinks I'm lazy
- He'll hate you if you do that
- The boss is in a foul mood today
- Mary's really happy now

Cause and effect

Example: "He makes me cringe just by speaking"

Response: "How does he make you cringe?"

Response: "How do you make yourself cringe when he speaks?"

Very similar to the complex equivalence, the cause and effect has the result that if an event takes place then another, unrelated event must also take place. If I know that, when the boss has his door shut it's going to be a bad day and I see the boss's door shut, I will notice opportunities to make it a bad day.

The cause and effect implies a relationship in time, so that when one event takes place, another will automatically follow. This is useful in the physical world, so that if I step off a cliff, I will at some point in the future hit the ground with a 'splat'.

When we apply the cause and effect rule to people, we often get into problems because people do not follow the same physical rules as inanimate objects.

- My boss makes me angry
- If you do that I'll leave
- We can't do that because it won't work
- If I do the presentation it will go badly
- There's no point trying, he won't listen to me
- I won't apply because they'll never give me the job
- Things always go wrong when she walks in here

Presuppositions

Example: "I'll do that after I win this contract"

Response: "How do you know you'll win that contract?"

Presuppositions are the components of the sentence which must be held true in order for the sentence to be grammatically correct. The presupposition works at the unconscious level at which your brain parses language, ready to be decoded and translated into meaning, therefore a presupposition is accepted as true even before you consciously understand what has been said.

When we process language, we process all meanings and hold them temporarily until one stands out by fitting the context of the information. Therefore, presuppositions are a very powerful influence tool.

- When this plan fails I'll say 'told you so'
- It will be easier when he leaves
- What will the next reorganisation bring?
- When are you leaving?
- Who are you going to fire next?
- You'll enjoy it once you do it
- Once you make a start you'll find it easy

Universal Quantifiers

Example: "He never listens to me"

Response: "Never?"

Response: "Was there ever a time when he did?"

A type of generalisation, the universal quantifier takes a single example and makes it apply to all cases or at all times.

Think of someone who says, "I always fail". There are two problems here; firstly, the person is only noticing times in the past when they failed and is filtering out times when they succeeded, because success would disprove the rule and would therefore mean that the speaker is wrong – and people don't like being wrong! The second problem is that 'always' means every time in the past and every time in the future, so by saying, "I always fail", the person is setting their perceptual filters to notice failure in the future, and they are then generating behaviour that is likely to lead to failure.

In short, by creating a universal rule, the person will create a self fulfilling prophecy. This is a very useful ability if you apply it to a belief like "I am always successful".

- Nobody likes me
- It's always the honest people who lose out
- Nothing's the same anymore
- Nothing works here
- Everybody's talking about it
- We all need to do this
- All our competitors are doing this

Modal Operator of Necessity

Example: "I have to take care of her"

Response: "What happens if you don't?"

Modal operators modify the verb and are often an indication that the speaker is basing their behaviour or thoughts on rules – beliefs about their behaviour.

The important question to explore here is "how did they learn those rules?"

People are very good at learning rules and will continue to follow them – or break them – long after the need for the rule has gone away.

- We shouldn't do that
- You have to get a good appraisal
- You must arrive on time
- You've got to laugh
- You should always be dressed smartly
- You must get that work done to day
- You can't leave yet

Model Operator of Possibility

Example: "I can't tell the truth"

Response: "What would happen if you did?"

Response: "What stops you?"

Response: "How do you stop yourself?"

Where the modal operator of necessity indicated the presence of a rule, this language pattern indicates the presence of a choice.

"I can't tell the truth" indicates that the speaker has imagined telling the truth, imagined something undesirable happening and has chosen to not tell the truth.

Often, the modal operator of possibility indicates that the speaker imagines something bad happening in the future and takes avoiding action now. If you are running towards a physical brick wall, that's a very useful ability. If the barrier has only been placed there by your imagination, it's not as useful.

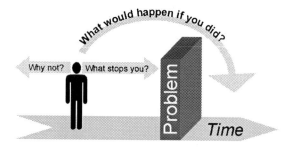

- □ I can't ring that customer
- □ I won't be able to complete that on time
- □ I can't apply for that job
- □ I can't finish that report on time
- □ I can't imagine that
- □ I can't tell him that
- □ I'll never to able to learn this

Milton Model

The Milton Model is also based on our fundamental grammatical rules but instead of using them to recover lost information, it uses them to lose information, allowing the listener to add their own experience or expectations in order to create meaning.

Using Milton language enables you to communicate in a very personal way to a diverse audience, and it is also the language used by mind readers, hypnotists and politicians.

Mind reading	You might think… You know… I know what you're thinking…
Complex equivalence	This **is** the life, hard work **is** the only way, that man **is** a nightmare
Presupposition	When are you leaving? When do you want to sign the contract? How many more times do I have to tell you?
Universal quantifiers	**All** salespeople are honest He **never** listens to me
Tag questions	This is the right thing for you to do, **isn't it?** Aren't they? Won't we? Is it not? Could it?
Lost referential index	Whilst **it's** true that….. **They** say that……
Double bind	Will you decide now **or** later…….?
Negative	I'm **not** going to tell you that….. I'm **not** being funny but…..
Modal operators	Should, ought, must, got to, have to, need to, will, want to…
Ambiguities	Annoys/a noise… see/sea… write/right… hi/high… wait/weight

When I worked in a large British telecommunications company, a colleague of mine was assigned a mentor as part of a HR mentoring initiative. In the period of time he was supposed to work with her, he never actually got to meet her once and therefore felt very frustrated when he read an interview with her in the internal magazine, espousing the virtues of the mentoring program.

He told me that the quote from her said how wonderful mentoring was, and how important a mentor had been to her, which made her hypocritical as she had never made the time to meet with him. I asked him to read the quote, and this is what it said:

"I cannot put into words the impact that having a mentor has had on my career. Certainly, if I had not had a mentor, I would be in a very different place today"

He repeated his assertion that this proved her guilt, and I asked him to read it again and tell me what it *really* said. As he read it a couple more times, the penny dropped. "It says absolutely nothing at all!" he exclaimed.

It was a perfect example of Milton Model language in action.

Modal operators

You saw modal operators in the Meta Model, and we can explore them in some more detail as they are a vital component of language for anyone interested in motivation.

A state has its own vocabulary. The words you use, your voice tone and the things you talk about are influenced by, and can influence, your state. Words themselves can be used as very powerful anchors.

When our thoughts become action easily, we are in a motivated state. Sometimes, we allow our thoughts to dissipate and fade away without translating into behaviour, or we think about something that we know we have to do, but we don't want to do it, such as cleaning the house.

Think about something that you do easily – something that you can always find time for or that you only have to think about in order to do it. What do you say to yourself as you think about it? You might use words like:

- Can
- Will
- Want
- Am
- Now

Now think about something that you're really good at almost getting round to. Something that is your job, or that needs doing, but you really don't want to do it so you always find a way to avoid it. What do you say to yourself as you think about it? You might use words like:

- Ought
- Should
- Must
- Need
- In a minute

Do you notice a pattern here? And is it possible to swap the words we use round in order to change the states? You bet!

Take something that you need to do, such as some admin work. Pay attention to how you talk to yourself about it. If, for example, you say, "I really ought to do that today" then actively change the words. Say out loud, "I am going to do that today".

Of course, you haven't done it yet, it is in the future and is therefore still an uncertainty. We can make the language even more powerful by shifting it into the past:

"By the end of the day I will have done that"

Now we have the problem that, "the end of the day" is not very specific. Which day? And when exactly does it end? We can go one better:

"By the time I walk out of the door to go home today, I will have done that"

There's no stopping us! We can still make the language even more powerful:

Stand up. Look up. Take a deep breath. Smile. Think about something you really love doing and really enjoy. Now say in a confident, musical voice:

"By the time I walk out of the door to go home today, I will have done that"

But be careful with this – you'll find yourself whizzing through all your outstanding chores like a whirlwind. We need to even the balance up.

Take something that you always end up doing, even though you think someone else should do it.

Sit down. Look down. Think about something you really hate doing. Now say in a nervous, flat voice:

"I really ought to do that soon"

I know what you're thinking... "If I can use this to manage my own state of motivation, could I use it with other people?" You are definitely getting the hang of this!

Listen carefully to the words that someone uses when they talk about something they really enjoy doing. Then make sure you use those exact words back to them when you talk about what you want them to do.

For example, when someone talks about something they had to finish off at work they might say, "I kept telling myself that I really should do it, I finally ran out of time and had to finish it off before coming here tonight". When they talk about going shopping at the weekend they might say, "so I said to myself ooh! I've just got time to pop into town". Now you have everything you need.

"You should stay at home instead of going to the gym, but you might get home and think 'ooh! I've just got time to pop down to the gym', and imagine how great you'll feel for having done that!"

You have also heard from them that they are motivated to take action by the pressure of a deadline, and they take action when the bad feeling of doing the work outweighs the good feeling of avoiding it.

When you get to the Time chapter, you'll find a useful version of the timeline technique that allows you to use this type of motivation productively.

The most important thing, as always, is to notice the words the other person uses, and use their words. Yours might make sense to them, or they might have the opposite effect. For example, 'need' motivates some people and stops others because it implies rules, so always pay attention to the person you want to develop a relationship with.

Trance

For many people, hypnosis and trance summon up images of swinging watches, covert influence and people doing things against their wills.

Pick up any serious book on hypnosis, or go to any serious hypnotherapy course, and you'll learn that there are many myths surrounding hypnosis and trance which are based on fear rather than reality. Here are a few ideas about hypnosis that you may wish to confirm for yourself.

Anyone can be hypnotised. People who think quickly tend not to respond to the slow paced, traditional trance induction as they get bored half way through. They respond better to fast inductions using pattern interrupts and suggestions. I can say that anyone can be hypnotised because everyone spends some time in a trance, every day.

It's even possible to say that we live in a trance, all the time. Very few people spend any significant time in total sensory 'uptime' - a state of total focus on the outside world. Typically, our days comprise both attention to the outside world and the daydreaming, thinking and remembering that are all trance states. Essentially, a trance state is where one or more of your senses are directed inwards. Every time you remember a telephone number, think about what happened yesterday or worry, your senses are directed inwards and you partially disconnect from the outside world. A deep trance is where all of your senses are directed inwards, although even in a deep hypnotic trance you will still hear the hypnotist's voice or a fire alarm.

If you think of a trance state as being a state of heightened focus of attention, then any time where you lose contact with the outside world as a result of intense concentration is a trance state. Being lost in a good book (like this one!) or daydreaming whilst driving are two common examples.

The magicians and witches of the middle ages were probably hypnotists. Magical spells and enchantments were most likely trances, exaggerated by fear and mass hysteria. In a modern world where dragons and unicorns are not as popular as they once were, the reality of hypnosis is much different, although the fears and doubts are much the same for some people.

So, the use of trance is natural and ethical, but not in a business context, right? Well, not quite. Remember that we move in and out of trance states naturally throughout the day, and that these states naturally coincide with other people's attempts to influence you. If you've ever agreed to something without being sure of what you agreed to, or if you've ever found yourself doing something familiar automatically then you've probably experienced a trance state at work.

Many people say that the presentation slot after lunch is the worst one to get because people don't pay attention. If you want to gain agreement to an idea, then this is the best slot to get! Some people plan their presentations so that the boring bit comes after lunch - in fact, that's when you should be closing the deal!

If you're in the middle of something that you're concentrating on and someone interrupts you, you may experience a moment of confusion. This is known as a 'pattern interrupt' because a mental pattern or program has been interrupted. Now, think about what you do when you interrupt someone to ask for something - do you ask first, or do you make small talk first? If you're interrupting someone to ask for something, get your request in early. Even better, make the request a question, adjusting your voice tone to make it an instruction.

"Can you sign my expenses?" gives the listener choice

"Sign my expenses" is perhaps a bit too direct

"Sign my expenses for me?" could work well

"Here are my expenses for you to sign" is an implied command

"Can you have a look at this report after you have signed my expenses?" is quite sneaky – it's a presupposition

Try it - and find out for yourself.

So, is this ethical? Well, you do it anyway, so you might as well do it consciously and purposefully so that you can be sure you're doing it ethically. You currently do this without thinking, so who knows what you get up to? In my mind, it's better to do this with a specific purpose or outcome in mind rather than to do it accidentally and achieve random results.

Right now, you probably daydream whilst driving and worry if you go through a red light. Just imagine - if you were to daydream during a meeting, you might find yourself influencing people in all kinds of ways to reflect your current state of mind rather than the one you want to portray. You might take an advanced driving course to refine your skills behind the wheel, so you could think of NLP as an advanced thinking course to put you more in control of the way you interact with other people.

By watching what happens when people naturally move in and out of different states of mind, observers have build up a repertoire of behavioural and linguistic patterns which tend to move people towards the state of inward focus which we associate with hypnosis.

If you ask one of your colleagues or customers a really good question and they go quiet for a period of time while they think carefully, you have induced a trance state. Their focus of attention is directed inwards, so they're not listening to you. We all get lost in our own thoughts, and an external guide can often help you to use these mental processes very effectively. The common name for such a guide is a hypnotist.

For you to use these tools ethically and professionally, it's important for you to understand the kinds of patterns that we're talking about, and that's why I'm going to share them with you. You'll recognise all kinds of patterns here that you use everyday, so this will help you to refine the skills you already have.

Cycling representational systems

If you rotate your focus of attention through your senses, you will find that your attention will become directed inwards. So, you can see these words, hear some sounds, feel the temperature of the air, see your hands, hear noises in the distance, feel the weight of your feet, see the colour of the paper, hear the words, feel that feeling inside and so on.

With corporate visioning being so popular, it's not uncommon to hear managers ask what people will see, hear and feel when they achieve a certain objective. You can imagine how easily you can build this pattern into a presentation or business report.

Awareness pattern

This pattern cycles your awareness from outside, to inside, to outside, and so on. Suggestions relating to states work very well with this pattern, so it's a good way to become more focused, energised or relaxed. Point out three things that are in your audience's direct sensory awareness, make a suggestion and then ask where their attention is focussed. Here's how it goes:

You can see the paper, you can hear the words, you can feel the weight of the book, you can realise how pleased you are that you bought it. What are you aware of now?

Personally, I think this is the most commonly used pattern in business today. Does this kind of presentation slide look familiar to you?

- It's been a tough year

- Profits have been hit

- We've all had to make sacrifices

- Your targets are increasing this year

And before you know it, you find yourself nodding to whatever change is being proposed. As Dale Carnegie said, "Get the other person saying yes immediately".

Pattern interrupt

Whenever you do something automatically, you are running a behavioural program that enables you to complete complex tasks without having to devote too much conscious brain power. Whenever you are lost in a pattern and someone or something interrupts you, your brain is stuck for a moment, unsure of how to complete the program. At this moment, you are open to suggestion. How many times have you been in the middle of something, or lost in a daydream, when a colleague has asked you a question and you've found yourself complying as if it were a command? Maybe you've also found yourself feeling bad that they made you do a certain thing, only to find that they have no memory of asking you to do it, merely that they mentioned it to you?

My wife does this all the time when I'm driving. She'll wait until I'm at a junction, concentrating on the traffic, and then she'll say, "I thought we were going to go the other way?" Before I know it, I've changed direction and she's now demanding to know why we're going the other way!

So, no-one's immune to pattern interrupts because we would be unable to function without our behavioural patterns. When your PC gets interrupted, it crashes, so just be grateful that it only takes your brain half a second to reboot and continue. Imagine what it would be like if you had to run the disk repair program every time someone interrupted you, or you went to sleep without finishing what you were doing!

Hypnosis scripts

There are many sources on the Internet of good scripts that you can use in hypnosis. Here's one that you can use for general relaxation, and to deliver a specific suggestion.

Before you see the script, a word on suggestions. Firstly, the suggestion must conform to the criteria used for Well Formed Outcomes, in that it must be stated positively and have no unwanted side effects. So, a suggestion that someone will give up smoking is very badly formed and will not have any effect. On the other hand, a suggestion such as "you will surprise yourself with how easily you forget to smoke" is much better, because it is well formed, and also because it's phrased indirectly.

A suggestion such as "you will be more confident" can be quite jarring, especially if the person believes they lack confidence. Rather than accepting the suggestion, they will reject it. A better way to phrase this would be to choose a specific example when the person would like more confidence, for example "you can find yourself breathing more confidently". You see the subtle difference? You're taking the emphasis off the suggestion, so that the person can integrate it more easily rather than questioning it. If you think back to the Milton and Meta Models, you're embedding the suggestion within a presupposition.

Now, it's old chestnut time. Does this mean that you can command people to do things against their will? Opinion is divided on this, and I stress the word opinion. In my experience, a state of hypnosis is just a state. It does not render the person vulnerable to instructions, nor place them at your mercy. As you will find out for yourself if you try this script, the person in the trance feels alert and awake the whole time, yet very relaxed and at ease. If anything interrupts them such as an unwelcome suggestion or a feeling of unease, they will open their eyes and be fully attentive. Whether people are in a trance or not, they can still tell what's good for them.

You move into suggestible states naturally throughout the day. Imagine a time when you're daydreaming and someone asks you a question. Often, you answer before you even heard the question and you wonder what you just agreed to!

Now for the script. Before you start to read this, prepare a suggestion and write it down so that you can weave it into the script seamlessly. Your voice tone, pitch and rate of speech are probably more important than the words, so that's something you can practice and play with.

"In this exercise you must be happy to learn about how to develop your relaxation skills and follow instructions exactly as asked – Neither taking too long to follow instructions nor anticipating what will be asked.

Now take a long deep breath and hold it for a few seconds. As you exhale this breath, allow your eyes to close, and let go of the surface tension in your body. Just let your body relax as much as possible right now.

Now place your awareness on your eye muscles and relax the muscles around your eyes to the point they just won't work. When you're sure they're so relaxed that, as long as you hold on to this relaxation they just won't work, hold on to that relaxation and test them to make sure THEY WON'T WORK.

Now, this relaxation you have in your eyes is the same quality of relaxation that I want you to have throughout your whole body. So, just let this quality of relaxation flow through your whole body from the top of your head, to the tip of your toes.

Now we can deepen this relaxation much more. In a moment I'm going to have you open and close your eyes. When you close your eyes that's your signal to let this feeling of relaxation become 10 times deeper. All you have to do is want this to happen and you can make it happen very easily. OK, now, open your eyes…now close your eyes and feel that relaxation flowing through your whole body, taking you much, much deeper. Use your wonderful imagination and imagine your whole body is covered and warmed up in a warm blanket of relaxation.

Now, let every muscle in your body become so relaxed that as long as you hold on to this quality of relaxation, every muscle in your body is totally relaxed.

In a moment I'm going to have you open and close your eyes one more time. Again when you close your eyes, double the relaxation you now have. Make it become twice as deep. OK, now once more open your eyes. …And close your eyes …and double your relaxation…good. Let every muscle in your body hold on to this quality of relaxation.

In a moment I'm going to lift your right (or left) hand by the wrist, just a few inches and drop it. If you have followed my instructions up to this point, that hand will be so relaxed it will be just as loose and limp as a damp dish cloth, and will simply plop down.

Now don't try to help me. Let me do all the lifting so that when I release it, it just plops down and you allow yourself to go deeper still.

[Gently lift their hand by the wrist and drop it onto their leg]

Take a long, deep breath as you let yourself go deeper still.

Now relax the muscles around your eyes to the point where they won't work... and pretend you can't open them even though you know full well that you can. As long as you hold on to this relaxation, you can pretend that they just won't work. When you're sure they're so relaxed that they just won't work, continue to pretend that they won't work and test them to make sure THEY WON'T WORK. Test them hard ......that's right.

We want your mind to be as relaxed as your body is, so I want you to start counting from 100 backwards when I tell you to. Each time you say a number, double your mental relaxation. With each number you say, let your mind become twice as relaxed. By the time the numbers get down to 98, you'll be so relaxed the numbers won't be there.

Now, you have to do this, I can't do it for you. Those numbers will leave if you will them away.

Now say out loud, the first number and double your mental relaxation. Say 100.

Now double that mental relaxation, say 99,..........now double that mental relaxation, let those numbers already start to fade. They'll go if you will them to. Say 98.

Deeper relaxed, now they'll be gone. Dispel them. Banish them. Make it happen, you can do it; I can't do it for you. Put them out, make it happen! Are they all gone?

Now really enjoy the skills and relaxation until I say something important to you, which I want you to take in at an even deeper level, easily and honestly if it's what you need.

[insert suggestion]

Now come back to this room when I've counted from 3 up to 1 and you've realised that you've learnt something important to you.

3...2...1"

I know people who use this regularly to help their partners fall asleep more easily. Some people even record it onto tape and play it to themselves to help them relax..

Whatever you choose to do with it, it demonstrates the immense power that you have with your voice and with the words you choose.

Self hypnosis CDs

A lot of people ask me, "Do self hypnosis CDs work?" as in will they help you to give up smoking or lose weight?

As you may have discovered by now – particularly if you have tried out these trance induction ideas with a friend – hypnosis is a dance, an interactive communication process. Hypnosis is not something that one person does to another – both must be engaged in the process for it to work.

Even the best designed CD cannot know when you close your eyes or breath out, therefore whilst the CD may have some very well crafted words, it cannot achieve the same results as a human being.

However, I do think that these CDs can work, but for a different reason. If you take half an hour out of your busy day to sit in a quiet place and think about something that is important to you, that is very powerful in itself. If you need a CD to give yourself a reason to take time out then that's as good a reason as any. Half an hour is probably more than most people spend in a month thinking about what is important to them.

Time

Our subjective perception of time is a very powerful and valuable resource that can be used to create change or to plan effectively.

When we talk about time, we use words that also apply to space – we say things like:

- Put it behind you
- Your future is all ahead of you
- Let's look ahead
- It's a long way off yet, we don't need to worry about it
- Don't look back
- I feel like it's on top of me
- I can see a time when this will be different

As you might expect by now, these kinds of words can be taken literally. If someone says that they have put an experience behind them, it's literally what they have done.

The way in which we interact with time also causes a few problems, in particular:

- We imagine future problems and act as if they are real now
- We relive a past problem as if it is still happening now

Rationally, you know that those reactions are unhelpful. You know that if something hasn't happened yet, you can choose or at least influence the way it turns out. You also know that if something has already happened, there's nothing you can do to change it. Of course, people do get stuck in patterns of behaviour that we can get them out of.

There's a whole branch of NLP called Time Line Therapy, in which a person's subjective perception of time can be used to make significant personal changes. You've probably noticed that all of these tools started out as therapeutic techniques, which means that there's not a lot of information around on how to apply the techniques in business.

The good news, as usual, is that you already use the principles of timeline, each and every day.

Essentially, you can use past timelines to change a person's perceptions of past events, or future timelines to plan more effectively for the future.

As with the rest of NLP, timelines haven't been invented, they're just patterns that people like you and I already use. We already have an internal representation of the flow of time that we interact with, and we already have both individual and generalised ways of interacting with time. Most people imagine their future being in front of them and their past behind them. If you ask someone to imagine a line that connects past, present and future, they will be able to point to it, even though they had never consciously considered it before. Think of a timeline as a graphical user interface for time, just like your PC's operating software. If you look inside your PC, you won't really find folders and notepaper in there. The interface is just designed that way so that it's easier to use.

Where do you imagine the future and past to be? As I said, many people imagine that the future is in front of them, and the past is behind them. Consequently, your parents tell you that you have your whole life ahead of you, and friends tell you that particular experiences are all behind them. They might even say, "it's all in the past now" as they point behind them, or wave over their shoulders. This is all extremely valuable information, as you are no doubt becoming aware.

My future is to my right and my past is to my left – I see all time laid out in front of me like a map. Everyone is subtly different, and it can be very powerful to explore those subtle differences. For our purposes, it's useful to work with the 'typical' model as everyone seems to have an understanding of it, even though it may differ from their own experience. The timeline concept in NLP is based on the exploration of a person's sense of time as a means of changing the impact of past events or planning effectively for future events. Here are a few exercises that you can use yourself in exploring timelines.

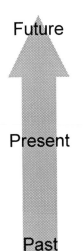

Future

Present

Past

Imagine a line on the floor that represents time, with the future in front of you, and the past behind you. The point where you are standing is 'now'.

Think about something you want to achieve and notice where it lies on the line – how far into the future it lies. It might be something quite ambitious, so you would like to achieve it but don't yet know how to, or how difficult it might be.

Walk forwards until just before the goal. Notice how that feels. Now step onto the goal itself, and notice how that feels. Finally, talk one more step so that the goal is completely achieved and notice how that feels.

Turn round and look back to the present moment, noticing all the milestones you passed on the way. Walk back to the present, taking with you everything useful you learned on the way so that the experience and knowledge can help you in the present.

When you get back to 'now', look towards the goal again. Has anything changed? Is it in the same place?

Of course, you didn't *really* travel through time, your brain just thinks you did. If you're keeping up with all this, you'll know by now that this is the same thing, in terms of your sensory experience. And what else do you have to go on? As Groucho Marx said, "Who are you going to believe? Me or your own eyes?".

This is a very powerful technique for unlocking potential and exploring future possibilities. Here are a few more ways that you can use this technique.

Overcoming obstacles

There is something you want to achieve, and you know that there are many obstacles or barriers to overcome. Use the basic technique, stopping briefly as you get to each barrier before you step over it. When you reach the goal, turn round and look back through the obstacles you overcame or problems you solved. As you walk backwards through each barrier, be aware of anything you learn or notice.

Exploring decisions

There is a decision to be made, but you find it difficult to make because it has long term implications. Imagine you are standing at the branch point of a number of timelines – one for each choice. Explore each one, going way past the decision point and experiencing the long term implications of that choice before returning to the branch point. Pay attention to any intuitive feelings you get whilst doing this. When you have explored all of the choices, take one step back and look at the time lines. Some may have disappeared, some may have moved. There's a good chance that one will be in the centre, or will be prominent in some way.

The Undo button

There is a decision you made in the past that you're not happy with. Turn round and face the past, looking back to that decision and noticing everything that has happened since then. Walk slowly back to the decision point, collecting up and taking with you everything that you have learned since then. When you reach the decision point, take one more step. Turn and face the future. With all of the experience you have brought back with you, what decision will you make? Move forward to the present, exploring the consequences of that decision. You might find that you still make the same decision!

Motivation

There is something you want to do in the future which involves work or effort now. It's difficult to get motivated now for something that isn't pressing, but you know that if you don't put the work in, you will regret it. For example, going to the gym now to be fit for your holiday, or working hard now to pass an exam in the future.

This is a slightly more complex version, so keep up!

Start with the basic time line procedure. Picture, in the future, your goal in the way that you would achieve it if you put the effort in now. Walk up to the goal and stop just beyond it. Enjoy the feeling of having achieved that in the way that you wanted to. Return to the present.

Next, picture yourself in the future when you haven't put the effort in – perhaps at the exam without having revised, at the presentation without having prepared or whatever. Walk forwards. There's a good chance you will feel resistance, and a feeling of impending doom as you walk forwards. This is good, use it. Stop at the goal and take plenty of time to fully experience your sense of disappointment in yourself. Really regret not having made the effort! Now, grab hold of this feeling as you walk back to the present and stretch that awful feeling of regret all the way back to the present so that you can experience it now in relation to your daily planning and time management. Ultimately, you have to make time for good preparation. Until now, there were more pressing demands on your time, and you wouldn't really devote much time and energy to this until it was too late. Well, this exercise makes it too late now!

Finally, imagine yourself in the present, making the time and effort to prepare well. Walk forward slowly, thinking about your daily and weekly routine and finding time to do the work you need to do. Continue doing this all the way up to the goal and notice how good it feels – both to have achieved the goal and to know that you made the effort and commitment necessary. Take this feeling and stretch it back to the present, pulling back that good motivating feeling and bringing it back with you so that you have it now.

What if?

There is a scenario that you would like to explore, tentatively. Use the basic time line procedure, but this time, do not bring the learning and experience back with you – leave it in the future as you explore each possibility. Step off the timeline as you walk back to the present.

Walk along different timelines to explore all the options you have before deciding, in the present, which is the best long term option.

So, how do timelines correlate to behaviour?

Here are a few examples, and when you've read through them, consider the relationship between your own timeline and behaviour.

Timeline	Behaviour
Future to the front, past behind.	Motivated by deadlines, long term planning tends to be obscured by short term needs. The past is gone and lessons from past experiences are not learned easily.
Future to the right, past to the left.	Deadlines have no strong meaning, the location of 'now' is relative. Good at connecting events that span long periods of time or planning long term projects.
Future to the front, past to the side.	Responds well to deadlines, learns from past experiences.

Those were easy. Here are some more examples taken from real people - see if you can spot the correlations.

Timeline	Behaviour
Future to the front, past inside.	Good at planning to deadlines but unable to recover specific detail from memories. Envious of people who had clear visual recall of past events.
Future to the right, past to the left with the line passing behind head where it splits in two. Images are on a branch that comes round to the front, sounds continue behind.	Easy going regarding deadlines. Envious of people who can recall conversations, could recall images easily but no sounds.

Future to the front, 'now' is in a large black ball off to one side	Works well with long term goals but has a great deal of difficulty focussing on current tasks and is easily distracted.
No future, past behind.	Highly responsive to the current situation, lives 'in the moment'. Doesn't easily learn from past mistakes. No plans for the future.
Future way off in the distance, present out in front, past begins in front and passes through body	No sense of urgency! Goals more than 24 hours away are so far that they're not important, and as soon as a goal gets close enough to worry about, it's already in the past and might as well be ignored as it's too late to do anything about it.

It's not useful to look at timelines and say, "the person behaves a certain way because of their timeline". Instead, think of the timeline as a graphical representation of their subjective sense of time, just as your computer screen is a graphical representation of the digital information stored on your computer's hard disc.

On your computer, when you drag an image of a file on the screen, the information on the hard disc changes accordingly. Similarly, when something changes on the hard disc, the image changes.

This turns out to be a very useful metaphor for the timeline, because we can manipulate a timeline and bring about instant changes in a person's sense of time.

As we do not have a direct sense of time, we perceive the passage of time through our other senses. When we change the image of the timeline, we are changing our perception of time, so by directly manipulating a person's timeline, you can change their response to time related events such as deadlines and goals.

Modelling

Modelling is a very important part of NLP. It is the basis for all of the techniques, because they were modelled from the minds of people who were very good at helping other people to change. Therefore, the techniques are not NLP in themselves – they are the results of NLP.

I mentioned this right at the start of the book and it's so important I'll say it again. I'm also very pleased with my art metaphor, so I'm looking for an excuse to tell you about it again.

Many people confuse NLP with its techniques – including many trainers I've seen. People who confuse NLP with its tools and techniques reduce NLP down to eye accessing and body language (which it isn't) and when they see NLP in action they say, "oh, that's just NLP". NLP is everything or nothing, depending on how you look at it, because NLP is the spirit of modelling excellence.

I've heard lots of people say, "I know NLP" because they've read a book and they think they understand the techniques. I've even heard HR managers in companies say, "Oh, we did NLP last year".

NLP is the process of developing evolving models of excellence. Can you honestly say you have reached a point where you can stop developing excellence in your business?

It's a bit like saying that art is just paintbrushes, or architecture is just bricks. The tools you will learn on a course, or read about in a book, are the results of NLP – they do not define NLP itself. A good NLP Practitioner will go on to model excellence in other people and create new tools in new situations. Someone who has not embraced this spirit of modelling excellence will use the tools in a prescriptive, inflexible way and – guess what? – sometimes they will work and sometimes they wont. People with the flexibility to model excellence and create new tools just keep on going until the problem is solved, and usually it doesn't look like they're doing anything at all.

In order to understand and apply NLP effectively, you really do need to understand the concept of modelling. People who just take NLP as its techniques find that those techniques work some of the time. By modelling the problem first, you'll find that the techniques work first time, every time.

If we take the fast phobia cure as an example, if you use it with ten people who have a phobia, you might find it works with half of them. This doesn't mean that the technique is only effective 50% of the time – it means that half of the people you used it with did not have a phobia. A common example is 'fear of flying'. I'll go out on a limb here and say that no-one is afraid of flying. Not a single person in the whole world is afraid of flying. There are, however, a lot of people who are afraid of crashing. There is no point doing a fast phobia cure on something like this because it is not a phobic response. A fear of crashing takes a great deal of imagination, and so the first step is to find out how the problem works by modelling it so that you can choose or create an appropriate technique.

In the world of electronics, there are good engineers and there are average engineers. The average engineers will fix a problem by replacing all the components until they find the one that was causing the problem. A good engineer will locate the problem first before changing the faulty component.

Good engineers observe behaviour closely. They know how a piece of equipment behaves when it is working normally, so they know where to start looking when it does not behave normally. Average engineers do not observe behaviour in the same way.

When I was an engineer, I learned to observe behaviour, because it was the only way to fix complex problems. If you don't know what the equipment does when it's working properly, how can you know what is wrong with it when it isn't working properly?

I find that this simple diagnostic approach is what is missing for the majority of therapists, consultants and coaches.

Psychologists study mental illnesses so that they can learn more about them. Unless you also study people without the illnesses, that information is useless. Schizophrenics, for example, can't tell the difference between what is real and what is imagined (whatever reality is). Unless we figure out how average people can tell the difference, we can't help the schizophrenics.

Far too many coaches are being taught prescriptive, off the shelf processes which do not benefit clients, because the client is not in the exact situation that the coaching tools were designed for.

If you want to improve the performance of a sales team, it's no use focusing on the under-performers. We need to figure out what the over-performers are doing first. NLP modelling is automatically systemic and ecological. By modelling a successful sales person, we can understand the mindset that works for that team, in that company, in that market, with those products and those customers. Therefore, by teaching that mindset to other sales people in the same team, we have an instantly workable process.

You are an expert. Anything that you can do really well without having to think about it is a talent. Maybe you've had the experience of watching someone do something amazing and asking them, "how did you do that?" to which they reply, "erm...I just did it. Doesn't everyone do it?"

Many people assume that this means the behavioural knowledge required to perform a complex task is locked away and is irretrievable. We get a glimpse of the knowledge through observing behaviour, but there is no way to extract the knowledge itself. Other people went on to guess at the behavioural programming, based on their observations. They made one key mistake - they tried to guess 'why' the individual behaved that way instead of asking 'how'. 'Why' is irrelevant. If I want to copy your talent for writing music, or sticking to a diet, or remember people's names at a party, I don't need to know why you do it. I just need to know how, so I can learn to do it.

Traditional 'body language' is an example of this, where a particular movement 'means' something specific such as arrogance or fear. Body movement is not a language in itself, it's a component of communication. The effects of 'body language' training are still with us today, lingering on in presentation skills courses that teach people how to stand so that they look confident. Isn't it better just to be confident, and let your body naturally communicate that?

The originators of NLP, John Grinder and Richard Bandler, decided that the behavioural psychologists were missing something important. Traditional therapy involved the students of a particular technique copying everything that its originator did. When they failed to get the same results as the guru, the obvious explanation was that there was something wrong with the client, or that the client was not ready to change.

This attitude to modelling – that to achieve the same result as someone else, you must copy everything they do – still lives on today in many ways. Good sales people become sales trainers, passing their wisdom onto new generations. Unfortunately, they often only teach what worked for them, with different customers in the past.

What Bandler and Grinder wanted to find out was the 'difference that makes the difference'. In modelling the hypnotherapist Milton Erickson, they wanted to discover what he did that achieved consistent results, and those techniques in turn provided an insight into the workings of the human mind.

Bandler and Grinder were first interested in excellent communicators in the field of personal change, so they went to talk to some of the most outstanding therapists at the time. They found that these people had certain things in common to do with they way that they communicated. By exploring these similarities, a model was developed of the way these people used language to influence patterns of thought and behaviour.

So, techniques such as anchoring and reframing are just NLP applied. They are not strictly NLP itself. NLP is the process by which we extracted those techniques from the minds of real people.

Modelling is as much a mindset of curiosity as an explicit set of tools that you must use as prescribed. This mindset will help you to learn interesting things from experts, from people you admire and from yourself.

You probably already know about learning styles. What are you? Have you done one of those online tests that tell you how you learn? Well, I suspect you already know how you learn. As Harry Hill said, "you can tell a lot about people from what they're like".

As with all 'personality tests', they're not true. They represent a way of thinking about and categorising a certain type of behaviour. If there were four learning types, you would see people everywhere fitting neatly into the four types. If there were eight, you would see… well you get the idea. Personality types are a filter through which you can view the people of the world. They are not true, in and of themselves because there are only two types of people in the world - those who think that there are two types of people in the world and those who don't.

When you watch your colleagues, clients, managers and friends, you will notice that they do certain things in a certain order. You will be able to watch the process by which they individually behave in order to achieve their goals.

There are a number of hallmarks of a talent that seem to be consistent:

- The person is able to get consistent results without having to think about the process or even being aware of it

- When asked, the person is a little surprised that the skill is worth modelling. They will often deny they are good at the task and will be surprised that everyone doesn't do it.

- When you first ask, "how do you do it?" they answer, "I don't know - I just do it"

There are many ways you can approach the modelling process itself, so here are a few ideas that you can use.

General hints

You'll find that the majority of valuable information that you get from your modelling subject will come when you're paying the least attention to them. It's a very good idea to record the conversation and listen to it several times to glean every last piece of content. Many people have said that the most valuable information came out after the interview had finished and they were 'just chatting', so that should tell you something about the style of interview that gets the most response from the subject!

You should aim to interview your subject somewhere that they feel comfortable, and preferably somewhere they would naturally use the skill that you're modelling so that they have easy access to it.

You may want to use the technique that Michael Parkinson uses when he interviews guests on TV. If you watch, you'll notice that he gets his guest fully associated into a past memory before he starts asking questions, and in doing so he gets a greater depth of emotional response than other interviewers. Just remember to spend a few moments getting your subject into a state where they are fully associated with the skill you want to model. You'll find that the whole process is then much easier.

And finally, remember to thank your subject and to share the results with them afterwards.

Success Factor Modelling

Robert Dilts is probably the most well known and prolific NLP modeller, having modelled people such as Walt Disney and Albert Einstein and produced models of generic skills such as leadership and creativity.

Dilts' Success Factor Modelling approach requires that you find a number of people who appear to share a common skill or talent. The whole modelling process is as follows:

- Interview the individual

- Interview the people they work with or relate to

- Watch them in their normal environment to confirm the model

- Check the model against their peers to benchmark their performance

- Check the model against your own peers to check current research or thinking

- Check the model against the individual or organisation's vision - their stated future direction

- Check the model against the individual or organisation's past - their legacy or habits

From all of these separate models you can then refine a model of the specific skill that can be used by anyone to achieve the same results.

Strategy elicitation and the TOTE model

A strategy is a specific sequence of steps that are necessary to perform a particular task. Simply, you take your subject through the skill, step by step, until you have built up a detailed map of the behaviour. For example, a skill for goal setting might break down into:

1. Visual construct of desired outcome
2. Kinaesthetic check for congruence of outcome
3. Visual recall of current situation
4. Visual construct of steps required to reach outcome
5. Kinaesthetic check for congruence of outcome

In other words, the person imagines what they would like to have, feels good about it, imagines the steps they need to take and, if it feels right, they do it.

The TOTE model adds an extra layer of formality to the basic strategy in that it adds criteria for starting the strategy and ending it. TOTE stands for Test Operate Test Exit, so to the above example it adds "how do you know when you want something?" and "how do you know when you've got it?"

You may also find that your subject has very specific criteria for the Test and Exit stages, for example someone who is scared of public speaking may know to get scared if there are more than 3 people in the audience. If there are fewer than 3, it doesn't count as a presentation so the 'get scared' strategy doesn't run (the Operate part). This can be a very useful change tool - shifting the criteria so that the problem strategy no longer runs.

The logical levels approach

Simply use the Logical Levels hierarchy as a structure for asking questions, so that you guide your interviewee through a sequence of thoughts and experiences. This approach works well for skills that are very broad such as 'leadership' or 'conflict resolution' as you can start at a very abstract level and gradually work down until you get to the specific strategies that drive the ability.

Environment

Where and when do you do this?

What is your state when you do this?

Behaviours

What specifically do you do?

How could you teach me to do this?

Do you set any specific outcomes when you do this?

How do you know when you've achieved them?

Capabilities

What skills do you have that enable you to do this?

How did you learn how to do this?

Beliefs

What do you believe about yourself when you do this?

How do you know that you're good at this?

Identity

Do you have a mission or vision when you're doing this?

What are you trying to achieve when you do this?

Who are you when you do this?

Remember to check you have a good level of rapport before you start - you may find it useful to frame the meeting with a statement such as, "When I've modelled successful people in the past, I've found the questions I'm about to ask really useful - if they don't make sense, that's fine - just use them as a guide to say what comes into your mind.

If I ask similar sounding questions, it's to give you a chance to build on what you've said already"

The curious approach

This one's easy, yet less structured than the other examples. You simply adopt a highly curious state and ask questions like, "Wow! That's amazing, how do you so that?" or, "Can you teach me how to do that?" Just explore the talent or skill freely and copy what your subject does, asking them to help coach you into the right state.

This approach also incorporates behavioural modelling in which you allow yourself to copy someone else's behaviour without consciously processing it. It's an excellent way to learn physical activities such as dance steps or martial arts moves.

You actually have a part of your brain that has the job of behavioural modelling. If you take a moment to get into rapport with the person you want to model, just imagine that your body is under their remote control. Don't look at specific movements, just defocus slightly and take in their whole body at once. You'll be able to copy the moves very successfully very quickly but if someone asks you how to do it, you might say, "I don't know, I just do it!"

Overall, modelling with NLP is an extremely valuable skill to develop. Often, when helping someone change something or solve a problem, just modelling the undesired behaviour will change it for the better. Perhaps this is as a result of bringing unconscious aspects of the behaviour to their conscious attention, perhaps it's as a result of reframing the behaviour as a talent rather than a problem. All I can say for certain is that it is a vital part of any coaching process that I undertake with a client.

Another important application of NLP modelling in business is talent management, or the replicating of talents within a team or organisation.

Most teams and organisations have a handful of 'star performers' who effortlessly excel – in sales, customer service, design, management, leadership or any area of a business where intuitive skills rather than business processes play an important part in an individual's performance. In other words, that applies to every area of every business!

By modelling your star performers, you can find out how they are able to achieve the results that they get. You can then help them to refine their own talent and you can also teach it to everyone else as a behavioural model for excellence.

By using this NLP modelling approach, you take a fundamental behavioural model that is already working in your organisation with your customers and your staff and you share it with everyone in that team. Perhaps you even share it between teams, for example transferring a model for customer service from your technical support team to your sales team.

Your organisation is already a proving ground for excellence, and you currently measure it through sales management, appraisals and pay rises. By adding the essential tools and principles of NLP modelling to this, you can accelerate the rate at which intuitive best practice develops in your business and benefits your customers.

The presuppositions of NLP

When Bandler and Grinder first modelled people like Erickson and Satir, they found that they had certain beliefs about their clients – beliefs that seemed to make it easier for the client to change.

In the context of NLP training, some trainers, regard the presuppositions as the 'rules' of NLP that you must learn by heart. My view is that they are like any other belief – useful, if they help you to achieve an outcome more easily. Therefore, think of the presuppositions as 'useful concepts to believe if you want to help someone to change easily'.

As usual, don't presume everyone wants to change.

The original language of the presuppositions was devised about 30 years ago in California, so it seems a little strange today, to say the least. You might see other versions and even other presuppositions elsewhere, these are the original ones as they were originally worded by Bandler and Grinder.

I'll translate each one into something that may be easier to understand, and I've given examples where I can of the impact that each belief can have. My translations are neither true not complete, they're just my translations. You might add your own to make them more complete for you.

The ability to change the process by which we experience reality is more often valuable than changing the content of our experience of reality.

It's easier and more useful to change your perception of the world than it is to change the world – especially when the problem is something that has already happened.

The meaning of the communication is the response you get.

Judge the effectiveness of your communication by what other people do, rather than what you think you say.

All distinctions human beings are able to make concerning our environment and our behaviour can be usefully represented through the visual, auditory, kinaesthetic, olfactory, and gustatory senses.

Everything that is in your head has a picture, sound, feeling, smell and taste – including abstract things like 'happiness', 'professionalism' and 'work'.

The resources an individual needs in order to effect a change are already within them.

You already have everything you need to help you get what you want, so the job of the NLP Practitioner is only to help you access those resources.

The map is not the territory.

The representation that you hold of the 'real world' is just a map, it's not the real thing (whatever that is) so any experience you have is a deleted, distorted, generalised version of what 'really happened', and anyone else will have a different experience. This also means that we can resolve any disagreement once we realise we are looking at different maps of the same territory.

The positive worth of the individual is held constant, while the value and appropriateness of internal and/or external behaviour is questioned.

Your value as a human being cannot be determined by your behaviour, which only represents part of your rich and varied capabilities. You are not stupid. Occasionally you may do stupid things.

There is a positive intention motivating every behaviour, and a context in which every behaviour has value.

Your behaviour is motivated by your desire to have or get something useful for you, and there is nothing intrinsically wrong with any behaviour, there's just a time and a place for it.

Feedback vs. Failure - All results and behaviours are achievements, whether they are desired outcomes for a given task/context, or not.

Some people translate this into 'there is no failure, only feedback'. In fact, I would add that there is no success either. Failure and success are judgements made against a desired outcome. The important thing is that you take action and notice what happens.

So what's the point of the presuppositions if they're not rules? Well, they happened to be the beliefs of people who were good at helping others change. So, if you want to help someone change, it is more useful to believe they can than they can't. Your beliefs shape your behaviour, so if you believe someone can achieve something by themselves, you might offer them support whereas if you don't think they have got what it takes then you might give them advice or tell them what they're doing wrong.

I would personally always choose a coach with the right attitude and beliefs over one with all the tools and techniques.

Think back to a time in your life when you were influenced by someone who you learned something from – perhaps a teacher, driving instructor or manager. Think of an example where a person's confidence in you made it easier for you to be successful, and think of an example where someone's lack of confidence in you meant you performed less well. You might also think of a time when you succeeded despite what someone else thought because of the belief you had in yourself.

So you can see that what you believe about a situation or a person will greatly influence your outcome. If your outcome is to help them change, the NLP presuppositions will be useful to you. What other outcomes do you often aim for, and what would be useful beliefs?

Let's take a common example – public speaking – and think about some useful and not so useful beliefs.

First, here are some unhelpful beliefs that are fairly common in business:

- I need to be an expert on the subject before I can be confident
- The audience are judging me as a presenter
- Presentations always make me nervous

And here are some more useful versions of those beliefs:

- I don't need to be an expert, I'm simply offering the audience my perspective on the subject
- The audience may or may not be judging me, as they are more interested in the subject matter than in me
- Presentations raise my energy level, and it's good to be a little nervous because over-confidence isn't helpful

Some people think that their beliefs are fixed and can't be changed at will. In fact, belief change is one of the easiest things to achieve with NLP and is often the best place to start. If you think back to logical levels, it is often easier to start by changing at the belief level than it is to change at the environment or behaviour level.

By helping someone adopt more useful beliefs for public speaking, you don't need to worry about changing their behaviour or propping them up with scripts or tricks which in the end, only give them even more to worry about.

A simple example is the Managing Director of an event management company who was quite a nervous presenter. It turned out that, when he welcomes the audience at the beginning of the conference, he doesn't think he has anything useful to tell the audience, so he doubts himself and becomes nervous.

Imagine you have just spent tens of thousands of pounds on a conference or corporate event. When the room goes quiet and the MD of the event company stands up to welcome everyone and outline the day, do you think that's of no interest to the audience? I think it's the most important presentation of the whole day! It sets the tone, gets the audience excited and lets the client know that the money was very well spent! Simply by changing that belief, all of the behaviour resolved itself.

I mentioned earlier that it's often useful to change a problem's criteria for operating rather than trying to tackle the problem itself, and this is a perfect example. He is still capable of getting nervous, he just doesn't need to run that behavioural program any more.

What about something like a fear of snakes? Personally, if I was lost in the jungle, I would want someone with me who is scared of snakes! If a snake came within ten feet of us, I would be the first person to know about it. The fear of snakes is not as useful in Birmingham, so there's no need to run that program there. This in itself is a useful belief. Just last night a friend of mine told me that she has a fear of falling over, and my response was, "great!" because, believe me, you definitely want to avoid falling over if at all possible.

These types of belief change techniques are called reframes, and a reframe is a very powerful conversational belief change tool. Simply by putting the behaviour or problem in a different context, you can change its meaning so it isn't a problem any more. Reframing works by changing the meaning of an experience. Notice we don't have to question the experience itself, just adjust how the person interprets it.

For example, if a colleague says "The boss always sends me to get the coffees, he doesn't like me" then there are a number of ways you can address this.

Firstly, many people will simply challenge the experience head on with, "Don't be silly, of course he likes you" which has no effect because it is a direct challenge and simply bounces off the listener's critical filters.

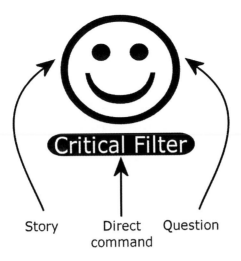

Story   Direct   Question
command

We could use the meta-model, asking questions like, "How do you know the boss doesn't like you", "How does asking you to fetch the coffees mean he doesn't like you" or "The boss *always* sends you?"

The Meta Model is a very powerful tool, yet in many everyday situations it can be a bit heavy handed. This is where a reframe is very useful:

- "Well, while you're fetching coffee you're not working!"

- "You're the only person he trusts to get the order right"

- "It's because he wants to talk about you behind your back"

- "You're the only person he trusts to bring the change back!"

So, you can see that reframing is often a more creative and light hearted technique that can bring about significant belief changes very quickly. Since those belief changes translate into behaviour, we don't have to do any more in order to help the person solve the problem.

Are there any other ways that you can adopt a useful belief for a particular outcome? By now, you should be expecting the answer to be yes… and it is.

First, think about your outcome and decide what it is you want to achieve. Let's say you want to resolve a dispute with a customer. What would be some useful beliefs for this?

Let's take a few examples:

- We will reach an outcome that we are both happy with
- We both have a valid point of view
- A bigger perspective will encompass both points of view
- I'm in no rush – patience will help me achieve my goal
- The customer wants to resolve this as much as I do
- I enjoy turning disputes into agreements

Imagine a circle on the floor and place the first belief in it. When you're ready, step into the circle and allow that belief to flow through you and, just for a few moments, really imagine that you absolutely and totally hold that belief. Imagine the meeting with the customer and notice your own behaviour and how it affects the outcome of the meeting.

Repeat the exercise until you have 'tried on' all the useful beliefs that you want to explore.

If you think of a belief as a state, you can use any NLP techniques that work with state to help you access a belief, for example anchoring, submodalities, hypnosis and so on. The end result is a state that is a combination of useful beliefs that will unconsciously shape your behaviour and make it much easier for you to achieve your goal.

End of part two

So you now know everything there is to know about NLP. Having read this far, you can confidently say to your friends and colleagues, "I know NLP".

As you will hopefully have realised by now, it's not that simple. It's much, much simpler.

In order to really understand, integrate and use NLP elegantly and effectively, you must let go of the tools and techniques. If your client, colleague or friend sees you doing a technique, you're not doing it properly.

The techniques, as taught on a Practitioner course, are designed in much the same was as the techniques you learn during your driving lessons. Emergency stops and hill starts are important technical manoeuvres that you need to know in order to drive, but they do not constitute driving in themselves.

Do you get in your car now and think, "I must remember to use some gears and look in the mirrors"? I imagine you're too busy thinking about where you're going to remember all the techniques involved in operating the car.

That's exactly what good NLP training is like. You use the techniques to learn the attitude.

So, having let go of the need for techniques, you are now in exactly the right frame of mind to learn some techniques.

Part Three

This part of the book takes us into much more detail of specific business applications. The applications are chosen based on what I hope the readers of this book will like, and what they will be like.

The content of this part of the book is largely derived from the NLP Master Practitioner modules that I created and run with PPI Business NLP.

Techniques by themselves are all very well, but for me the real power of NLP is the ease with which you can adapt the techniques to everyday situations to get consistently powerful results.

This part of the book will set you off in the right direction with some ready made ideas for applying NLP. How you take it further is up to you.

Leadership

Leadership is a topic that's talked about extensively in business today. For some, leadership has an ethereal, mystical quality that cannot be understood and that you must be born with. For others, leadership is a specific set of behaviours and skills that can be taught at business school. Some years ago, a MBA qualification would open boardroom doors whilst today you'll be lucky if it opens the broom cupboard.

There's no doubt that the nature of business has changed. From another point of view, all of the key principles are as important today as they have ever been. The most important of these is, perhaps, leadership.

Words like 'driver', 'pilot' or 'pathfinder' are often used to describe the leader's role, yet for many entrepreneurs and corporate leaders, the position can be a lonely one. Being a leader means having the courage of your convictions, the faith in your journey to go it alone. Only when you stop and look behind do you find that there were people following you. In this context, a leader's role is more like a lighthouse.

To say that a leader leads people seems obvious, yet it is important to note that it is the people who choose to follow, not the leader who makes them.

An excellent leader has a wide range of specific tools in his or her toolkit. They include group influence, mediation, goal setting and, above all, the ability to inspire other people to take action.

In this chapter, we are exploring those tools that create the behaviour of leaders – the behaviour that casual observers mistake for intangible leadership qualities.

Our first task is therefore to define leadership, so that we have a common frame of reference for the concepts and tools that we will explore.

How do we define a leader, and how is a leader different to a manager, entrepreneur, mentor or visionary?

One way to define a leader is through the people that they lead. It seems that having followers is not a prerequisite of the skills of a leader, it is more a means of identifying a leader and distinguishing him or her from something like a visionary or entrepreneur.

Certainly, we can see examples every day where leaders introduced to an organisation to revolutionise it are thought of very differently when people no longer want change.

A business leader, known for his previous work as a 'hatchet man' might be brought in to 'prune out the dead wood', for which he is praised and rewarded. What happens when he carries on pruning?

Another business leader, brought in to smooth out a period of transition and change, might be very good at stopping the organisation from changing and providing stability. When the organisation needs to change, she is seen as living in the past and holding the business back, forcing it to stagnate.

So, the success of a leader is very much dependent on the perception of their actions, given the business context in which they operate. The ability to innovate, stabilise or inspire could be perceived as either good or bad, given the context, therefore we could say that these kinds of abilities must be secondary to what lies at the core of leadership. How could some of a leader's abilities be perceived negatively?

Positive perception	Negative perception
Inspiring	Manipulative
Innovative	Obsessed with change
Good at making tough decisions	Ruthless
Strong	Autocratic
Leads by example	Controlling
Democratic	Weak

So, what could we say are the core qualities of a leader that transcend the context and provide the framework for this chapter?

We could say that, for our purposes, leaders have:

- The ability to conceive the future and translate it into a roadmap for others to follow
- The ability to stick to a course of action regardless of what other people say or do
- A high degree of self belief and self reliance
- The ability to engage the skills of others and build a team that can deliver their vision
- The ability to communicate in an engaging way to a wide range of people
- The ability to focus on what is important
- The ability to identify and gather feedback about their progress
- The ability to engage the resources available to solve problems
- An acceptance of the rewards and risks of their position
- The ability to plan rather than trusting fate
- Personal ownership of their actions, successes and failures
- The ability to recognise when something has failed, and the ability to do something else instead
- A strong sense of congruence, honesty or ethics

So, successful leaders will set a course of action and follow it, accepting that sometimes people will love them and sometimes people will hate them. They are able to engage all resources in any context to move forwards and they take personal responsibility for their actions. If a plan fails, it's no-one else's fault but their own.

Notice that, while a leader may have strong ethics, you might not agree with them. That could be what defines the people who choose to follow that leader.

You can see that these qualities could equally apply to an entrepreneur, the difference being that an entrepreneur is often focussed on achieving the outcome himself, using his own skills. The successful leader is focussed on achieving the outcome by engaging the resources and skills of other people.

Even when the leader seems to be struggling against the tide, he or she will still have some followers to depend on. Another key skill is therefore to identify who those people are and to develop relationships with them that stand the test of time. You'll often find that a good leader has a good right-hand man – or even a whole crowd of them.

Your personal outcome

What is your goal or mission as a leader? What is it that you want to achieve?

The first step in being able to lead other people is being able to lead yourself. The first step in leading yourself is to know what your goals are, to know what you want to achieve as a leader. Whilst this may seem obvious, it's surprising how many people find themselves placed in a position of leadership and do not take time to review their own goals and ambitions before focussing on the people or organisation they are asked to lead.

For any goal, we can use the 'Well Formed Outcomes' approach to clarify the goal and make it more achievable. For a goal to be 'well formed' it must satisfy the following four criteria:

Positive

Your goal must be something you want, not something you want to avoid.

Under your control

You will never achieve goals that you are not in control of. For example, getting a promotion is not under your control, whereas gaining the skills to get promoted are much more under your control.

Real

Success is not a goal because it is too vague. A Well Formed Outcome has something that you can see, hear and feel as its target. You may even be able to smell and taste something too.

If you don't know what your goal looks, sounds and feels like, you'll never know what to aim for, nor when you've got it.

Ecological

Many goals in life have side effects. For example, a promotion carries both a pay rise and greater responsibility. If your goal has any negative or detrimental side effects that you have not fully considered, you will sabotage your own attempts to achieve it.

Setting priorities

Now that you have a clear representation of what you want, you are more likely to get it. In order to achieve a complex outcome, you will need to engage many resources – some of them yours, and some of them belonging to other people. Every complex goal comprises a number of steps that you must organise efficiently in order to achieve your goal as quickly and easily as possible.

The best place to begin planning anything complex is at the end, looking backwards.

Just imagine a leadership goal and think about how the steps you have to take in achieving it. Perhaps some steps are uncertain, or involve other people so it's difficult to see exactly how things will turn out.

Now imagine that you have achieved this goal and, as you look back to the day you started working towards it, you notice the milestones you've passed, decisions you made, people who helped you and so on. As you look back from the future, you notice that the uncertainty you had looks very different, because you only see the choices you did make.

Remember the milestones you see, and notice the order in which you get things done – these will be your priorities.

Articulate a simple vision

So, you know where you're going and you know what you need to get done first. The next step is to get people on board so that they can help you to achieve your goals. In order to do this, you don't have to spell out everything that you need people to do for you. Many leaders in organisations fall into the trap of believing that people in the organisation need to be directed. They are very capable of managing themselves, all they need is to be shown the way.

There are many presentation tools that you can use to structure the way you communicate your vision, yet the simplest and most effective is for you to be honestly and openly passionate about your vision.

After all, if your goals don't excite you, how could you expect anyone else to follow you?

When you first communicate with the people you are leading, it is their chance to make their mind up about you. When you think of the leaders you have seen in the past, what kind of things were you wondering when you first saw them? Were they things like:

- Do I trust you?

- Do I believe you?

- Would I follow you?

- Do I agree with your opinions?

- Do I agree with your goals?

- Do I like you?

- Can I respect you?

- Will you listen to me?

- Can I work with you?

So, if you have ever considered any of those when meeting a new leader for the first time, other people will think about them when they meet you.

As a leader, you are in an unusual position when you meet people in the organisation you are leading. They're not just meeting a new colleague, they are looking to you for guidance, to be a role model, to walk the talk.

It's therefore vital that you embody your guiding principles, values and even your destiny at all times. If that sounds like a tall order, don't worry. You'll have done all of that by the time you reach the end of this chapter.

Identify your team

You can't do this alone. One area where leaders differ from entrepreneurs is in the teams they build around them.

Entrepreneurs tend to work alone until they need key technical skills to achieve their goal. Leaders tend to build networks of people who extend their reach into the organisation they're leading, developing a leadership culture that allows the leader to operate more effectively. Your team are your eyes and ears as well as your arms and legs in the organisation!

Effective leaders achieve tasks through relationships with other people, rather than focussing on the task directly. Therefore, it's vital to build a team of people around you who extend your own capabilities, rather than surrounding yourself with an insulating layer of people who protect you from bad news.

Far too many organisational leaders fall into this category through good intentions. They create a team of people who they like and who support them in what can be a hostile environment. These people then work hard to keep you safe and protect you from bad news. Of course, by the time you realise you need to do something about the bad news, it's too late.

Whilst it may not be as comforting, you will be a more effective leader if you build a team of people who complement your natural skills and leadership style.

You can use a range of psychometric tools to do this, ensuring you build a balanced team in terms of their individual strengths and characteristics. NLP metaprograms are an ideal tool to use in this way, ensuring you get the right balance. Here's a quick reminder of some useful metaprograms and their behavioural impact for your leadership team. Your job is to act as a mediator or communication centre between these different views of the world.

Options	Comes up with new ideas, challenges existing processes and questions the status quo. Use these people to create new ideas or change old habits.
Procedures	Maintains existing procedures, implements new ideas. Use these people to get things done properly.
Internal	Self directed and needs minimal supervision, but needs to be kept on track. Use these people for business projects that need completing, regardless of external pressure or dissent.
External	Needs external supervision or input. Use these people to interface with the outside world – stakeholders, staff etc. as they are receptive to external information.
Towards	Goal oriented. Use these people to set ambitious goals and objectives, regardless of what is achievable.
Away	Problem oriented. Use these people to double check plans and limit goals to what is achievable.

You can also imagine a team meeting in full flow and pay attention to the interactions with people. As you sit back and watch the meeting in progress, you will notice some areas where people conflict because their roles or characteristics overlap. In other areas, you will notice gaps where something is missing. Make whatever adjustments are necessary as you continue to fine tune the team and become aware of some of the characteristics or skills that complement your own, yet you may not have thought about before.

Imagine yourself in your ideal boardroom, at the head of your ideal boardroom table.

Think of a number of different tasks or roles that are integral to your leadership vision.

Turn to each empty chair and imagine someone performing that role. Imagine engaging in a conversation with that person, and then think of the qualities that you notice in that person.

What one piece of advice do you hear from each team member?

Continue until all the roles are filled and the team is now sitting round the boardroom table.

Finally, create a movie of the first team meeting in progress. Sit back and feel the atmosphere in the room, noticing the group dynamics and helping them to feel a sense of excitement and anticipation about the team's future success.

If appropriate, identify real people who would fit into your "dream team".

Identify your customers

It's important that you identify who your customers are. For now, forget all this talk about stakeholders or even shareholders. They will be happy if your customers are happy. In the past, customer service training focussed on the concept of internal and external customers, and treating everyone who relies on you as if they were a customer.

The modern language of 'stakeholder' is useful in differentiating people who have a vested interest in your success and people who actually depend on you and, in return, pay the bills.

So, by customer I simply mean 'The person who pays the bills'

Identify your stakeholders

Now we can ask 'who has a vested interest in your success?' Traditionally we might think of shareholders, investors, creditors and so on. What about your family? Your friends? The families of the people you employ? They are important for two simple reasons:

1. They want you to be successful
2. They can help you to be successful

How can your family be successful when they have nothing to do with the business? How can the family of an employee help you to be successful? I don't have to tell you the answer – you already know.

Think of a salesman who enjoys a good standard of living. Imagine that his wife likes it too, and does what she can to help him work more effectively. Perhaps she encourages him, supports him when he talks about problems, reassures him when things aren't going so well.

Now, I do not advocate using personal relationships to influence people. What I strongly advocate is that you recognise that everyone who touches your business is part of the system that supports it. Whether you think people are relevant or not does not matter. What matters is that you recognise how the system is maintained, and what you need to do to keep the system in balance. I've seen sales managers cancel days off for their sales staff just to go to a meeting. How does that sales person's family react to that, and what effect does that have on that person's motivation and continued employment?

In one situation, I spent about two hours on the phone with a sales manager who wanted to cancel the holiday of two of his staff because his manager had called an important meeting. He wanted to prove to his manager that he was a powerful leader, and that he could command his team to do anything. Of course, this isn't the army, so he can't get people to do anything they don't want to do. Both of the sales people concerned had no intention of cancelling their holidays, and a nasty situation was looming.

Finally, I managed to get the sales manager to see the light with a reframe, by asking him, "How does allowing these two people to miss the meeting prove that you are an even more capable and effective manager?", to which he replied, "I don't see how it does." Notice he didn't say, "It doesn't". Then I suggested, "You are proving that you have built a strong team that does not rely on any one individual. You have built a team with the flexibility to adapt to changes, so that you can allow people to have personal lives too. You are proving that what matters is not the people in the team but the way it is lead."

You may or may not agree with that, yet what it achieved was that the manager backed down, the sales people went on holiday and the meeting went ahead. It turned out to be a pointless meeting, so imagine what would have happened if he had found a way to force his whole team to be there.

Identify barriers

So you have your plan, your goals, your targets and your strategy. Having those things does not mean the world will step aside and let you have your own way.

Sometimes, events will conspire against you, and there's really not much you can do about that. You could have a contingency plan, but the big problem with that is that the very act of contingency planning requires you to accept an outcome that is not what you want.

Throughout history, great leaders have had no plan B. They have only planned for success.

For our purposes, there are some much more important barriers that will prevent your success – the barriers within you – fear, uncertainty, doubt, disbelief will all stop you more surely than anything the world can throw at you. How can we discover those barriers and banish them?

Here's one exercise that you can use to explore unconscious barriers. In this exercise, you don't have to know what the barriers are, you simply have to be open to feeling their presence first, and you might figure out what they are later.

Start by identifying a timeline on the floor, running from past through present to future. Stand on the line at a point that represents 'now'.

Identify the point at which your goal or outcome has been successfully achieved.

Walk forwards towards the goal until you feel yourself encountering the first barrier. Make a note of what it is, then take one step further, just past the barrier. Say the first thing that comes into your head about the way you overcame the barrier. Notice when this barrier occurs.

Take a moment to feel the effects of having overcome that barrier before moving to the next one.

Continue until you reach the goal, and then step a little further.

As you look back to the present, notice everything you achieved and the barriers you moved past in order to achieve your goal. Notice how it feels to be where you are now.

Finally, walk slowly back to the present moment, walking through each barrier, remembering each action you took to overcome the barrier and bringing back all the learning and experience to the present moment.

As you turn and face the future again, what seems different?

Identify your key resources

What are the critical resources that will help you achieve your outcome? They might include Money, People, Skills, Time, Space or something else.

You can identify the degree of control you have over each resource and the degree to which it is important in achieving your outcome. For example, a personal skill may be highly important and is totally under your control. Money may be critical but not under your direct control, so you will have to find a way to exert indirect influence over the budget holder.

You can draw out a chart like the one below for each resource that you have. Mark the point on the chart of the amount of control you have over that resource, and also the impact that it has for you to achieve your goal.

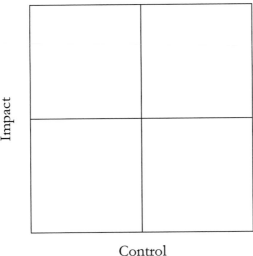

Control

As you look at the charts for all your resources, do you notice anything that is helpful to you?

For example, you may need to get more control over your key resources, or you may find that the resources you think you have are not the ones you need to achieve your goals.

For resources which are not under your direct control, such as money, you can plan a way to either reduce their impact or increase the degree of control you have.

This is a very important process, because so many leaders fail through wasting their time trying to control resources that are not under their control. Another outcome of this exercise is to be clear on what resources you already have, and to find out how to make the best use of those.

Effective leaders do not always wish for more resources; they make the most of what they have.

Communication plan

How will you communicate, both formally and informally? How will you recognise every action as a communication in itself? How will you take every opportunity to set the tone of your leadership culture?

Think about:

- Your state
- The purpose of your communication
- Content
- Feedback

It's important to recognise that your followers will not judge you by your track record or your business plan – they will judge you by what you do, right now. More specifically, they will judge you by how you communicate with them. Now, you might say that your followers aren't important, the people you really need to impress are the City, or the shareholders, or the board or whoever. But guess what? If you don't impress your followers, you're not a leader. You're just someone else doing a tough job. You need these people to put your plan into action, and they are probably the most important resource you have.

Many years ago, I worked in an organisation that had a regional director who was mysterious and authoritarian. He was mysterious in that no-one knew much about him, thanks in part to his protective secretary and in part to his frequent trips to the golf course.

At one company Christmas party, a colleague of mine, Paul, noticed the director talking to staff and seeming to have a good time. On leaving the party, Paul said to the director, "Goodnight Bob". The director's reply was, "In my office, Monday morning". Monday came and Paul went to Bob's office, and Bob said, "the only people who call me by my first name are friends and senior managers, and you will never be either of those".

What happened next? The news spread like a rash, and practically everyone in the company dropped out of the social club and boycotted social events. Bob issued a memo saying that attendance of social events was compulsory! He never undid the damage that he caused in that one moment. Bob was a manager. He had no followers. Paul, just a lowly engineer had many followers, and he controlled the outcome of those events.

Make your mark

How will you make your mark, stake your claim and establish yourself as a highly visible leader?

When a new leader takes over in an existing environment, he or she will often do something to make their mark. It might be to hold a launch conference where they can make an inaugural presentation, or it might be to fire some people and introduce some new policies.

Making your mark is a way of publicly defining your leadership style, so whatever you choose to do, be aware of what it says about you to the people who will choose to follow you.

Make difficult decisions

What makes a decision difficult? Is it:

- An emotional connection
- Imagining what might happen as a result
- A lose/lose outcome
- A complex outcome involving many people

Or something else?

One characteristic of strong leaders is that they don't hesitate when making difficult decisions. Here are two exercises that will help you to achieve this.

Dissociation using perceptual positions

Choose a difficult decision, where you think you will benefit from having some distance from the situation.

Fully associate with the situation, the people and the decision as you think it through or describe it to someone.

Move to a 2nd perceptual position, watching yourself process the information and make the decision. In this 2nd position you are someone else involved in the outcome of the decision.

Move to a 3rd perceptual position as a neutral observer. Observe the 2nd position and notice how you, in the 2nd position, respond to the decision maker in the first position.

Move back through 2nd position and finally into 1st position, taking with you anything you have noticed or learned.

You now need to make a decision. Notice your feelings and congruence as you do this.

Repeat this as many times as you need in order to make the decision comfortably.

With this new insight, what seems like the right thing to do?

Timeline to test outcomes

If you are unsure of the long term implications of a decision, this is a good exercise.

Simply imagine a timeline with the future in front of you. Notice the decision in the near future and walk towards and through it. As you walk, notice how it feels to have made the decision, and continue to walk forwards for as long as you wish, noticing any new feelings that you have.

When you feel that you have gone far enough, turn and look back at the decision, noticing what has happened since then, and where you are now. Walk back to the present, taking anything you have learned back with you.

As you look at the decision now, what seems like the right thing to do?

Test the status quo

How do you know that the current culture and environment are 'right'? Some new leaders automatically accept the situation, others automatically try to change it. It's important that you change what needs to be changed and leave alone what needs to be left alone.

You will always have preconceptions about an existing situation – whether you are aware of them or not. It's important to notice how these preconceptions affect the way you communicate with people. You will communicate your beliefs and intentions as clearly as if you had them written on your forehead.

Now that you realise this, how can you use this to your advantage? The first step is to check your preconceptions and be aware of them. There is nothing wrong with the preconceptions that you have, instead think about how they align with your goals.

When you first walk into the environment that you are leading, you will no doubt ask many questions in order to learn about the current situation. The questions you ask will be loaded with presuppositions that transit your beliefs, such as, "are you still doing it *that* way?" or , "why are we losing so many customers?"

These two examples imply to people that there is something wrong with what they are doing. In the early stages of your leadership, people will be listening to what you say more carefully than ever, so this is the perfect time to change the beliefs you want to change and preserve those that are useful.

Often, new leaders only think about what they want to change. It is equally important to think about what you must maintain. Any organisation has activities and attitudes that both help and hinder business performance. There are activities that you succeed because of, and those that you succeed in spite of.

So, in applying NLP to leadership, we can formulate:

- Questions that will help you **test** individual and collective beliefs about the organisation
- Questions that use presuppositions or embedded commands to **change** cultural beliefs
- Questions that use presuppositions or embedded commands to **reinforce** cultural beliefs

Here are a few examples to get you started:

Test

- □ "Tell me about…"
- □ "I'm interested to hear more about…"
- □ "Tell me how this works…"

Notice that these are more like commands than questions; this avoids putting the listener into the state of mind where presuppositions are most powerful and prevents your beliefs from infecting them.

Change

- □ "What's wrong with…?"
- □ "What do you think we should do about…?"
- □ "Are you still doing it *that* way…?"

Many years ago I worked for a large company that, out of the blue, sent round a memo with employee questions and answers. One question was, "Is the company planning to make redundancies?" to which the answer was, "the company has no plans to make redundancies at this time". Hang on! Why did you feel the need to tell me that? And who mentioned redundancies? And what do you mean 'at this time'? What about next week?

So, I saw the writing on the wall and left a few months later. A few months after that, mass redundancies followed and the company was split up and either sold off or absorbed into the parent company. I think the memo was a mysterious omen of some kind.

Reinforce

- □ "What's good about…?"
- □ "You have a lot of experience in this, what do you think about…?"
- □ "What works well now…?"

In a potential change situation, what people really want to hear is, "Everything's fine! You're doing a great job! I like you! Is there anything you think we can do better, while we have this chance to reflect on our performance?"

The questions you ask, your behaviour and how you make your mark will communicate this to your followers more quickly and effectively than if you stood in the car park waving a flag.

Create a dashboard

It's important that you have a simple and effective means of tracking progress as you establish yourself in your leadership role. The dashboard in your car gives you a summary of all the information you need.

You also have a natural feedback mechanism, yet you may not even be aware of it. Simply, it's the way you know when everything is all right.

Earlier in the book, we talked about sensory filters:

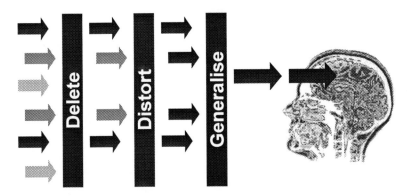

You unconsciously gather huge volumes of sensory information in order to generate the feeling of 'everything is OK'. When some of that information is missing, or isn't what you need, the feeling changes to 'something isn't quite right'. For many people, they do not become consciously aware of the process until the feeling becomes 'Danger Will Robinson!' (It's what the robot in Lost In Space used to say when it sensed danger, just in case you never watched the TV program).

You can use this knowledge to build an organisational feedback process that matches your own sensory filters. This has two major advantages for today's busy leader:

- You don't have to spend all day reading reports
- You will know the instant something goes off track

Here's how you can build yourself a dashboard.

Choose three situations; one you know is working, one you know isn't working and one that you are concerned but undecided about.

Since this exercise elicits unconscious information, it's very difficult to do it yourself, because you don't know what you don't know. I'll tell you the process anyway, so that you can make a start.

In each situation, elicit a simple strategy that concentrates on the key feedback criteria that generate your response to each situation.

If you look back to the chapter on modelling, you will find an outline of how you can elicit a strategy in this way.

You will now have three simple strategies – use them to create explicit feedback mechanisms.

For example, let's say that your strategy is primarily visual and that colours have some useful associations for you. Rather than having to plough through spreadsheets to figure out what today's cash flow position is, it would be much easier to have someone else do that and just show you traffic lights for 'OK', 'Needs attention' and 'Danger!'

If your strategy is primarily auditory, don't waste time trying to interpret graphs. Have someone else do that and tell you what the result is.

What you are doing is helping the people in your organisation to communicate with you more effectively, which is ultimately better for everyone.

Be true to yourself

Successful leaders are highly congruent with their stated goals and ambitions. Their state and beliefs align with their outcomes to create a powerful presence which helps them to share their vision, gain commitment and deliver results through their relationships with others.

Leaders who are not true to themselves create incongruence and confusion around them. There is no point soldiering on with something that you think needs to be done, even if you don't agree with it. Your incongruence will affect the people around you and translate into their behaviour. Your confused thoughts will become their confused actions.

- What do you believe as a leader?
- What do you believe about yourself?
- What do you believe about your followers?
- What do you believe about your customers?
- What do you believe about your stakeholders?

By beliefs, I mean what you know to be true. For example, you might believe that your followers choose to follow you, or you might believe that they have to do what they are told. You can imagine how different beliefs translate into behaviour.

We can apply the logical levels concept to this to help you think through your beliefs.

Take one of your beliefs about yourself as a leader:

- With this belief what are you capable of?
- With those skills, what do you actually do, day to day?
- Where do you do that? Who do you do it with?
- And what kind of leader does that belief make you?

It is important to understand your own beliefs and how they influence your actions. If you think of your beliefs about leadership and your leadership role as a whole, what is important to you about being a leader?

Another way to ask this is, "what aspects of your job would you continue to do, even if no-one paid you for it?"

Staying true to your values means that you will stay on track and achieve goals that are good for the organisation and good for you.

Ascent, the adventure coaching experience, is an ideal way to develop the personal leadership skills that keep you on track.

You can find out more about Ascent at www.ascent-experience.com

What if?

Earlier, I mentioned contingency planning and the importance of not admitting defeat, even before you start. If you had a contingency plan, what would it be?

- An exit plan?
- A "find a scapegoat" plan?
- A golden handshake?
- A clause in your contract?
- An honourable defeat?
- Another job offer?
- A succession plan?

Most people only plan for the start of things – it's a habit that often leads to worry. What would happen if, instead of planning for the start of your leadership term, you planned for the end of it?

Think about how a politician's career would be different if they planned their exit from public office as carefully as they plotted their rise to power!

So, what if it all goes wrong? Leadership is a very context dependent set of skills. A tough leader in one organisation is a hatchet man in another. A supportive, collaborative leader in one organisation is an indecisive fence-sitter in another. If you're joining an organisation to complete a task, what will happen when you have achieved your goal?

It's often better to plan your exit, especially if you are thinking of your long term career plans.

And how do those plans affect your attention and congruence in the job you're doing? How can you create an effective 'What if?' plan that maintains your focus on your outcomes?

Leadership destiny

Until now, we have concentrated on your goal for leadership – a particular outcome that you need to achieve. Certainly, for many leaders there will be such a specific outcome that they need to work towards. What many leaders in companies miss out on is their own development.

In dedicating themselves to the needs of the business, many leaders lose sight of their own long term goals and many don't notice how far they have wandered off track until it is too late.

What we now need to do is put the whole of this chapter into the context of your long term personal goals.

For this, we can use another timeline. Handy things, aren't they?

From a starting point in the present, walk forwards into the future, exploring your development as a leader. The first step you take will represent your entire first 30 days in office. Every subsequent step takes you further and further into the future. You can stop whenever you feel that you have explored far enough.

As you stop, turn and look back through their journey and ask yourself, "with the experience I now have, what kind of leader have I become?" Don't think about it, just be aware of the answer that comes into your head.

Review your current position and think about any changes in the past that are necessary to create a fully congruent and successful future.

Finally, walk back to the present, taking with you the experiences that you have had.

As you return to the present, face the future once more and ask yourself, "what will I do differently now that I have had this glimpse of my destiny?"

The final step, of the exercise and of this chapter, is simply to be, in every thought, word and action, the leader you are destined to be.

Ascent

Ascent is a unique adventure coaching experience that helps you to explore your purpose, your goals and the barriers that stop you from achieving your true potential.

Aimed at the individual, the Ascent experience leads to powerful personal leadership skills and a sense of purpose that is naturally inspiring and compelling for the people around you.

Ascent deals with one of the essential contradictions of life, that you can't forget something by trying to forget it, and you can't relax by trying hard to relax. After a certain point it has to be about letting go, about unlearning. Sometimes, you know more by learning less.

When you know you are on the right path, you know it will lead you to the right destination. Whilst we focus on your goals during the Ascent process, what you really discover is how to live your life in pursuit of those goals.

Ascent was born from a unique concept, with unique exercises and is the only program like it running anywhere in the world. Ascent integrates powerful, insightful coaching with reflective exercises and the outdoor experience to bring mind, body and spirit together in a way that you will never have felt before.

If you want to experience the hero's journey for yourself, visit www.ascent-experience.com and see what others have said.

Suggested reading:

Alpha Leadership	Dilts, Deering, Russell
Balanced Scorecard	Robert Kaplan
Balanced Scorecard in a week	Mike Bourne
Faster than the speed of change	Paul Lemberg
Good to great	Jim Collins
Leadership by the book	Kenneth Blanchard
Who says elephants can't dance?	Louis Gerstner
Visionary Leadership skills	Robert Dilts
Six Questions	Peter Freeth
How to win friends and influence people	Dale Carnegie

Sales

Some people say that sales is the lifeblood of their business, generating a vital supply of new orders. Some people say they don't need to sell, their product or service should speak for itself. Some people are wise enough to realise that both are true, and that you don't need to call yourself a salesperson to make it easy for your customers to do business with you.

Let's reduce the concept of sales to its most essential elements. Sales is the art of making it easy for your customers to do business with you. If you do not adopt the simple attitudes and apply the practical tools of this chapter, you may find that your customers still trade with you but that it's not as easy as it could be, or that there is frequently friction in the relationship that just saps time and energy.

Another way to define sales is 'the art of helping people make good decisions'. From the simplest sale to the most complex, this basic skill is at the heart of a sales professional's toolkit.

There are many different sales models, ranging from tactical, transactional sales at one end of the spectrum, through complex solution sales and on to outsourced and service sales. Each has its own unique demands and requirements, yet we can see common threads of essential sales skills running through the different sales models.

This chapter concentrates on that thread of core skills. As you move from transactional sales to solution or service sales, the sales process relies on more people – designers, project managers, bid managers, commercial managers, consultants, engineers to name only a few. Therefore, the further towards the service end of the spectrum you sell, the more skills you have to acquire in areas such as leadership, communication and even coaching and delivering powerful presentations.

You may already be an experienced sales professional. You may be an entrepreneur, business owner or self employed consultant who believes that you have little experience of sales. In fact, you already have a wealth of experience that we can draw upon in applying the information in this chapter – experience that is invaluable both to you and to your customers, and experience that will help you to achieve consistently better results in all of your customer relationships

Outcomes

Once again, we start with a Well Formed Outcome. Thinking about developing this idea for sales, every meeting you go to and every contact with a prospect needs to have a clear outcome. It's amazing how many sales people go to meetings with the objective 'to meet the customer'. It's no wonder that some sales people often feel that the customer is in control of the sales process.

Many sales people focus on activity rather than results. They focus on being busy, meeting lots of customers and writing lots of proposals instead of focusing on the results that they need to get. By keeping busy, some sales people allow the customer to take control of the sales process. I would suggest the following definitions of a sales led or buyer led process.

- Sales people draw information from the client and match the client's needs to their product
- Buyers draw information from sales people and match it to their own needs

In an active sales situation, the sales person controls the process. This requires the sales person to have two key areas of knowledge; how to manage the sales process and what it is they are selling.

Now, we put a lot of emphasis on writing your goals down. What you can also realise is the importance of sharing those goals with other people. You'll find that your goals connect with those of your peers, customers, colleagues, friends and competitors to impact reality in a way that you could not have predicted.

You can use this form of language for communicating your goals:

- What I want is …
- What I need from you is …
- How do you feel about that?

It's good to get into the habit of telling people what you want, and realising that most reasonable people are happy to help you get it.

It's also important to tell your customers what you want from them, otherwise they don't know what to do. I've met many inexperienced sales people who say, "I can't tell the customer that I want them to buy something at the start of the meeting, they might say no!"

Let's just pick that set of beliefs apart. Firstly, what do you think the customer thinks you're there for? Because you're lonely? Because you like the coffee? The customer wants to find out if you have something worth buying and he wants to do that as quickly as possible. Secondly, if you don't tell the customer what you want, he doesn't know what to pay attention to and how to sort the information he is receiving from you.

Finally, if the customer does say no, you need to find out as quickly as possible so that you can find people who might say yes. Your respect of his time will also create a good impression that might help you in the future.

Don't be tempted to change the final question to, "what do you think about that?" Sales is about forming emotional connections, and if you avoid your customer's emotions, so will he and he will never get excited enough to buy your product.

So, what I want is to sell lots of books, and what I need from you is for you to tell all your friends and colleagues how useful you found this book. How do you feel about that?

When you start to practice this regularly, you may be surprised at just how helpful other people are.

Sales models

We can compare three broad models; product, solution and service. You may use different terms for these sales models – the important thing is that you recognise the qualities and requirements of each model.

Product	Service	Solution
Physical	Intangible	Combination
Transactional	Ongoing contract <3 years?	Ongoing contract >3 years?
Risk on customer	Risk on supplier	Shared risk
Try before buy	Buy before try	Combination/ongoing
Assets owned by customer	Assets owned by supplier	Assets owned by Joint Venture

It's important to recognise that although these three models all follow the same basic sales cycle from start to end, solution and service sales cycles are typically longer, more complex and involve more people, both on the supplier's and the customer's side of the deal.

Solution sales cycles are often further complicated by the setting up joint venture companies, jointly owned and staffed by the supplier and the customer. In these cases, it is often hard to tell who the customer is and who the supplier is in terms of the companies who make up the venture. It's more like a partnership, where they both agree to work with the same customers and the same suppliers.

Comparing sales with marketing

Some people see sales and marketing as the same thing, some see them as being poles apart. It's useful to draw a few distinctions between the two to highlight how they complement each other.

	Marketing	Sales
Communication	Broadcast	Unicast (one to one)
Direction	Transmit	Interact
Purpose	Demand creation	Demand fulfilment

Here's another definition of marketing that you might find useful:

"Selling to people you haven't met yet"

Routes to market

How do you get your marketing message to potential customers?

What routes to market do you exploit?

What routes to market would not be appropriate for you?

What does that tell you about your beliefs or approach to marketing?

Buying motivation

Robert Cialdini (author of Influence: Science and Practice) has some views on how people are influenced which are relevant to sales.

Reciprocation

If you do someone a favour, they feel more inclined to help you in return. Do you ever get charity letters that include a free pen or other cheap gift?

Consistency

People will stick to a decision they have made, even if it means bending over backwards. Therefore, the model of sales which builds on commitments exploits the consistency rule.

Social proof

In the absence of personal experience, people will follow other people. Case studies and reference customers exploit this rule.

Liking

People buy from people they like – it's what sales people have been saying since the first caveman and cavewoman left the wheel dealership saying, "What a nice sales caveman"

Authority

In the absence of personal experience, people will follow authority figures. Did you ever wonder why toothpaste and washing powder are advertised by actors wearing glasses and white coats?

Scarcity

People perceive that limited supply equals higher value. This is why carpet and furniture showrooms are always having the last day of their big sale.

Pre-qualification

Before we get onto the sales cycle itself, we should do some background work. It's useful to be congruent in your role as a salesperson, and probably the one area that all sales people agree is important is product knowledge.

The logical levels model is a very good way to explore something like this, and it can help you to create alignment through the levels, leading to greater congruence in yourself.

Starting at either the top or the bottom, explore each of the five levels, discovering how you think of yourself at each level and how each level connects to and through the others. Finally, play back your responses and check for congruence.

If you have a strong sense of identity but are less certain about your products or customers, start at the top. If you are clear about your customers and products but not as certain about how this fits into your personal or brand image, start at the bottom.

Identity – your brand image
Beliefs and needs – you, your customer and your product
The skills you have
What are you selling? How will you sell it?
Your customers, the market environment

The result of this exercise could be regarded as your personal brand.

Your ideal customer

Imagine yourself, sitting in a typical business meeting with your ideal customer, talking with them and agreeing on an outcome. Notice that this isn't a 'dream customer' but a realistic ideal. It's not a customer who signs a huge order with no effort and also gives you the keys to his weekend cottage in the country. This is an ideal customer who accompanies you through the sales cycle, tests and challenges your sales skills and encourages you to develop as a sales professional. At the conclusion, both you and the ideal customer are wholly satisfied that this has been a good working relationship where you have both benefited equally.

Notice anything about the way the ideal customer sits, moves, dresses, speaks or does anything that characterises them.

Notice what the customer is doing to help you, and what they are doing to help you develop your sales skills. Notice any subtle changes or events which are important clues that you might otherwise miss.

Finally, imagine a movie of the first meeting in progress. Sit back and feel the atmosphere in the room, noticing the dynamics and feeling a sense of excitement and anticipation about the outcome of this meeting.

Can you think of a real person who fits this role?

Put yourself in their shoes

This is a perceptual positions exercise that helps you to plan your sales approach from your customer's point of view.

Just imagine the first meeting with your ideal customer and run through it, creating every detail as if it were happening right now.

Now move to where the customer will be, and step into their position. In this 2nd position, watch the whole sequence again, watching and hearing yourself as if you are the other person. Notice how you feel, and any new information that you become aware of.

Move to a 3rd position on the other side of the room. You might imagine stepping outside of the room and watching through a window, as a casual onlooker. Watch the whole sequence again, paying attention to the interaction between positions 1 and 2. Notice any new information or insight you have in this position.

Finally, move back to the 1st position, in your own shoes, and run through the whole scene again, integrating everything that you learned in the other two positions.

How do you feel about the meeting? Did it turn out the way you wanted it to? If not, you can go around the 1st, 2nd and 3rd positions again until you get the result you want. Notice any difference between the approach you end up with and the way you started.

What are you selling?

What is your primary product? If you work in a service business, think about your product as the outcome of your service. For example, good head-hunters think of the candidate as the product.

Chunk up to what your product does for people, first by imaging yourself as the customer or end user of the product:

- What does the product do for me?

- And what does that do for me?

- And when I have that, what does that give me?

- And what does that mean to me?

- And so on....

Finally, think about how the value or meaning of your product connects to product features. Come up with some feature/benefit statements, phrased as "benefit because feature".

Why would you say it that way round when years of traditional sales thinking says "feature means benefit"?

Let's work through the process. My chair has four legs which means that.... which means what? By the time I have told you the feature, you have already created an internal representation and from that you have derived a meaning. If my benefit now matches yours, we're OK. If my benefit does not match your feature, you will either disagree or have to go back and create new meaning – both of which break rapport.

Now, let's take the other version. My chair is really stable because... because what? Do you feel the difference? By telling you the benefit, your thinking moves up to the level of values.

For example, You get a high level of skills integration because of our modular approach to NLP training.

Compare that to, "Our modular approach to NLP training means a better level of skills integration". To you, it might mean that it fits into your diary more easily.

Finally, the word 'because' creates a cause and effect rule, linking that benefit to a feature of your product.

Try it both ways and see what happens.

The sales cycle

Some people draw the sales cycle as a straight line. Some people draw it as a curve, with the emphasis on prospecting and closing with a lull in between. Some people draw it as a funnel and some people draw it as a arrow. Put those representations out of your mind for a moment, because for us it is a true cycle – feeding and sustaining itself and generating its own momentum.

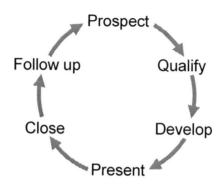

Prospecting

The first stage in the sales cycle is finding people who are likely to buy from you.

There are many methods of prospecting, from high tech approaches such as online networking through to traditional approaches such as talking to real people to find out if they want your product.

Networking

How do you currently network? Do you network purposefully, visiting conferences, networking events and business groups, or is it an informal process where you just bump into interesting people?

What can you do to network more purposefully, as a way of generating more prospects?

When networking, it's very important that you can tell other people what you do as clearly and concisely as possible. The Logical Levels model is an excellent structure for communicating this kind of information as it engages the listener's brain and leads it on an inviting journey.

You can start at the Identity level and work down, constructing a short phrase that is easy to remember and flows well. For example, "I'm a leading business coach who helps large and small organisations, teams and individuals get better results, more consistently.

| Identity - Who you are |
| Belief - What's good about that |
| Capability - What you can do, your skills |
| Behaviour - What you actually do |
| Environment - Where or with whom you do it |

New forms of networking have appeared in the past few years including online networking and speed networking. If I were to be really strict I would say that these are strategies devised by people who are afraid of picking up the phone and prospecting the old fashioned way – by talking to people!

Cold calling

Sooner or later, any salesperson has to pick up the telephone and call a potential customer. Many people call this 'cold calling' and this can make the process unnecessarily difficult for many sales people. It hardly sounds inviting, does it?

Whether you make sales calls from a list or to follow up on warm contacts from an introduction or networking event, at some point you do have to pick up the phone.

Some sales people excel at making sales calls, however many find it very hard. Whilst many sales people find it difficult to get into a routine with their sales calls, there is often a process that we can uncover using NLP modelling techniques.

For example, if you get variable results when making sales calls, you may have the right skills but an inconsistent process. If you get consistent but undesirable results, the process is working perfectly and it's the content you need to change.

Easily making sales calls is such an important aspect of the sales person's job that I'm going to share with you an article I wrote for a magazine on exactly this subject

How to love your sales calls

Making prospecting calls is one of the most important, and most feared parts of a sales person's job. The other day, I received this email from a sales person I worked with recently:

"I would just like to say a BIG, BIG thanks, I feel totally transformed, my 'phone fear' has disappeared. Its really quite weird, but I don't hesitate to pick the phone and ring people, in the past 10 days I've picked up 4-5 briefs. When I see an opportunity I just grab it.

I've noticed a big difference in my day too, I just don't know where the hours go, and I wish there were longer hours in the day to fit everything in. This will make you laugh, the last few days I've had lots of admin work, and haven't been able to get on the phone, I actually heard myself saying that 'I wish I was on the phone more' can you believe it?"

What would it be like if you felt the same way about your sales calls? Now, in order for you to be succeeding at your job, you must already be making sales calls, so I'm not talking about teaching you the basics here. I'm presuming you already do make calls, but maybe you tidy your desk, answer your emails and make a cup of coffee before you get yourself into the right mood. Maybe you stop after ten calls instead of stopping when the clients have all gone home. Maybe you make it harder for yourself than it needs to be.

Maybe you already love sales calls and you're already getting great results, in which case – why are you reading this? Get on the phone!

A change like this can happen very quickly. The longest this has ever taken was about an hour, the shortest about one minute.

But how? Well, the exact process varies from one person to the next because every person I've ever worked with creates this situation in a slightly different, unique way – and so will you. Having said that, there are some general principles and patterns that I can tell you about that you can use right away to improve your approach and therefore your results.

Firstly, stop cold calling. It's difficult, time consuming and produces poor results. Instead, spend some time each day calling people you haven't spoken to before and finding out how you can help them.

Secondly, At the moment you pick up the phone to dial, what picture pops into your head? What does the voice in your head say? Do you begin your call by apologising, or does your voice tone demonstrate the pride you take in your job? Just work through these simple steps, giving yourself time to think this through very carefully:

Imagine yourself sitting at your desk at the time you would begin making sales calls. As you imagine starting to dial, what picture pops into your head. Specifically, whose picture? If you find sales calls consistently difficult, I'm guessing the picture is of someone you don't have much in common with who doesn't look pleased to hear from you. If you find calls randomly difficult, I'm guessing there's no coherent picture. In either case, that's good news.

Next, imagine you're about to call your best friend or someone you like very, very much. You know exactly what I mean. As you dial, what picture pops into your mind? Now, stop and think about yourself – are you smiling? Are you sitting upright? Are you dialling eagerly? When you speak, does your tone of voice reflect this?

So, if you imagine someone who doesn't want to talk to you, simply imagine reaching out and grabbing the picture, screwing it into a ball and throwing it over your shoulder. Then simply draw a new picture of someone who looks like you, who you have something in common with and who looks pleased to hear from you, or at least open minded. Imagine calling that person and notice how your voice tone is different.

Practice this a few times, just repeating the process over and over. Imagine starting to dial, see the face of someone you want to talk to, hear your positive voice tone, notice how that feels nice to talk to someone who enjoys talking to you.

Thirdly, what do you say to yourself before, during and after the call? If it's in any way critical that's not helping. Often, the voice in your head has really valuable feedback but you don't hear it because it just sounds like nagging or criticism. Think again about sitting down to make your calls and this time pay attention to what you are saying to yourself. Change the voice tone to something more neutral, like a news reader, or to a voice that you like – even something sexy! Now, listen to what the voice tells you – is the information more useful? You can also ask questions back. If the voice is critical, say, "Thankyou! Now, how does that information help me?" or, "Thankyou! Now, what do you suggest I do differently?" Oddly enough, you'll find the same approach works very well with that person in the office who always offers you helpful criticism.

Last of all, you can't really control what happens during each call as you are not in control of the person at the other end. They might be busy or tired and you know the importance of respecting their state. So, no matter how each call goes, it's important to treat each call as if it's your first. There are many ways that you can quickly control your state, and the simplest for our purposes here is through your focus of attention. Think of a time in the past when you felt really confident and in control of yourself. Remember that time in all the detail you can, recalling what you saw, heard and felt. Maybe you even remember some smells and tastes. When you have all that, think of a word, colour or piece of music that seems to represent it. Repeat this a few times so that the trigger becomes associated with the feeling. Now, in between calls simply replay the trigger and your state will switch to the confident, in control state.

After you have practiced all this for a day and then slept on it, your brain will build it into an unconscious calling routine for you so you won't even have to think in order to get good results. What's this based on? The principle that you are already following an unconscious process which is working perfectly for you. The process is fine but the results need a little tweak. By taking conscious control over the process and making some slight adjustments, you'll find that you can get surprising results, very quickly. How quickly? You'll only find out by finding out!

Starting the meeting

What's the best state to be in for your first meeting? This is an excellent exercise to think about when your customer is walking you from the reception area to their office or meeting room.

Choose three states that you think would be useful in your meeting. Let's say that you choose attentive, thoughtful and enthusiastic. You remember that you can effectively manage your state through physiology and focus of attention, so we can use both to elicit a state easily.

It's good to access states whilst you're moving, so just go for a walk. As you walk, think about a time when you felt attentive. Remember what you saw, heard and felt. As you walk, think about your posture, your breathing and your pace. Notice how fast you walk, how heavy your feet feel and so on. Do the same for the other two states, and then finally imagine combining all three states together. You'll find that by doing this – even on the way to the coffee machine – you will be able to access extremely useful states, very easily.

Now imagine doing the same thing as you walk with the customer to the meeting room. As the two of you get into rapport, they begin to access the state that you are demonstrating.

You may have read or heard elsewhere about body language, and my personal opinion is that it is not useful to think of your body as having a separate language. In any case, by copying your customer's posture, you are matching their state. If their state isn't useful, yours won't be either. There's not much point agreeing with a resistant, dismissive customer!

Choosing your own state allows you to lead the customer to a state that is more conducive to a productive business relationship that will benefit you both.

Set a context

Tell your customer what you want, and what you would like from them.

"The reason we're meeting is … and by the end of this meeting I want to have …"

By doing this at the start of the meeting, you help your customer to pay attention to the information that is most useful to them. You might say that you already do this when you set an objective for the meeting. What most people do is set an abstract objective such as 'agree a way forward' or 'agree next steps'. As you'll know by now, that's meaningless as far as your brain is concerned because it is too abstracted from sensory experience. Here's a different example to think about:

"The reason we're meeting is so that I can find out how this product is of value to you, and by the end of the meeting I want to have a decision from you that we can either progress to a formal proposal or not."

You already know that good communicators frame their communication, so that the listener can get into the right state first, for example, "let me ask you a question…" puts the listener into a state to understand and answer a question.

In my experience, the things you learn on a typical negotiation training course are not negotiation – they are haggling. Haggling is what you have to do at the end of a decision process when you don't tell the other person what you want soon enough. Negotiation is when you tell the other person what you want right at the start, so that they can then figure out what they need in return.

I bring this up because so many sales people meet with, and present to customers in order to inform them and then wonder why the customer acts surprised when the sales person asks for an order.

I get lots of sales calls, and I particularly like the ones from a famous business directory with coloured pages where they call to check that they have the correct details for me in my free listing. When I ask if they are trying to sell me an upgraded listing, they say, "oh no, we just want to check your details". Then they ask me to look at the website so that I can see a more prominent listing of a company who has paid for a highlighted advert. Again, I ask if they are trying to sell me an upgraded listing, and again they say, "oh no, we just want to check your details" at which point I start to get annoyed.

If they were to ring me up and say, "Hello, I want to sell you an upgraded listing, and this is what it will do for you" then I would be happy to listen.

Anchoring

Even a pen or a brochure with your logo on can be an anchor. Mind readers use anchoring extensively to 'predict' which card or object their audience will choose.

The mind reader first sets up an anchor for a pleasant state and then transfers that anchor to a particular object. The volunteer then chooses an item at will, and feels drawn to the one that they feel good about.

Could you use the same techniques to help the customer choose your product?

Traditional marketing training puts a lot of emphasis on consistency in branding – could this be an application of anchoring?

Rapport

Whilst we don't normally recommend artificially copying someone's posture and movement in a meeting, it's worth playing with occasionally to find out what happens. Often, it's unnoticeable and helps to create a harmonious relationship more quickly.

I find that the degree of rapport you have is a good barometer. If you find that your posture suddenly changes, it's worth thinking about what's happened that reduced the level of rapport. It can be as simple as using a particular word. For example, if the customer uses the phrase 'road map' and you translate it to 'route map' then you can create a slight disharmony that can become magnified throughout the course of the meeting.

All of these techniques are catalysts – helping you to accelerate the development of a relationship. They will not help you create relationships with people who do not want to work with you.

Questions

What questions do you want to ask in a meeting? Most sales people will ask questions to find out information. Really good sales people also ask questions to help their customers think in different ways. Which questions would you ask to guide your customer into a resourceful state?

Remember that in NLP we ask questions for other reasons than to find out information. We also ask questions to focus attention and change state. Tag questions are a form of hypnotic language that shifts the listener's attention away from the command and onto the question, aren't they? This forces a more receptive state, so that the suggestion or command is more readily accepted, isn't it?

We can also use questions to convey suggestions indirectly. For example, instead of saying, "that won't work" you could use, "that's an interesting idea, can you explain how it will work in practice?"

When you ask questions of this type, the customer will talk themselves out of their objections without you having to do any work.

I coach a number of managers in a large engineering company and one of them was having problems with production meetings. When trying to solve production problems, someone would come up with a suggestion and the manager I worked with would instantly try out the idea in his mind, visually, and find a drawback which he would immediately state as an objection. Arguments and ill feelings usually followed, as people saw him as 'negative'. I suggested that instead of saying that the idea wouldn't work, he make a note in his diary of the difficulties he saw (to slow his thinking down) and then ask questions about the implementation of the idea.

What then happened was that the person with the suggestion would have to imagine the same outcome in order to process the question and would realise that the idea was unworkable in practice. The person would talk themselves out of the idea and the manager was regarded as being much more supportive. An interesting consequence was that, although the ideas were unworkable in their original form, they frequently had the seeds of other ideas within them which then went on to become really good, practical solutions. By questioning the idea instead of dismissing it, he found that the group came up with more creative solutions more quickly – so not only did he improve his own professional image, he also solved the original production problem more effectively too!

Stories

Stories are a very powerful sales technique because they are not true or false, and customers can choose for themselves how they relate to the story.

There are broadly two types of story that are useful here; the change story and the teaching story. A change story has a start state that the customer can identify with, an event or action and then an end state that the customer would like to move to – for example:

"My last customer was uncertain about this product too, yet after he had a chance to talk to his colleagues he formed a really clear idea that helped him to get real value from it."

A teaching story has a lesson or moral embedded in it. By identifying with a character in the story, the listener goes through the same experience as that character.

Case studies are good examples of stories that can be in either form.

Wiping the slate clean

You might want your customer to lose any preconceptions about you, your company or your product. They may even be having a bad day that you would like them to forget about, just for a few moments.

The Swish is a NLP technique for interrupting habitual thought patterns and leading someone's mind in a new, more useful direction. At the Practitioner level, it seems like one of the strangest, least applicable NLP techniques. In fact, it's one of the most flexible and easy to use in a wide range of situations, if you understand how it works and how to use it.

Every day, in every office in the country, swish patterns are already in use in business. Every time you turn over a page in a report, a flipchart pad or move to the next slide in Microsoft PowerPoint, you are using the same structure as the swish pattern. Now that you know that, you can use content, layout, colours and slideshow affects to enhance the impact of the swish.

The structure of the Swish is simply:

Current state > Interrupt > New state

So anything that you do that follows that basic structure will work to replace an existing or habitual thought pattern with a new one.

Qualify

Qualification is the process of deciding if you want a particular piece of business, and is vital in prioritising the way you apply your resources to the sales process.

The most important thing about having a qualification checklist is having the determination to use it consistently so that it helps you to ask the questions that you might take for granted.

There are many examples of off the shelf qualification checklists, many of which are copyrighted so I can't tell you about them here. Many of them cover pretty much the same qualification criteria, arranged to form a neat acronym that can be copyrighted for commercial benefit.

Money	Does the customer actually have the money to spend?
Effort	Is this worth the effort? Think about geography, strategic fit and so on.
Authority	Are we talking to the person who will make the buying decision?
Need	Does the customer really need to buy this?
Solution	Do we actually have the right solution to the customer's needs? If not, will the customer find out before we get a chance to close the sale? Probably!
Competition	What is the competition doing? How do we plan to beat them?
Originality	What is unique about our solution? And how does that meet the customer's buying criteria?
Timescales	When will this close? Is this a short term or long term project?
Size	How much is this worth to us? How much profit do we make? Is it worth going for?

The value of having, and using, a qualification checklist like this is that it forces you to ask yourself the questions you need to be asking the customer.

It's amazing how many sales people don't qualify properly, and I believe that this is mostly down to the way that their performance is measured. Sales people who are focussed on sales targets generally qualify ruthlessly – as if they value their own time above everything else. Their focus is on what deals they can close now and what those deals are worth to them. If a deal is huge but won't close for a year, they ignore it.

Many sales people working in more relaxed environments take a more strategic view of qualification, which means that if someone asks them a question they don't like, they say, "it's strategic". For example:

Sales manager	"What's this deal worth?"
Sales person	"£500"
Sales manager	"So why are you wasting your time on it?"
Sales person	"It's strategic. It will lead to more business"
Sales manager	"Hmmmm"

In situations like this, it's common to find sales people measured on activity rather than outcomes. In other words, they are motivated to look busy rather than to sell. As long as they are working on lots of deals they can always blame something else for their low closure rate.

You might think that this is a tough view of sales, but remember that sales can be a tough job. Some people say that long term, strategic projects require a different approach and I would say that, in my experience, the people who perform well in any sales situation are the ones who do the basics well, who follow a consistent sales process and who are in control of that process.

Qualification is possibly the most important step in the sales process, because it keeps you on track. Once again, some people say that sales is an interaction between sales people and customers rather than something that the sales person owns, so I will just ask you one final question. As you think about your long term business plans, do you want to develop the business that you want or the business that your customers want? The answer to that question tells you how much control you need to take when qualifying.

Of course, you want your customers' business, but at what cost? Successful companies have a business plan and they find the customers who help them to achieve that plan. The alternative is that you find people with money and give them whatever they want. That approach may work in the short term, but in the long term it pulls you in so many different directions that you end up being unable to support any of your customers. This is the problem that many small businesses face when they chase customers rather than focussing on building the business they want.

Identify requirements

Spending time finding out what people want will deepen relationships in many areas of your life. In a sales context, you can find out what is important to your customers in the context in which you do business.

I designed a workshop for a global communications company that was training its sales people to sell more complex solutions at a higher level – selling to CEOs rather than IT managers.

The sales training company that were running the majority of the training were doing a good job of telling the sales people what to do – exactly what the sales people already knew they had to do. They had to understand politics, meet the CEO, influence strategy and so on. All great stuff. And all the sales people would say "I know I have to do that, but nobody is telling me *how* to do it".

The workshop I designed and ran for them during the training course was designed to help them form very deep connections, very quickly in order to really understand a customer's unspoken needs. You can try out this exercise in your own team meetings to find out what happens, and you can also use the techniques that it covers to develop deeper relationships with your own customers.

Here is the workshop script, in full.

You'll spend a lot of time during these two days understanding what customers tell you – about their business plans, political structures, budgets and so on. Yet talk to any seasoned, exceptional sales professional and they'll tell you that being really successful is no longer about understanding what the customer tells you – it's about understanding what the customer doesn't tell you.

Being a really effective communicator is about reading between the lines, hearing what isn't said and seeing what the customer doesn't expect you to see, because it leaks out his beliefs, fears and true intentions.

Who likes watching Derren Brown on the telly? Have you seen any of his tricks where he can tell if someone is lying, or which hand they're holding the coin in? The thing about these tricks is that you can already do them – if you open yourself up to the unconscious communication that radiates from everyone around you. You already know that 93% of communication is outside of the simple world of words, yet many training courses focus only on the words that the customer gives you.

Years ago, sales people used to be trained to make small talk with customers. There were sales people who had intimate knowledge of their customers' families, hobbies and golf handicaps, yet they didn't sell anything. We learn by making connections, and those connections often take the form of a purpose. For example, you know what a Mars Bar is for, so you know how to know when you need one. We do the same thing with relationships, especially those fleeting relationships that we experience in business. We remember people by what the relationship is for. Guess what? If the customer remembers you as that nice person he talks to about golf, he will come to you for exactly that. If he thinks about your relationship in the context of buying telecoms services, that's what track his mind will switch onto when you meet or talk. And if he thinks of you as someone who helps him to solve real business problems... well you can guess the rest. The important thing here is context, so right from the very first meeting, you need to keep your conversation within the context of his business and his business problems – problems that you are going to help him solve.

When people make decisions, their words only rationalise a decision that has already been made, emotionally. By tuning into those emotional signals, you'll know what the customer wants before he does. If the customer has an emotional response to something, that's a good sign that it is important! If you challenge that decision or opinion head on with facts and figures, all you're doing is embedding the customer deeper into that emotional response. In short, your efforts to change their mind actually convince them more.

I know what you're thinking – "show me how!" and in this short slot I can only show you a couple of ideas that you can take away and use immediately. By the way, as well as being able to read your mind, you can also use these ideas to improve the quality of your personal relationships too!

OK, let's practice something really simple first. In a moment I'm going to ask you to pair up and do a really quick exercise – 5 minutes each is plenty of time for this.

What I want you to do is have your partner tell you about a current, real problem they have that they feel some emotional connection to – maybe frustration, disappointment, confusion, whatever.

You may want to get your notepad and right now, think of a problem you currently have and make a note of it. It can be anything at all – whatever you have in mind write now.

As they tell you about it I want you to ignore their words completely. I know that, as nosey human beings, we like to get tied up in the content, offer suggestions, fix people's problems and so on. Irritating, when people do that to you instead of listening, isn't it! I want you to completely ignore their words and instead focus on only three things, and I want you to notice what they do when they talk about a particular aspect of the problem, or experience a particular emotional state. What I want you to pay attention to is:

- Their voice tone

- Where they look

- What they do with their hands

That's all there is to it! So, really quickly pair up and I'll call you back in just over 10 minutes. When you're done, stay with your partner for the second part of the exercise.

The feedback from the audience included points such as:

- I couldn't pay attention to all 3 aspects, only 1 or 2
- I noticed how every time my partner said x he did y
- I found it hard to not listen to content
- He looked around a lot
- She moved her hands a lot
- His voice tone changed when he talked about his feelings

Excellent. You've noticed some really good things there, the kind of things that really excellent communicators notice intuitively. Now we'll do part two of that exercise.

Go back to the person you worked with last time and summarise their problem back to them to check your understanding.

I want you to each play back your partner's problem, concentrating on using the exact voice tone they used, looking where they looked (as if they were looking at something real) and moving your hands in the same way. If they showed you a direction, or an obstacle, or a picture, just reflect that back. You don't have to understand what it means, you're just respecting the fact that it means something to them. Don't try to understand or summarise the problem at this point. So play back your partner's problem concentrating on their voice tone, eye movement and gestures.

Each take a turn to do that, and again you only need a couple of minutes each.

Feedback from the audience included:

- ❏ I felt like my partner was really listening
- ❏ I felt comfortable with my partner
- ❏ I felt that my partner really understood me
- ❏ I was surprised that I do all of that when I talk

What you have done by noticing your partner's voice tone, eye movements and gestures is pick up on the key non verbal communication channels. You have started to focus on the 93% of communication where someone's true beliefs, reactions and intentions are communicated. By focusing on those three things, you will pick up far more valuable information than all of the business plans and organisation charts in the world will tell you.

I think it's a bit unfair that we should spend time exploring your problems and not let you solve them, so the final thing we're going to do is solve a problem only by asking questions about it. Remember, it's not your problem so it's not your responsibility to solve it. All you need to do is change your partner's perspective of the problem.

Think about this in a customer scenario. When you are talking to a customer who is telling you about a business problem, it matters. It means something to him because he has an emotional response to it. As you're learning during this workshop, the problem isn't really about software compatibility, user capacity or even customer satisfaction. The problem is about emotions – triggered by politics, power, threats, perceptions, promotions and so on. If you sit in front of your customer and really listen in the way you have practiced here today, you will create a greater depth of rapport and empathy than you can imagine. The problem with this is that the customer will automatically associate you with the problem – specifically, just because he has told you about it and you have listened, he will think you can solve it.

So let's try out a few questions that we can use to clarify the problem. These questions work in a particular way, changing your partner's perception of the problem. When their perception changes, they will see solutions that had previously been hidden from them. I want you to question the problem using only the questions on the slide. It doesn't matter if you ask the same question more than once, you will get a different answer each time as the problem changes.

If your partner says something that has "I can't" in it, reply with "What would happen if you did?"

You have 5 minutes each for this – and if you solve the problem with the first question, just talk about whatever you like! Remember to ask these questions gently, as if you really care about the person's problem, and as if you know that they already know how to solve it, they just haven't realised it yet.

- What is important to you about solving this?
- Imagine it's a year from now, what has changed?
- Imagine it's a month from now, how does it feel different?
- What stops you from solving this now?
- What would happen if you did?
- What does a good solution look, sound and feel like?
- What do you really want to do about this?
- Think of someone who would handle this really well. What would they do?

Feedback from the audience included:

- It really helped me to think through the problem
- It helped me to find my own solution
- It changed my perspective of the problem
- I feel differently about the problem

Now, you might be thinking that this is all very well for face to face meetings, what about the times when you call someone over the phone? Well, it's exactly the same with just a small difference. This 93% of communication that is unconscious is made up of two components – visual and auditory – which need to reinforce each other for communication to be 'congruent'. We normally perceive congruence as confidence, certainty or honesty. When we speak to someone over the telephone, we only have the auditory component, so where does the visual component come from? We make it up! We make it up based on our own expectations, and on the auditory component. When you're making sales calls, you unconsciously visualise the person you are calling. If you have never met them, you visualise something based on your prior experience. This is why calls often go exactly the way you intend them to – when you're feeling confident the call goes well, when you are nervous and doubting yourself, the call goes badly.

You've all done so well that I think we should wrap up this part of the workshop with one final exercise, that will take you only a couple of minutes each. I want you to use only your intuition for this. I know you all have a strong intuition, and I know how aware you are of what happens when you trust it, and what happens when you don't. With your partner, I want you to simply trust your intuition. Don't rationalise it, don't explain it, don't find reasons for it. Just tell your partner what you feel their problem is really all about, and give them one single piece of advice. Don't sit there and analyse it. Don't worry about whether it is right or wrong. It doesn't have to make any sense. Just say what you feel is right.

Feedback from the audience included:

- The summary was absolutely spot on
- My partner discovered something really important that I hadn't even mentioned
- The suggestion was really accurate
- My partner told me what I already knew I had to do

You see, the 93% and 7% don't just work in the way we communicate outwards – they also apply to the way we take information in. What you have just done, by trusting your intuition, is allowed yourself access to more of your brain than just by focusing analytically. So if you really want to pay attention to someone, stop listening and allow yourself to really hear.

We've got time for one last exercise, so let's put together everything you have learned so far. I want you to pair up again and imagine that you're making a telephone call to someone who you want to arrange a meeting with. You can do this exercise with your eyes closed if you really want to simulate being on the telephone – that's up to you.

What I want you to do is think of two people now. The first is someone who you find difficult or obstructive, who you struggle to communicate with and who never gives you what you ask for. The second is someone who you get on well with, someone who you feel is always helpful and always sounds pleased to hear from you.

What you're going to do is randomly pick one of those two people and really imagine that you are about to call them to arrange a meeting. Imagine what they look like, imagine their voice and imagine how you feel when you are preparing to talk to them.

As you imagine that person, imagine you are calling them and when they answer, tell your partner whatever you normally say when you make a call. It's not a role play, so your partner does not have to pretend to be that person – you just say whatever you normally say as you imagine talking to the person you have chosen.

Do this a few times, each time selecting one of your two people at random and taking a moment to really imagine talking to them.

Your partner's role is very simple – just listen carefully and guess which person your partner is thinking of. After they have made a few 'calls' tell them what differences you noticed.

Feedback from the audience included:

- It was really obvious!

- My partner was convinced there was no difference, but I heard it right away

- My partner's nervous voice tone made me feel nervous

- My partner's confidence made me feel really receptive

- My partner's aggression made me feel intimidated

We've worked with lots of sales people, helping them to really enjoy making sales calls. One common thing that sales people do is to imagine the person they're calling being impatient or even rude, so they're apologising even before the other person picks up the phone. The solution is to simply imagine you're calling someone you look forward to talking to! The difference in your voice tone will make a huge difference to the state and response of the person you're calling.

So, during this part of the workshop, what have we achieved? Well, instead of hearing just 7% of the customer's communication, through their words, we have started to focus on 100% of their communication. It's in that hidden 93% that what they are really trying to tell you is conveyed. By paying attention to that, you will learn more about what is really important to them, and that creates greater empathy and strengthens the connection between you. That strong connection allows you to ask questions that normally you wouldn't get away with, and those questions help you to change the person's perception. Changing the other person's perceptions is the basis for changing their opinions, needs and beliefs, and that is the basis for creating a very powerful business relationship.

Through these simple ideas, you can build stronger relationships, influence state and you can change people's minds. You can understand people like never before, and they will want to tell you about what is important to them, because they feel good about telling you. What more could you want!

Identify values

Our behaviour tends to be guided by what is important to us. Therefore, if you want to understand someone's behaviour, you must first understand their values. This is surprisingly easy – you just ask someone what is important to them.

This is very important with respect to customer service. All too often, sales and service people give the customer what they ask for instead of what they need.

I once had this conversation with a customer:

"I don't like my current account manager"

"What don't you like?"

"She doesn't listen"

"What is important about listening?"

"So I don't have to repeat myself - it's a waste of time"

"So is time important?"

"Yes"

"What is important about that?"

"Because I've got lots to do"

"So is action important?"

"Yes"

"And why is that?"

"I like to get things done, to get results"

"So time and action are important. Is 'efficient' a good word for that?"

"Yes, that's it!"

"OK, so what DO you want in an account manager?"

Did you notice that this gets different results to just saying, "OK, we'll get you a new one...."?

If we only listened to what this customer didn't want then we could wheel one account manager after another in front of him and he'd never be happy. This would actually annoy him even more, even though we'd be trying our best to make him happy. Instead, we now know what is important to him and we can satisfy his needs much more easily. Finding a word to describe the value is good, as it gives you instant feedback - when the person you're talking to says, "yes! that's it" then you've 'hit the nail on the head' - by describing his value accurately you've proven that you understand it.

He went on to tell me what he does want, so now we can give it to him, so everyone's happy.

Develop

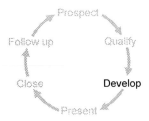

Now that you have qualified the deal, you need to understand the customer's needs in more detail and develop a solution for them.

Understand the customer's needs

The Meta Model and Milton Model are two excellent questioning tools that you can use to gather information and at the same time change or reinforce beliefs.

You can use Meta Model questions to test a customer's beliefs or experiences without influencing them, for example:

"What would a good solution look like to you?"

"How will you know when you are ready to make a decision?"

"What are you looking for in this type of product?"

"What do you need to hear from me that will be most useful to you?"

"What can I tell you about the product?"

You can also ask questions that contain presuppositions or embedded commands to change or reinforce customer requirements. Analogue marking – a change in voice tone or a gesture to mark out the command – is indicated in italics.

"How will you know *you are ready to make a decision*?"

"How do *you see my product standing out* against our competitors?"

"When *you are ready to go ahead*, what will you need from me?"

If you want to change a customer's mind, it's important to remember to pace before you start leading. Even Dale Carnegie wrote about this in 'How to win friends and influence people' when he advised a salesman to agree with a customer who preferred a competitor's product.

So pace first...

"You're right, that product is certainly popular with some people and is a good choice..."

Then lead...

"for people who don't need the extra reliability and low servicing costs of my product"

A more subtle way to introduce this type of change is to set up an anchor for good and bad experiences. You can get the customer to talk about products or suppliers he likes and also those that frustrate him. You can anchor the two states with:

- A word
- A voice tone
- A posture
- A gesture
- A location (spatial anchoring, useful when presenting)
- A pen
- A facial expression

So that when the customer talks about your product you play back the 'good' anchor and when he talks about your competitors, you play back the 'bad' anchor. A simpler and often more congruent way to do this is, after you have a good level of rapport, is to simply agree non-verbally (smile, nod etc.) with the customer when he talks about your product and disagree non-verbally (frown, fold your arms, break eye contact) when he talks about your competitor. If your level of rapport was good to start with, the customer will begin to feel bad when he thinks about the customer.

Is this manipulative? Watch a conversation between two people who are in rapport. You will notice that when they agree, they non-verbally support each other. When one says something that the other doesn't like, you'll see frowns, folded arms, downward looks and so on. It's a natural process. If you knew nothing about NLP, cared personally about your product and took it personally when your prospects mentioned your competitors you would respond in exactly this way, randomly.

By using this natural communication system purposefully, you are protecting the relationships that are valuable to you. It's up to you whether you do this consciously and purposefully or unconsciously and randomly.

If you've read my book 'Six Questions' you'll know that there is a deceptively simple question that you can use to embed a person more strongly in their beliefs and perceptions. If you are coaching someone or helping them to change, it's usually the worst question you can ask. If you're helping someone to be even more convinced of a course of action, it's a very useful question. The question is '"Why?"

There. I told you it was deceptively simple.

The question 'why?' presupposes that everything the other person just told you is true. You might hear a colleague say, "I can't finish that report today" and when their boss asks, "why not?" the answer is, "because blah blah blah". The "blah blah blah" can be completely meaningless, yet it will be accepted as true because it is preceded by the magic word that we use to teach each other rules... "Because".

So if a customer says, "I don't think I can order your product" then absolutely positively never ever ask, "why?" If a customer says, "I have some concerns about my current supplier then always ask, "why?" just to air their concerns and really help them to think them through.

Influence and persuasion, for me, are not about getting people to do things they don't want to do. They are about noticing the subtle shifts that people make as part of their natural decision making processes, magnifying and amplifying those shifts and using them to help the person move in a particular direction with greater certainty, so that you get a decision that benefits both you and the customer.

Perhaps a useful belief about sales is that if a prospect is actively looking to spend money on a product, their decision criteria are going to be highly subjective. If that's the case, then whether they choose your product or someone else's is a matter of taste. People are very good at making up rational sounding decision criteria to disguise their subjectivity, but in the end it comes down to which product they get a good feeling about. If the customer is going to buy a product anyway, why shouldn't that product be yours?

Products and services

You'll notice that I keep talking about products, and you might be selling your services. You might even be self employed, in which case you are selling yourself.

I'm going to be picky on this and say that whatever you are selling, you must think of it as a product. Calling it a service or a solution is a way of avoiding the harsh reality of having to give the customer something tangible in return for money. In order to reach a decision, an equal exchange has to take place.

Think about a situation where you buy something. You don't buy money, yet you think of the value of a product in terms of money. When you pay a bit more than you think something is worth, you might rationalise your choice as being about 'quality'. If you pay a bit less, you might feel good about getting a bargain. What if you pay a lot less? You might think there's something wrong with it. If you pay a lot more? You might feel like you've been had.

Therefore, the challenge for the salesperson is not to make the product seem like a bargain – it's to make it seem like good value for money so that the customer gets a fair and equal exchange for their hard earned cash.

Now, back to products and services. When you provide a service such as coaching, accounting, consulting or recruiting, your customer is buying a tangible result. Many people who sell services such as consultancy don't know what that result is, so they don't know how to sell consultancy. They way they get round this problem is to sell consultancy by doing it, perhaps with a low cost pilot study or a free taster session. Of course, the recommendation is that the client needs more consultancy...

Good recruiters think of the candidate as being their product. They research the product to have good product knowledge, they market the product and when they find the right opportunity they sell that product in. Lazy recruiters just throw CVs at a prospect to demonstrate how many candidates they have on their books, and that's no different to a lazy salesperson who gives out brochures rather than uncovering a prospect's needs and presenting the right product to meet those needs.

So am I against coaches giving away free trial sessions? The short answer is yes, because it requires no commitment on the client's part, and no sales skill on the coach's part. To me, that's a recipe for an unsatisfying commercial relationship.

Create value

In order to understand value, you of course have to understand what the customer will do with the product and that involves actually talking to the customer – something which some salespeople would rather avoid.

If you don't uncover the client's interests and needs, you will just have to list features at them in the hope that some of those features 'stick'. You could probably go to most car showrooms and still experience this approach. Many industries have a cultural belief that since the staff turnover will be high, there's no point training sales people to be any more than a talking brochure, so sales people get product training and little else.

In my mind, sales is an art and a profession, and it's a genuinely pleasurable experience for the sales person and customer when it's done properly.

So how do you understand what the product is worth to the customer?

Price

A more economical car will save me money on petrol. A smaller car will save me money on insurance. A digital camera will save me money on film processing.

Telephone services, electricity, insurance and so on are all sold using this simple approach. Spend money with us and save money overall.

This approach has one major drawback – sooner or later, a competitor with newer, more cost effective technology will come along and you'll no longer be the cheapest. If you have done nothing to solidify customer relationships, you'll be in the difficult position of reducing prices and losing profits.

Many companies have been put out of business by this strategy.

Value of solution

You can simply associate a value to the solution you're selling. Whilst more complex than selling on price, it's worth it because you are creating a direct link between a product's features and a customer's needs, and expressing that link using the universal language of money.

A faster computer will save me time which is worth money to me. Of course, it's hard to quantify how much time, but I know how frustrating it is to sit and watch my computer process graphics while I'm creating a book cover. I also know how much I would spend to solve that problem.

When you explore the value of the solution, you will often uncover hidden needs – criteria which turn out to be vital which the customer had not even thought of.

Cost of problem

Many sales systems help you to create a cost for a problem which gives you a direct value to sell against. For example, you have an office with 100 staff (Situation) who have difficulty getting to the office due to local traffic and parking problems (Problem). This means that staff absence and turnover is high (Implication) which costs the business £100,000 per year (Value) Therefore, any solution to this problem which costs less than £100,000, or pays back within a reasonable time period, ought to be a 'must have'.

Many years ago, in a former life, I designed a new network for a company that makes flight simulators. Their old network was so slow that it actually caused a project to run over, incurring huge financial penalties. Although the delays only amounted to a few minutes a day, over many thousands of man hours those delays added up and cost the company millions. They had to do something, and it involved spending money. The eventual cost of the network, whilst seeming like a large amount of money, was small in comparison to the value of a contract. The network cost £400,000 and a flight simulator costs £35 million.

The only real obstacle was the buyer's fear of getting such a high profile decision wrong. After reading this book, you will have many ways to help people overcome that kind of fear, my personal favourite being to literally pluck the fear out of thin air and move it behind the person's head, into their past where it can't do any harm.

Opportunity cost

What is the cost of not buying? It could be a missed opportunity or the loss of the value of the solution. What about an opportunity that is in limited supply? What if you miss the opportunity to buy something and one of your competitors buys it instead? What about the cost of missing a time limited discount?

Of course, some sales people might exploit this in order to help you reach a decision quickly. You'll notice how many shops always have sales that end this weekend.

Creating financial and emotional value

What's in it for the customer? The pleasure of making a good decision? Publicity? Political power? Making sure he can't be criticised for making a wrong decision? What about peer pressure? Is that something else that some sales people use to their advantage.

People might buy for a number of reasons:

- Influence
- Achievement
- Affiliation
- Security
- Power
- Relationships
- Results
- Image
- Recognition

If you can identify and name these values, you will create a very powerful rapport between yourself and the customer. Often, when you first meet them, you will know what is important just by looking at and listening to them

Remember...

... customers want good value. I see lots of websites advertising 'too good to miss' promotions. When you buy the book, or training course, or CD, you get a "free $200 value e-book" Right. I'm really convinced that e-book was worth $200 and I just got it for free.

If you actually fall for that kind of trick, I'd like to hear from you as I currently have just a few remaining copies of my Ultimate Success Formula CD with a free £200 value e-book.

Regular meetings

In a long sales process, it's important to continually review your progress and to ensure the customer is still fully engaged in that process. You can simply ask, "are we still on track?" or you could use something like this simple pacing tool, which is partly based on timeline.

When many people introduce meetings, they start 'now' and move forwards into the future, describing what will happen. The future is uncertain, whereas the past cannot be changed, and is a much better place to start building agreement.

Instead of starting 'now', start at the first point of shared experience and work up to the present moment. When you notice nodding or other signs of the audience entering an agreement state, move gently into the future and suggest what will happen next, that takes you towards your outcome. You can either talk through this or use a flipchart or notepad to draw a timeline. You could even anchor or mark out a timeline by walking or moving an object on a table.

Present solution

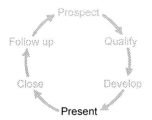

Having understood the customer's needs, you are now ready to present your solution and move towards the closing stages of the deal.

You may have to present your solution to the customer literally – by putting together a presentation to a group of decision makers. In the Presenting Impact chapter you will find a lot of information that will help you to do this well, including some ideas on overcoming any objections that are raised during your presentation. For now, we can concentrate on a simple presentation, where it's just you and the customer talking informally.

Setting an outcome

Create an opening statement using the principles of Well Formed Outcomes, then phrase it as if you were looking back from the end of the meeting, for example:

"By the end of this meeting I would like us to have made a decision on what the final solution will look like"

When you do this, the customer knows exactly what they have to pay attention to, so they will feel more comfortable and receptive and will have better quality information on which to base their decision.

Testing for agreement

The simplest way to test for agreement is to ask and listen to whether your customer says "yes" or "no"!

Tag questions are very useful here, aren't they?

"This is what you have in mind, isn't it?"

If you are feeling adventurous, you can shift verb tense in the tag question for a very powerful effect:

"This is what you have in mind, wasn't it?"

When you use these kinds of questions, you can use the ecology check from Well Formed Outcomes. In other words, watch the customer carefully and notice if they agree or not!

Questions and objections

Many objection handling techniques are based on the presupposition that the objection is real.

If the customer has a genuine objection, then a number of things must be true:

- The customer has thought about owning the product

- The customer has imagined a barrier to owning the product

- The customer is sufficiently engaged to tell you about it

So, if an objection is genuine, then it can be thought of as a buying signal, or at least a sign that the customer has moved into 'buying mode'. If I'm buying a car and I want to check if my child's pushchair will fit in the boot, I must have imagined trying to get the pushchair in the boot and logically, if I am trying to get a pushchair in the boot, at some point in the past I must have bought the car.

Of course, not all objections are buying signals, in that customers will raise objections for other reasons. It's always a good idea to slow down and give yourself time to think about an objection before you choose whether to respond to it or not.

Simple objection handling process

1. Pause

2. Restate the objection

3. Clarify the objection

4. Pause

5. Answer honestly and directly

Feel Felt Found

A good old fashioned technique for handling objections based on uncertainty is the Feel Felt Found technique, which goes something like this:

"I understand how you feel. Bloggs & Co felt the same way and they found that by spending more money they became much more comfortable".

Even though it's a very old technique, you'll see it uses some basic principles that you'll recognise from NLP – empathy, rapport, pacing states and even timeline.

How could you adapt this technique? Does it only apply to kinaesthetic customers? Or does it engage emotions in some deeper, universal way?

Red herrings

When you really think about it, there are many reasons why customers ask questions other than to get an answer, for example:

- To take pleasure from putting you on the spot

- To look good in front of their boss

- To relate a question that has been suggested by a competitor

- To stall for time

- To have a reason to say "no"

I'm sure you can think of many more reasons. The important point is that if you run off to find answers to the customer's question without first checking if it's a real objection, you are wasting your time and theirs.

When you have developed rapport with a customer, you might both feel bad about upsetting each other. In such a situation, the customer will often come up with many elaborate ways of saying 'no' that seem like valid objections yet just waste time.

"I'll think about it" or "I'll need to talk to my wife/husband/boss" really mean "no" and should be treated as such.

Think about it. Let's say you have spent a lot of time building a sales process, and when you present the product and ask for the business, the customer says, "Does it come in green?"

At this point you might feel frustrated that the customer didn't mention this before, so you go off to check with your technical or marketing people and the deal is delayed yet again. If the customer just said, "no" then you could choose to either walk away or to pursue what is missing in either the customer's perception or your own understanding of the customer's needs. That saves time on both sides, and either course of action will be more effective than answering a question that the customer didn't want answered anyway.

A dangerous situation arises when you are in a competitive situation and the customer asks you questions relating to a competitor's product. Often, the sales person with the best customer relationship will prime the customer with questions to ask the other bidders. Sometimes these are subtle and relate to features that the competitor's product supports but which yours does not. More often, the questions are clumsy and instantly give away information about the buyer's affiliations because they relate to proprietary features or trade marks.

If you respond to tenders, this is also one of the most important things to look for, because it will tell you who wrote the tender. Just because the tender selection process seems to be objective, don't presume the playing field is level. End users know exactly what they want and who they like, and they are usually masters at manipulating the finance department's rules on supplier selection.

Any time you are asked a question or see a written requirement that doesn't seem to be quite in plain English, it's worth typing it into Google in quote marks to see what comes back.

Probably the simplest way to flush out most red herrings is to use the simple objection handling process mentioned above, because the clarifying step will reveal a question that has no real need behind it.

Future pacing

You can use a conversational timeline to lead the customer past the decision point so that they can be comfortable with their decision and won't 'undecide'

Buyer's remorse is traditionally seen as the customer changing their mind, but I don't believe this to be the case. When we make a complex decision, we often cycle between choices, mentally trying out each option to experience how it feels. When someone presses us for a decision, we reveal the current state of that process, not the end state. After that point, we don't change our minds – that cycling process just keeps on running as it hasn't been given the time it needs to complete naturally.

Do you ever sit and ponder over what you're going to order at an all you can eat buffet restaurant? You can have it all! Compare that to the angst that people go through as they sit examining a menu – 'if I have the beef I can have red wine but the chicken looks nice but then I couldn't have red wine and I quite fancy red wine tonight'.

So the logical chain of thought goes:

Red wine > Beef > Chicken > Red wine

And you go round and round in circles until the waiter comes over and you are forced to make a decision which you then sit and think about until you actually get your meal and start eating, because at the point at which the waiter takes your order, you still haven't made a decision. You order based on whichever point you're at in the loop, but you have not really reached a decision.

In sales, it's worth bearing in mind that people do not change their minds – they just carry on processing a decision that they have not yet made. We don't change our minds because we are remarkably consistent creatures. Inconsistency or indecision is an illusion – the reality is that we force people to put choices into words that have not yet been made.

Traditional sales practice says you should avoid getting your customers into 'owning mode' and instead keep them in 'buying mode'. Ikea seems to disagree with this, and the founder of the company is now richer than Bill Gates. What do you think?

In real time, we go through the following stages: Information, Decision, Buying, Owning. Ikea take you through the process in reverse order. How do they do that? What effect does it have? How could you use the same principle?

Information	At this point, you don't even know that you need the product or that it exists. You need to gather general information in order to create your decision criteria.
Decision	Now that you have gathered enough information, you are ready to make a decision using your natural decision process.
Buying	Having made a decision, you are interested in finding out how to acquire the product. You want to find out about payment options, delivery, if it will fit through your front door and so on.
Owning	The product is now yours and is part of your everyday life.

Other furniture shops fill warehouses with sofas and have a few tables and plants scattered around to make the place seem a bit more homely. Ikea create entire rooms, complete with real TVs. If you go to Ikea, take a moment to watch the young couples sitting in these sets experiencing a shard hallucination that they are in a real 'dream home'. You'll hear them say things like, "our wedding picture will look nice on the wall, and that clock your mother gave us will just fit perfectly on that shelf".

If you think about it logically, if you own something you must have bought it, and if you bought it you must have decided to buy it. When external events simulate a future outcome, our brains are very good at filling in the missing steps. It's as if we create a false memory of buying the product which presupposes that the customer made a decision to buy it in the past.

In the old days, we would call this the 'puppy dog close'. Once you get to hold the puppy, you don't want to give it back.

Now you know something they didn't know in the old days. You don't even have to give the customer a puppy, they just have to imagine having one!

Negotiation

Many negotiation courses teach you how to arrive at an agreement in a commercial decision process. In fact, what most negotiation courses call negotiation is really haggling – the small part at the end when you find a price you're both happy with. In fact, this type of negotiation requires both parties to move from their original position or compromise so in fact it always results in a lose/lose deal. What can you do to create a win/win?

There are many different definitions of negotiation that we could use. We could say that negotiating is "reaching an agreed settlement between two or more parties" or we could define it as "reaching a compromise between conflicting needs". For our purposes, we can define negotiation as:

"The art of getting what you want, even when you don't have direct control over the person who will give it to you."

This may or may not be your usual working definition, so just regard it as a useful context for this part of the book and in doing so accept the simple premise that underpins it:

You are more likely to get what you want if you know what you want and are flexible in how you get it

As a general rule, the earlier you tell people what you want, the less you have to negotiate at the end. In my experience, what most negotiation courses teach is the haggling you have to do at the end of a decision process when you didn't tell the other person what you wanted early enough.

Negotiation is such an important part of the sales process that we should spend some time exploring it in detail.

Preparing to negotiate

So, let's start with the most obvious aspect of a negotiation - you negotiate in order to get something. What makes it a negotiation instead of a demand or request? The belief that you have to give something back in return.

Let's explore this interesting aspect of negotiation first; that you don't always have to give something back. Or, at least you might not always be aware of what the other person is getting in return.

Think back to when you were a child. You constantly made demands on your parents - for their time, their attention, their money and for all the things they gave you. Was this a negotiation? Or was it an unfair trade?

Of course, your parents got something in return and, as a child, you instinctively knew that you could ask for the moon on a stick and your parents would still get more out of the deal. At least, you acted as if that were true, and herein lies the first secret of negotiation and influence:

Act as if you fully expect to get more than you are asking for

Of course, this presupposes that you know both what you want and what you are prepared to settle for. In all kinds of transactions, people have two expectations; what they would like and what they would settle for. What I see, time and time again, is that people end up getting exactly what they would settle for. There's an important lesson in that.

A few years ago, I worked with some consultants who were in the early stages of building their consultancy business. The consultants were having to make sales calls and ask potential clients for meetings. One girl was having trouble with this, and said that she couldn't get people to agree to meetings although she generally got agreement to send a brochure.

Think about modelling strategies – if the result is consistent, there must be an underlying process.

I asked her what she was aiming for and she said, "Well, what I would really like is to get a meeting", so I asked what she would settle for and she said, "Well, I would be happy if they let me send them a brochure".

People tend to get exactly what they aim for, so if the result is not what you want, it's worth checking the real outcome.

Planning your strategy

In order to execute any plan you need a strategy. In other words, after you have decided what you want, the next step is to do something. The question is - what?

Planning a strategy is not the same as doing something. Ultimately, people can only give you what you want if they know you want it. Therefore, the next secret of negotiation and influence is:

The easiest way to get what you want is to ask for what you want

And do it in the most direct way possible. Other people cannot be relied upon to understand hints and gentle nudges, or roundabout requests, or tact, or any of the other ways that we make ourselves feel less self conscious about expressing our needs. If you do not habitually tell people what you want then you have no right to get it!

Here's a good way to ask for what you want:

"What I want is… And what I need from you is… How do you feel about that?"

Understanding needs and outcomes

Possibly the most important skill for helping other people get what they want is to be able to understand their needs, even when they aren't very good at expressing them. Think of a time when you've had really good service in a shop or restaurant and I bet it has something to do with the other person predicting your needs or exceeding your expectations.

It's easy to imagine that you are exceeding your customers' expectations by giving them more than they have asked for, but beware of giving them 'more' according to your criteria than to theirs. For example, in choosing a removal company to help me move house, price is not my main selection criteria once it falls into a broadly competitive range. My main criteria are reliability and care - I want the removal company to turn up on time, move me efficiently and not break anything. In order to get this, I will pay more than the lowest price as long as the price is 'in the ball park' i.e. in the range limited by the supplier's competitors or market.

If a removal company tries to win my business by offering a discount, I will probably rule them out. If a company gave me a list of previous customers I could speak to, I would probably be more impressed, but I probably wouldn't call anyone. If the person who comes to provide the estimate gives an air of confidence and capability, I will probably choose that company.

Therefore, in exceeding your customers' expectations, it's vital to know what their criteria are, and how they are different to your own.

In negotiations, everyone wants something in order to get something else - people want cars to go places, they want furniture to sit on and they want money to buy things. The objects of the negotiation are not an end in themselves, they are a means to an end. A very useful step in the negotiation is for you to find out what ends are served by the negotiation. This will make you more flexible and more effective.

The only time I've ever seen customers really unhappy is when they were given what they asked for instead of what they wanted. Therefore, always find out what people *really* want instead of simply giving them what they ask for.

It sounds obvious, yet many sales people don't know how to find out what their customers really want. With your NLP skills, it should be no problem at all.

Common negotiating tricks

You already know all the tricks people use in negotiations, because you've already heard them all or used them all yourself. Let's have a look at the more common ones.

"But that's all I can afford"

This may be absolutely true, or this may be a ruse to get you to discount or meet someone's price demand.

If this is true then the person genuinely cannot afford what they want and should not be looking. If this is false then it's a nice try. In either case, standing up to this will force them to either back away or offer more. You may choose to offer discounts to people who genuinely can't afford your product, if you really want to. Just don't confuse that with being fooled by this simple trick.

From the other point of view, sales people will tell you that their price is already at rock bottom and they can't afford to discount any further. In that case, you have to decide if you are looking at products that you really can't afford, or if this is a trick. In either case, walk away and see what happens.

"You'll have to ask my husband/wife/boss"

When you reach a stage where the other person wants to think or back off, they will often defer to a third party who has more authority than they do. As with all the tricks, this works both ways. A salesperson will defer to a boss - real or imaginary - to make a decision, and may even come back from that conversation with a tempting special offer if you sign right away. Don't be fooled by this.

A buyer will often find the final decision is just too much pressure and will defer to someone with more authority - often a trick to give themselves time or to back away completely.

"That's expensive, I only paid x last time"

That was last time, this is this time. If the previous supplier was willing to give away the product or service at a ridiculous price then that's their lookout. It's always better to negotiate a little good business than lots of bad business.

"The other guy said it would be cheaper"

Other guys have a tendency to do that. If you can't find this other guy then give the customer the chance to walk away. Of course, this trick forces you to defend your colleagues. If you don't give in then you are undermining what your colleague said - or at least what a potential customer with a desire for a discount said they said.

"I'll meet you half way"

A very reasonable and fair sounding offer that gets you to pull your selling price down or your buying price up. You can't say no, because it sounds so fair. Or can you?

"How much for just this bit? And this bit? And this bit?"

Breaking a package down into components is an excellent way to erode the price. I knew someone who bought a furniture set using this trick. He said he didn't want the footstool, so why should he pay for it. After the deal was closed, he said, "You might as well throw in that odd footstool - you've got no use for it now!" Remember - if your product or service is a package, keep it that way. You can achieve the same result by asking a supplier to itemise their quote.

"I just don't want to pay that much"

Well, at least they're honest. What can you do? They've effectively given you an ultimatum. You either accept their price or walk away. In fact, what they're really telling you is, "I want your product or service but you haven't created enough value yet". You have a simple choice - either build up the perceived value or remove cost in order to meet their target price.

Percentage based service fees are often difficult to defend, and it's often why legal fees are fixed - it makes it harder to negotiate them down. Surely, the same amount of work is involved in selling a £100,000 house or a £1,000,000 house? Therefore, why should they charge a percentage? By quoting a fixed rate, they avoid this problem.

You could calculate your percentage behind the scenes and then offer the client a fixed price service - remembering to list all the components of the service that constitute the asking price.

Of course, there is another alternative. Maybe if they don't want to pay that much, they should be looking at a cheaper product.

Time or availability limited offers

If an offer is valid today, it will be valid tomorrow - if they want your business enough. You'll see this in general terms, in retail — "sale must end Saturday" - and you'll see it in specific terms too – "if you agree to this now then I will do x". Remember –"now" is a very flexible time, so don't allow yourself to be put under pressure. There are very few products in this world that are so variable in price that you can't afford to make a proper decision. The same applies to "buy now, limited quantities available". Remember, there's only a limited quantity of everything on the planet, so it's not a good reason to give in!

"I'll think about it"

This means "no". Treat it as a "no" and act accordingly. Either write off the negotiation or challenge them directly – "what can I do to help you make the right decision?"

"No"

This means maybe, but you haven't completely convinced me yet. The key is in their behaviour, not in their words. If they are still talking to you, they're still interested.

Next time you're in a motorway service station, look out for the people selling credit cards. Watch the way that potential victims say no but still don't walk away, and the sales people respond to the behaviour, not the words by continuing to talk.

You'll recognise a pattern in the way you can handle all of these tricks and objections. There's no need for fancy, complicated tactics or tricks. You only need one method to successfully handle any tactic that you suspect is a trick or ruse. Just walk away. If you are unable to walk away then you have been forced into a weak position and you will be taken advantage of. Even if you get lucky, you'll still feel like you were taken advantage of.

Consider the situation when you buy a house. When you first walk into the estate agent's office to look for a house they tell you that you are in a strong position because you are the buyer and it's a buyer's market. Previously, they told their client that it's a seller's market so sellers have the power.

When you go to view houses, the estate agent is trying to find out personal information about you and your lifestyle so that they can help you to fall in love with the house. They know that first impressions are critical and they exploit this. By falling in love with the house, you move into a weak position and the estate agent excludes their competitors. At the same time, the estate agent shifts the seller into a weak position by telling them the market is slowing down, that the buyer is in a good position to proceed etc. The estate agent will now negotiate a price that will lead to the fastest completion - and the fastest commission payment for the estate agent. Like any business, the estate agent needs cash flow. Having paid for all the advertising and business overheads up front, the agent needs to secure the commission as soon as possible. A difference of £10,000 on the house price might make only £100 or £200 difference to the estate agent. On a £250,000 house, the agent would rather have £2,200 now than £2,500 next year.

By shifting both the buyer and seller into weak positions, the agent can now manage an agreement on price that secures the fastest completion of the sale. The agent can push the buyer's price up because it's their dream house and the seller's price down because the market is slowing down. The job of the estate agent is therefore to move into a controlling position. Their criteria is time. To the buyer and seller, price may be more important. The could lead to a conflict of interest in which people feel they paid more than they should have done, or accepted less than they should have done. No-one is happy in this situation, and the estate agent can always blame 'the market'. At the end of the negotiation, the estate agent will always close the negotiation by saying, "really, you did well to get the house at all, the way prices are going up" and, "really, you did well to sell the house this year before the market dies down".

Of course, this does not represent the ethical and professional approach taken by the majority of estate agents in this country. This story can merely serve to remind you to always take personal control of negotiations that affect you and your family.

Just remember to ask yourself this simple question:

Can I afford to make the wrong decision?

If the answer's yes, then go right ahead. If the answer's no, give yourself the time and space that you need to think it through.

The single most powerful negotiating tactic

"   "

Can you guess what it is?

Silence.

Concessions

What if a negotiation is stalled and neither party is making any progress? Should you make a small concession in order to get the negotiation moving again?

Imagine you make an offer on a house and the reply is a simple "no". What do you do next?

Imagine you're negotiating a business contract and the customer seems to want everything for nothing, yesterday. What information do you already have that puts you in a strong position?

You would be amazed at how many sales people - in retailers and in all businesses - will give away discounts with almost no effort on your part at all. In all but the most commoditised of retail outlets (where staff have no authority) you will find that the price on the ticket is not fixed, and that the salesperson will give away a lot before you even ask! When he's finished giving, you can start asking.

Remember - always be polite and let the other person concede first.

What is negotiable, anyway?

We get so used to negotiating on price that it's easy to forget what else is negotiable. This ties in very closely with a customer's buying criteria - always aim to negotiate on elements that are important to you but less important to the other person.

What is negotiable for you in your work situation?

For example:

▫	Price	▫	Supply	▫	Marketing
▫	Time	▫	Demand	▫	Publicity
▫	Risk	▫	Service	▫	Commitment
▫	Quality	▫	Delivery	▫	Credit

If you're negotiating a pay rise, what are you trading in return?

If you're negotiating a fee for professional services, what are you trading in return?

So, what is negotiable? Everything!

Creating a "win-win" outcome

A win-win outcome is one in which you get what you want and the other person gets what they want.

Here's a simple question:

In any negotiation, is it better to compromise than to lose the 'deal'?

If you put a lot of effort into creating win-win outcomes then you are wasting your energy. Simply let the other person take care of what you want, taking care to notice any imbalances in the negotiation that would give either of you an unfair advantage. For example, if you were starving you might accept £10 for your grandfather's Rolex watch. This is clearly an unfair bargain, in which the other person has exploited a perceived weakness on your part. You have responded to that perception - not the reality that the Rolex is worth £1000, whether you're starving or not. People often 'lose out' in negotiations by linking together elements that are completely unrelated. The value of the watch is completely unrelated to your state of health. The price that you will settle for is related to the state of your health, and this reminds us of another secret to successful negotiation:

Price and value are different things. Never confuse them.

So, a win-win situation is one where both parties feel that they got a fair deal. That doesn't necessarily mean a compromise on price, for example:

You want to buy a new TV. You're not the kind of person who wants the latest model so you look around for end of line bargains. You find a shop that has last year's model. It's effectively new, but it doesn't have all the features of this year's model. After some haggling, you get the shopkeeper to reduce the price of the TV by £200. You walk out the door with a great bargain and a big smile on your face. The shopkeeper is smiling too. Who got the best deal?

Trading value

So, price and value are not the same. What is the price of a bottle of water? Now, what is it's value? To the manufacturer, the retailer, you and a man lost in the desert.

The price of an item is the amount of money being asked for it. The cost of an item is what you lose by buying it. The value of an item is what it's worth to you.

People who make a fortune at car boot sales, buying rare art and china and reselling it at auction, are exploiting the difference between price and value. They have expert knowledge that helps them to do that, so you need some help if you are to achieve the same results.

The most tempting and common question is, "why do you want that?", to which the answer is always, "because I do". There's nothing to be gained in understanding people's past reasoning as you can't change it. There is something to be gained in understanding people's thinking processes as they can be influenced.

Possibly the single most powerful application of NLP in sales is in modelling a customer's decision process so that you can insert your product information into the natural strategy that the customer runs when they make a good decision.

Closing the negotiation

When a negotiation is a simple transaction, it's easy to recognise the start and end and to act accordingly. Not all negotiations are as clearly defined, and it's very important to recognise the point at which you need to stop negotiating.

It's vitally important in any commercial negotiation to ensure that the other person is satisfied with the outcome, otherwise you risk having them change their minds later on. When people make decisions, you need to make sure they stay made.

The simplest way to achieve this is to ask questions about the decision itself:

"You're happy with that outcome?"

"Have we covered everything that is important to you?"

"Is there anything else that you would like to discuss?"

The next part is very important, so make sure you remember it:

Ignore what they say in response to these questions. Only pay attention to what they do.

Next, talk them through the process that follows on after the decision. Push the decision into the past by walking them through all the steps that will happen next.

"OK, so now that we've reached that decision, let's just talk through what happens now"

This is a vital closing step. People unmake decisions because those decisions are not fully made - they still linger in the present and have elements that are not fully resolved. By talking through the next steps, you force the other person to think through the implications of the decision. If any unexpected side effects are going to occur, this process will flush them out so that you can deal with them. In other words, the other person may have made the decision without fully weighing up the implications, this step helps you to guide them through a more effective decision process than the one they naturally use.

If the decision was a wholly good one, then this process simply pushes the decision into the past and focuses the customer on the action they now need to take as a result of the decision.

Close

The point at which the decision is made and the deal is agreed.

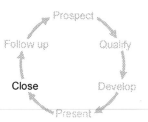

What closing techniques do you know or use?

Summary close

Summarise the process and the customer's decision criteria, then ask for the order. Some sales trainers are critical of this approach, saying it doesn't work any more. In fact, it can work extremely well because it is another form of pacing. If your summary is accurate and phrased in a generalised way, it can create a powerful agreement state. Here is an example:

"So, we have talked about the demands on your business and the services you have tried in the past to meet those demands. We talked about what you look for in a training provider, and I outlined some of the ways that I think we can help you achieve your targets more easily. Is there anything else that we need to cover before you're happy to go ahead?"

Weigh up pros and cons

Draw a line down the middle of the paper and list the pros on one side and the cons on the other. If there are more pros than cons, why not buy? This one is as old as the hills...does it still have any value?

Half-nelson

A range of old-school closing techniques that leave the customer with no choice but to sign the order. Do they still have a place in a modern, professional sales process?

- Do you want to sign the order now or later?
- Do you want this delivered on Tuesday or Wednesday?
- Do you want it in red or black?
- How do you want to pay?
- How many would you want?
- When would you want the first delivery?

These were a little clumsy at first, but they seem to have developed into more subtle presuppositions. Is there a way that these techniques could still be useful?

Just ask!

We could say that all of the above examples are ways to avoid asking for the order. What would happen if you just asked?

Metaprograms

How could you use metaprograms to create a closing strategy?

One metaprogram that confounds a lot of sales people is the procedures/options one. Good sales people are often procedures oriented, and they are good because they follow a process and get consistent results. When they meet an options oriented buyer, their intention is to close down options, yet the buyer keeps creating new ones. How frustrating! The key to closing an options buyer is to create more choice! Someone with an options orientation doesn't like to make a final decision, because it narrows his choices, therefore it's important to frame the decision as the first step that creates more choices in the future.

Procedures oriented buyers are much easier to understand, because once you find out what their buying process is, you just have to follow it properly.

The reference source can cause some difficulty too. Externally referenced buyers will rely on testimonials, references, brochures, word of mouth and so on. Internally referenced buyers will only rely on their own experience. If they have never heard of your product, how can they gain the experience they need to buy it? In this case, you can begin with something the customer does know about and shift slowly towards your own product by inference. For example, if you were selling coaching to an internally referenced training manager who didn't know what coaching is, you might start by talking about training, then moving to the demands of high performers and senior managers, then to bespoke training, then to individual training, then to coaching. At each step, your lead is what the customer already understands and approves of.

Mutual agreement

The best time to close is when both parties want it to happen. When the customer is ready to buy and the sales person is ready to sell, that's the best time to close.

Are sales people always ready to sell?

Can you think of any examples of when the customer wanted to buy something that you weren't sure about?

Follow up

What you do after the deal is closed, both to develop the relationship and to build future prospects.

Reassurance

A good decision is one that stays made. What do you need to do to reassure the customer?

When people change their minds (buyer's remorse) it's often when they have physically decided (i.e. bought the product) but in their minds the decision is not yet fully made. If this is the case, what can you do to ensure the decision is made to the customer's satisfaction?

In coaching or change work using NLP, the final step of the process is always to future pace and check for congruence. What the coach needs to do is get the client to imagine the behaviour that had been a problem and check that the client's physiological response indicates that an internal change has take place. In other words, if I just cured your fear of spiders, I want you to imagine seeing a spider so that I can check you look relaxed.

Future pacing is a vital part of the sales process because, even though the order is signed, you can never be absolutely certain of where the customer is in their decision process. Much better to check that it's the right decision, for everyone's benefit.

Prospect generation

Every customer is both a new prospect and a source of new prospects.

What questions can you ask to feed into your prospecting activities?

For example:

- Who else can you recommend I talk to?
- Where do you network?
- Who are your competitors?

Win/loss analysis

Many sales people are afraid to ask why their customers buy from them, in case they change their minds. In fact, it serves two important purposes. Firstly, it helps the customer to become even more comfortable with their decision by reviewing it. Secondly, it strengthens the relationship by getting the customer to talk about what they like about the company, product or sales person.

What many companies do is to only review the process when it goes wrong, and then it turns into a 'drains-up' or 'witch hunt' . Remember – there is no failure, only feedback. This also means there is no success, only feedback. Always be learning, and in particular, appreciate all the times your customers help you to learn from them.

In general, the earlier you win a deal, the harder it is to lose. Knowing at which point the decision was made is very useful information that will help you to review and refine your sales process.

You can explore this in conversation, or you can use a simple timeline to explore the sales cycle and identify the point at which the deal was won or lost.

- At what point was it won/lost?
- What would have made a difference?
- What will make a difference next time?

When you use a timeline to explore an experience in this way, you will often get strong feelings that you may not be able to explain immediately. When you find the point at which the decision was made, you will 'just know' so simply trust yourself to be right and to find an explanation later when you have finished processing the unconscious information that is available to you.

Keeping motivated

How do you reward yourself? Some people set themselves targets with a treat on completion. Others commit to something big like a new car and think it will motivate them to work harder to pay for it. Which works for you?

Many companies still think that sales people are motivated by money. I have never found this to be the case. If money plays a part, it is that good sales people seem more comfortable making a direct connection between value and money, and that they are not afraid to talk about it.

Many people starting their own businesses struggle with the sales process because they are afraid to talk about money, as if it is a taboo subject. They are afraid to ask for good rates, and they often undersell themselves.

Remember what you read earlier about customers wanting a fair and equal exchange – if you charge £200 per day your clients will expect a service that is only worth £200 per day. If you charge £2000 per day, you will find it easy to differentiate between two types of people in your target market; the people who can't imagine your service to be worth £2000 and the people who expect to pay for high quality.

Setting your rates is more about market positioning than about the reality of the market. Choose how you want to be perceived before you discount your rates.

If money is the universal language of business, sales people are comfortable speaking it. Whilst they might not be motivated explicitly by money, they are very aware of the amount of money they need to get the things that do motivate them such as status, respect or just a nice lifestyle for their families.

Recommended reading:

The Two Minute Message	William Freemen
World Class Selling	Jim Holden
SPIN Selling Fieldbook	Neil Rackam
Selling with Integrity	Sharen Drew Morgon
Sales on the Line	Sharen Drew Morgon
Rethinking the Sales Force	Neil Rackam and John Vincentis
Power Base Selling	Jim Holden
Persuasion Engineering	Richard Bandler and John La Velle
Influence: Science and Practice	Robert Caldini
Getting Partnering Right	Neil Rackam et al
Cold Calling Techniques	Stefen Schiffan

Executive Coaching

Coaching is a fast growing service industry, yet the principles and practices of good coaches have always been with us. Mentors, consultants, inspirational leaders and good friends have always played a role in the development and achievement of successful people, so what is it that makes coaching a discipline worth pursuing in its own right?

Firstly, a coach is focussed on performance. The client dictates what area of performance he or she wants to work on, and the client owns the measurement criteria. In the most simple terms, the coach must add value to the client in order to make money.

Therefore, we could say that the role of a coach differs from that of mentors and friends firstly because it is a commercial relationship and, like any other, must demonstrate tangible value.

In order to achieve this, the coach must first have a basic understanding of the commercial demands of the client's working environment. Many counsellors and therapists who have tried to move into business coaching have struggled with this first stage, simply because they find it difficult to build rapport with the type of clients that executive coaches work with, and they often focus on health or stress issues as a result.

The coach does not need to have the specific technical knowledge of the client's business, because the coach is not there to advise or suggest a course of action. The coach is not a consultant. The consultant's job is to analyse data and provide answers. The coach can only provide questions.

Of course, it is inevitable that when the coach understands the client's business, this will colour the relationship and at times the coach may take a more directive role, so it's important to recognise that this is a consequence of the coach's experience, not the purpose of the relationship.

So, what defines executive coaching? At the most obvious level, an executive coach is a business focussed coach who works with executives, professionals, entrepreneurs and senior managers. Whilst these people are not necessarily any different to any other employee of their organisations, they do have different demands from more stakeholders, and they often have a much greater need for confidentiality and commercial sensitivity. Balancing the needs of employees, regulators, the board, shareholders and customers is often a demanding and stressful job, and an executive coach can often help someone at that level to balance those demands with their own needs and interests.

The feedback that I get from clients working at this level certainly supports the view of an executive coach as a sounding board. I used to think that this was a bit of a cliché, yet what I am told by MDs, CEOs and people in senior positions is that they have no-one else they can talk to about important issues.

From a NLP perspective, a critical part of many people's decision and learning strategies is to verbalise an idea and hear themselves say it out loud. Certainly, many people do get themselves stuck when they are unable to verbalise a concern or idea for fear of how it might sound.

From a CEO's point of view, they cannot talk to anyone in their business about ideas that affect staff without starting rumours. As a general rule, anything that you put into words will be accepted by other people as your real opinion. I personally find this fascinating, as often, in meetings, I will take whatever is the opposing view to the one being pushed, just to even up the balance. The people in the room are then certain that it's my real opinion, so when we meet again and they take a different point of view they say that I have changed my mind when, in fact, it was never made up in the first place.

Therefore, a CEO sees an executive coach as to talk through ideas with prior to them deciding on their real course of action. The executive coach understands and is able to ask intelligent questions, and the CEO gets the chance to try out ideas without changing anything.

The role of a coach is getting broader every day, partly because greater awareness of the potential of coaching leads clients to explore the coaching relationship more, and partly because many more professionals are redefining themselves as coaches. Everyone - from therapists to consultants, via small business advisors and sales managers - is rebranding themselves as a coach.

Coaching could be described as the process of unlocking human potential. We are all born with more or less the same mechanical parts and the same blank canvass of a mind. How does one person go on to achieve great things whilst another just coasts through life? I believe that everyone achieves great things, within their own frame of reference and when viewed without the bias of what we publicly and temporarily regard as great.

A hundred years ago, no-one would have cared about Bob Geldof wanting to help some starving people in Africa, because very few people would have known about it. Today, television, the Internet and the newspapers bring the world's achievements and failures to our doorstep, giving us a global benchmark for our own lives.

If you haven't cured cancer, abseiled down a volcano and cloned a human before breakfast, you haven't lived. Fifty years ago, climbing Mount Everest was an amazing feat of human achievement. Today, it goes as unnoticed as a stroll in the park, yet anyone who does it - or runs a marathon, or teaches a child to read, or bakes a cake, or holds the hand of someone they love - deserves the praise and recognition of the world.

As a coach, you are touching the lives of people who may go on to cure cancer, or they may even go on to spend their spare time helping children to read. What matters is that you helped them set aside their doubts, free their spirits and unleash their potential to achieve anything that they set out to achieve.

Useful beliefs for a coach:

Your beliefs as a coach are the foundation for the skills you develop and the way you behave with your clients. It's important to identify the beliefs you have, and to adopt any that will be useful to you. You can bear in mind that there are many ways to adopt a new belief temporarily if that would help you to achieve a result with a particular client.

Here are some beliefs that past course delegates have suggested:

- The client has all the resources they need to change
- The client has already changed
- Where the client is now is exactly the right place for change
- Coaching is a learning process for both the coached and coach
- The client can get to where they want to be
- The client does want to change
- I am capable of helping this client
- The client has the resources they need to change
- The sky is the limit
- I can add value to the client's own experience
- Everything is possible
- The client will choose the right outcome for them
- It's worthwhile
- Both the client and the coach gain from the experience
- I believe in my intuition
- I can dare to dream
- It's up to the client to change
- There's no one answer
- There are no wrong answers
- The relationship is a 50/50 responsibility
- The problem is the solution
- The client has something to offer the coach
- The relationship has a tangible value to the client

Resourceful states for a coach:

Why should state be important to a coach? And should a coach just be confident and strong?

Aside from the fact that a coach is a human being, you will find that your client cycles through many different states during a coaching session. Yesterday, I met with a client who experienced three very distinct states during our coaching session. When he was explaining what had happened at work since we last met, he was nervous, sitting forward in his seat, wringing his hands and with an unsteady voice tone. As soon as he finished recounting the past and focused again on the present moment, he sat back in his chair, the tension drained from him and his skin changed colour as he warmed up.

We were talking about frustration, and I said that frustration is the state you experience when you are attempting to direct energy, to achieve something, and that energy is being blocked by a barrier. People are good at finding ways to move external barriers, but internal barriers such as fears and beliefs are much harder to move. In this case, his frustration was the result of a barrier which was out of his control – a very common situation.

After we spent some time exploring the issue, he realised that the barrier was completely under his control. Specifically, he realised that he couldn't control someone else's behaviour, he could only control his response to it. His frustration at a lack of recognition from his manager was directly related to the fact that he hadn't asked for recognition!

I asked which of his two children he would give more attention to; one who was performing well at school, always did her homework and was quiet and hard working, or the one who struggles, who avoids his homework and who is easily distracted. Of course, he would leave the one who was OK to her own devices and focus on the one who needed the most help. Guess what was happening at work? He was the quiet, hardworking student and his manager didn't give him recognition because he didn't appear to need it. This reframe helped him to understand his manager's behaviour and find ways to change it.

At the instant he realised this, he literally lit up like a light bulb. His face was glowing, he had a huge smile on his face and he was radiating so much energy that I felt fantastic just sitting in front of him, soaking it up.

When you are coaching, you could think of the metaphor of teaching a child to swim. As the child gains more confidence in their strength and ability, they begin to swim further without touching the bottom.

There comes a point where the child can swim, but keeps close to the side just in case. As they swim along, you'll notice they reach out and touch the side, every so often, just to make sure it's there. As a coach, your job is to be the side.

At other times, it's easy for clients to slip into their comfort zone and run through the same script they give everyone else to rationalise and defend their problem. When everyone else is understanding and patient, it can be good for the coach to surprise the client with a fierce or challenging state.

Here are some states that past course delegates have suggested:

Playful	Intrigued	Focussed
Cheeky	Fierce	Pushy
Mischievous	Detached	Quiet
Magical	Guiding	Assertive
In control	Challenging	Passive
Confident	Open minded	Intrigued
Happy	Positive	Enthralled
Listening	Knowledgeable	Empathic
Questioning	Patient	Flexible
Curious	Caring	Safe

Defining coaching

What is coaching? How does it compare with being a mentor, trainer, teacher, therapist, counsellor, consultant, adviser or just a good friend?

There doesn't seem to be a clear, simple definition that everyone agrees on. In practice, coaching seems to span a range of disciplines from counselling to management consultancy. With such a wide range of styles and client types, perhaps there will never be a definition that everyone is happy with. It seems that in creating a definition, most people describe what a coach does rather than what a coach is. My attempt is "a coach is someone who helps you get what you want in the context of a professional relationship"

Here are some definitions from past course delegates:

- Helping people come up with their own answers
- Facilitating objectives
- Helping people become more self aware
- Whatever feels right
- Supporting people as they move from one place to another
- Creating a safe environment for change
- Developing skills
- Helping people identify a direction then achieve their goals
- Improving efficiency
- Helping functioning people function better
- Helping people to get what they want

Forms of coaching

There are many forms of coaching, and many terms that coaches use to describe their work, including:

Executive	Career
Business	Leadership
Life	Team
Sports	Sales
Performance	Spiritual
Wealth	Personal
Fitness	Adventure

Which are you? Which is your natural role?

What makes this true for you? - is it your background or your aspiration that defines you as a coach?

As coaching becomes more popular, clients will get used to these different terms and will associate them with particular styles of coaching. In the past, many coaches have tried to differentiate themselves in the market by creating new names and new styles, but this often works against them because a client searching for a coach can't easily decide what they do and so will move onto the next website or directory entry.

As a first step in communicating with clients, it is often useful that they can clearly understand what you do, even if you feel that it is inaccurate or does not portray your full range of capabilities. You can correct that misconception later – something you can't do if they are already talking to someone else.

You might even consider first deciding what kind of clients you want to work with, and build your coaching style on top of that.

Why does coaching work?

You might be surprised to find the 'why' question in here, since from a NLP perspective you might think it's more useful to find out how it works rather than why it works. When you are talking to prospective clients, they will not be thinking in terms of 'how' coaching works, because they don't care. Do you care how colour television works? Do you care how your computer works? Most people only care when it doesn't work, and then they ask, "why doesn't it work?"

So when you are talking to prospective clients, it is useful to be able to answer this question because it is part of the process by which people build buying criteria.

Here are some reasons that past course delegates have come up with:

- It offers a different perspective
- It asks the questions the client should ask
- People like success
- It broadens the client's horizons
- It's under the control of the client
- It clarifies the client's options

- It overcomes inertia
- It forces the client to think
- It forces the client to make time to think
- No-one has perfect knowledge
- Because the client believes in it
- The client has already chosen to change
- It's goal oriented
- Because the client wants it to

The final idea is mine, and it's based on the client's expectation. If the client expects the coaching to work, they will find a way to help you. If they don't want it to work, there is nothing you can do about it.

The characteristics of successful coaches

What are the characteristics - beliefs, states or behaviours - of successful coaches? Past course delegates suggested:

- Empathic
- Good listener
- Hears
- Gains trust
- Gives feedback
- Open
- Comfortable with silence
- Can be directive
- Flexible
- Good questioner
- Non judgemental
- Can be either detached or engaged
- Objective
- Is confident in self and has confidence in the client

It's important to add commercial and business skills to this list. We focus on the technical qualities of the coach, but the coach needs some other skills to get into a position to use their technical skills. First, the coach needs to be able to find clients and form professional relationships with them. Even a coach operating within a company with a 'captive audience' needs these skills – perhaps even more so, to overcome the resistance of buyers who believe they have no choice and will therefore resist it.

You could think of a coach's skills as operating in layers, with some skills needed before others can be employed.

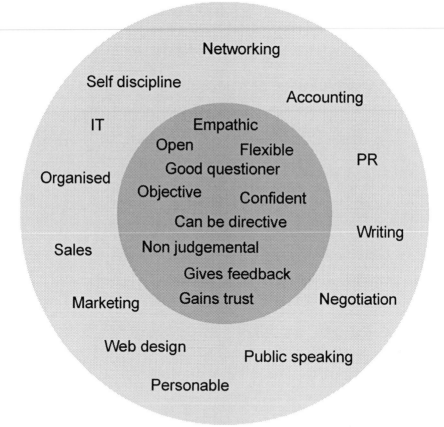

You'll recognise that there are skills in the outer layer that are common to anyone running a business, and this is a mindset that successful coaches have. Not all coaches, or people running businesses, have accounting or marketing skills, so some of these skills are often outsourced to people like accountants, lawyers, marketing consultants and so on.

In the way that we see small businesses grow, either the coach can focus on coaching and outsource the outer layer, or the coach can concentrate on building the business and outsource the inner layer, by hiring employees or associates. Both types of business model function well to give the business owner more of what he or she wants from it. A lot of coaches do a bit of both, outsourcing a function like accounting or web design and also working with a small number of associates or partners.

The perfect coach

Here's an exercise that we run during the masterclass which has a useful message for any coach.

Client: Present a question to explore with the coach of your choice. You can choose from the list in 'forms of coaching' or from the characteristics of successful coaches - or both. You simply choose what kind of coach you would most like to explore your question with. Help your coach to associate into the role of your chosen coach.

Coach: Find out what kind of coach the client would like to work with, then associate into that role as fully as you can. Help the client to explore their question 'as if' you are the coach that they have requested. This may mean that access resources that you are not used to, or it may mean that you behave in a way that you are not used to. Your flexibility may be tested in this exercise, so use whatever tools and techniques you need to stay focussed on your role.

Here are some suggestions for tools you can use to associate into a state, belief or behaviour:

  □   Imagine a circle on the ground that is filled with the resource. When you are ready, step into the circle and allow the resource to flow over and through you.

  □   Imagine someone who, for you, embodies this resource. As you imagine them standing in front of you, step into them and experience the world through their senses.

- Recall a time when you have accessed this resource in the past. Have your partner amplify this state and anchor it.

- Change the environment and your physiology to reflect the necessary resource.

So how is that important to a coach? When you are working with a client, it's very tempting to launch into the coaching session in your normal style. Over time, you will find whether that works for the client or not if they stop paying you.

When you first meet a new client, it's useful to ask, "how do you want me to coach you?"

Good coaches spend time setting up a feedback mechanism at the start of the relationship so that it's easier for the coach to give the client feedback in the future. Asking the client how they want to be coached will tell you a lot of information about their expectations and needs and so will help you to coach them more effectively.

It doesn't mean the client is right, but it does give you a valuable insight into their expectations and their comfort zone. For example, when coaching in companies, these are the kinds of responses I get:

- I want to tell you about management situations that have been difficult, so you can tell me what I should do differently

- I want to think through my approach to management situations so that I can perform at my best

- My colleague has upset me and I want to know what to do about it

- My colleague has upset me and I just want to feel calm again

- I want to further my career, so I want you to tell me what I'm doing wrong

- I want to further my career, so I want you to tell me what I can work on

- I've done everything that I know I can do, I need your help to come up with new ideas to try out

I don't coach them in the way that they have asked, I always help them to find their own resources and answers because I don't want them to become dependent. Their answers do give me valuable information about their current state, beliefs and expectations that help me to coach them more effectively.

When to intervene, and when not to

When a client requests the services of a coach, we could assume that we are required to coach, or to intervene, whenever we talk to that client. Sometimes, the coach simply fulfils the role of sounding board, where the client needs to verbalise a situation in order to organise it in their own minds. At other times, the client will cycle through a number of 'stuck' states and an intervention from the coach would be useful in helping the client to move forwards. How do you tell the difference, so that your interventions are most impactful and effective and you avoid the problem of 'doing techniques' to your clients?

One way to do this is by noticing and tracking the client's mental processes as they speak. Cycling or repetition indicates a 'stuck' state which you can 'unstick' with an intervention. When the client is in free flow they may be organising new thoughts or concepts to create meaning and understanding, in which case you probably don't need to intervene.

Asking good questions

One definition of a coach is 'someone who asks good questions'. What are some really good coaching questions?

Of course, for you to be a really effective coach, you have to bring some of your personality to the role. The process will not do the coaching for you. As a coach, you cannot stop your personality, beliefs, values and expectations creep into your work. Merely by being aware of this, you are already becoming much cleaner in your approach. If you cling steadfastly to the belief that you do not influence your clients' thoughts and actions at all, then you are not coaching them.

Part of your job as a coach *is* to influence your client's actions, yet to do so in a way that is congruent with your client's own choices and pace of change.

By recognising that you already do influence your clients, and choosing to do so positively and congruently, you will become an even more powerful coach than you already are

While all questions influence remember the difference between questions that elicit clean information and those that lead.

If we look at NLP's linguistic tools, the NLP Meta Model is invaluable when you want to elicit information to expand the client's awareness whilst influencing the client as little as possible and the Milton Model is invaluable for guiding and influencing the client in a subtle, indirect way.

Feedback

One characteristic of effective coaches is that they spend a significant time establishing feedback criteria and mechanisms with their clients.

There's a nice exercise that you can do to demonstrate the nature of feedback in a coaching relationship:

Client: Throw balls over your shoulder with the intention of hitting a target. You need to tell the coach what feedback you want and you need to help the coach to tune the level of detail of their feedback so that it is most useful to you. You may find that the type of feedback and the level of detail change during the exercise.

Coach: Help your client to hit the target by providing them with the feedback they need. Only give the specific feedback, at the level of detail as requested by the client.

This exercise is interesting because many people, in the role of coach, want to tell the client what to do. They also focus on the client rather than the target, so when they look and see that the ball missed the target by a metre, they miss the fact that that's where the ball ended up, not where it first landed.

The person in the role of client often goes through a period of frustration in this exercise when the information they ask for doesn't help them to hit the target. For example, the client will often ask a question such as, "how much harder do I need to throw the ball?" to which I usually answer, "three". It's a meaningless answer to a meaningless question.

Even if the client asks to know where the ball landed in relation to the target, I will often say, "37 degrees". Again, without the client specifying a frame of reference, the information is meaningless. Only when the client has specified a clock face or compass system, and asked for distance either in centimetres or to be shown will the feedback be useful.

An important point in the exercise comes when the client realises that all feedback is useless until they have calibrated their own behaviour. Until the client knows how it feels to throw the ball short, they cannot accurately throw the ball harder. The client starts to focus on using just one joint such as their elbow, instead of changing their throwing style with each attempt. By reducing the number of variables in the system, the client can get more consistent results with the help of the coach's feedback.

That, for me, is a pretty good definition of coaching in itself.

Measurement

How will the client know that the coaching relationship is working? How will the coach know that they are being effective and that progress is being made?

It's important to set up measurement criteria at the start of a coaching relationship. It's not always necessary to set up objective criteria, and we could argue that there is no such thing anyway. Ultimately, what will convince the client that the relationship is valuable is that their subjective experience changes, and they are able to get results in their lives that they did not get previously. For example, they may find themselves being more confident, assertive or relaxed in situations that they used to find difficult.

It's important to set up these subjective measurement criteria because they also give the client an outcome to aim for. When the client next goes into a meeting expecting to be more confident, their attention will be more focused on that outcome and they will notice how much more confident they are. If you do not set up the criteria first, they will be more confident but may not notice it, so they will not immediately attribute their success to the coaching.

Meta coaching

One of the paradoxes of great coaching is that you need to be able to both maintain an objective view of the conversation whilst, at the same time, be totally focussed on the client. In NLP terminology, a good coach has to be in 'uptime' and 'downtime' at the same time. How can you achieve this?

It's a good idea to adopt a coaching process that you are comfortable with. That does not mean religiously following the GROW model – it means finding a basic structure that allows you to focus on the client without losing sight of the direction of the conversation.

Some people think that models such as GROW are a coaching process in themselves. A good coaching process needs many more components than what is contained within GROW. For example, you need to set up the right environment, review progress to date and make sure the client is relaxed and comfortable before you can even think about anything else.

A lot of people ask me, "do you use GROW?" to which I answer, "no, because GROW is not a coaching model."

Models such as GROW, ARROW and so on do not encompass everything that a good coach does and so like all models, they are only a reduced representation of the real thing. Coaching models do not define coaching – they are a greatly simplified representation of coaching that allows someone to learn part of the process. They are like the scaffolding that is used in building a house. Once the house can stand on its own, you take the scaffolding away.

Any model cannot be as accurate as the real thing it represents. As soon as a model becomes 100% accurate, it's not a model any more – it's the real thing.

So choose a process – any process – that you are comfortable with and that lets you focus on the client. Once you have the experience you need, you can come off the script and still guide the client towards the most positive and rewarding outcome.

Basic structure of coaching intervention

There are many coaching models that you can read about, and some that you can buy off the shelf. NLP doesn't prescribe a coaching model, only a change model, so it's important to understand how this fits into a wider coaching context.

A coaching intervention has a fundamental process that we can usefully explore.

Proprietary coaching models

It's useful to appreciate the range of proprietary coaching models that exist so that you can choose what works best for you. You will also find that each proprietary model creates its own marketing demand and occasionally clients will ask for a particular approach by name.

Proprietary models include:

- ARROW – Aims, Reality, Reflection, Options, Way forward

- GROW – Goals, Reality, Options, Way forward

- TGROW – Theme, Goals, Reality, Options, Way forward

John Grinder, co-developer of NLP, suggests the following phases for a coaching intervention

1. Gain rapport/ contract

2. Establish frame

3. Elicit information

4. Establish goals

5. Create action plan

6. Get commitment

7. Follow up

As you know by now, Bandler and Grinder have never been gifted at coming up with snappy mnemonics!

Here's another model I came up with a while ago: SURE. It's based on a style of coaching that removes the obstacles to achieving goals rather than just setting a goal and leaving the client to get on with it. The concept is based on my observation that people achieve goals naturally when there are no obstacles, so you don't need to force clients to set goals – you only need to remove the obstacles that stop them from naturally taking action. Once that's done, all the coach needs to do is get out of the client's way.

Set Context

This happens at the start of the relationship, or at the outset of any specific courses of action such as the resolution of problems. At this stage, the framework and rules are established and the client states the type, format and frequency of feedback required.

Understand Situation

At this stage, the client states any problems or outstanding issues and also describes the desired outcomes or ideal situation. The aim of the coach at this stage is only to gain understanding of the environment around the coaching relationship. The coach does not intervene at this point.

Resolve Issues

Before moving to desired goals and outcomes, any outstanding issues and problems must first be resolved and moved into the past. If outstanding problems are ignored, they can often resurface to sabotage any attempts the client makes to get better results in the future.

Establish Action

With the framework and feedback agreed, the context and environment understood and all relevant problems moved aside, the coach and client can now concentrate on the future. Desired outcomes and goals can now be transformed into behaviour and action, with any necessary tracking and feedback built in at this stage. The goal of the coach is to help the client generate so much motivation and self belief that feedback and tracking of progress is usually unnecessary. With motivation established, the coach just needs to get out of the way.

With so many coaching models around, how can you choose the right one to use? Duh! There isn't a right one, because no model can ever be a complete representation of the process – that's what makes it a model.

When a model reaches the stage of detail and complexity that makes it an exact copy, it isn't a model anymore. Since every conversation you have with a client will be different, you can never produce a model that is complete because it will either be too specific or too generalised to apply to any one coaching session.

What SURE demonstrates is that you, the coach, can make up your own model if it's useful to you.

Modelling your own process

It can be very useful to model what your own natural coaching process is. Just as with the client's problem, I would advise you against learning an off the shelf coaching process until you know what your own is.

You may also want to model state and beliefs in order to reproduce the full set of skills yourself. Here are some questions that you might ask in modelling a behavioural process:

- What do you do first?
- Is there anything you need to do before that?
- Then what?
- How do you know to do that?
- How do you know that worked?
- How do you know to do x instead of y?
- How do you know you've finished?

Have a look at the chapter on modelling for more information on the tools you can use to model a coaching process.

During the Executive Coaching Masterclass, we have modelled delegates' coaching processes and come up with a 'master list' from which you can select the most useful components for your own coaching situation.

Research	Background on client
	Did the client freely choose coaching?
	Research on their company or environment
Setting the scene	Is the client ready to be coached?
	Rapport
	The coach/client contract
	Confidentiality
	Define coaching
	Coaching style
	Boundaries

	Ethics
	Expectations
	Framing
	Outline of process
	Commitment
	Client's values
	Coaching tools e.g. psychometrics, career options
Topic	Area to work on
	Diagnostic tools (e.g. wheel of life)
	Values
	Check understanding
Goal	Well Formed Outcome
	Measurement criteria
	Boundaries
	Timescales
	Success criteria
	Check understanding
Current situation	Check current state or situation
	Reality check/where the client is now
Barriers	Explore barrier
	Explore limiting beliefs
	Challenges
	Why hasn't client already achieved the goal?
	What has the client already tried?
Techniques	Apply tools or techniques to solve problem, remove barrier or limiting belief

---

Options	Generate options
	Tools e.g. 6 step reframe
	Resources required
	Resources available
	Influence/control
	Well Formed Outcome
	Evaluate options
Plan	Next step
	Evaluate plan
	Measurement criteria
	Time limit/SMART
	Commitment
	Check plan achieves goal
Review	Summarise process
	Confirm agreement
	Commitment
	Test (Future Pace)
Follow up	Follow up
	Review progress
	Test progress against goals and values
Evaluate	Send the invoice!
	Evaluate success of coaching program
	Case study
	Testimonial
	Referrals
	Marketing

As a result of this, you will shortly see the RSTGCBTOPRFE coaching model being used by all of the best coaches, as we continue in the great NLP tradition of incomprehensible acronyms.

Modelling problems

Imagine your central heating breaks down and you call an engineer. Would you like him to start taking the boiler apart before he first asked you what the problem is? All too many coaches – and NLP Practitioners – start diving in with techniques before they have first identified the problem.

When I was a telecoms engineer, 20 years ago, the first thing I learned was a basic diagnostic process, and it is my experience now that there are too many people being trained in tools like coaching and NLP who are not being taught the most fundamental diagnostic procedures first. The only option they have is to keep applying techniques until something works.

A lazy engineer will keep changing components until the boiler starts working again. A good engineer spends the majority of the time observing – either observing the fault, observing normal operation or observing to check that his intervention has worked. As a coach, unless you observe or model your client's behaviour, your interventions will have random success at best.

Earlier in this book, there is a chapter on modelling which you can use as the basis for modelling problems.

Since your client is alive (I presume) they must be doing almost everything right. If they are consistently finding an aspect of their life or work difficult, that tells you they have a working process and either the content or the context is not appropriate for their outcome.

Let me put that into English. In order for anyone to get a consistent result in anything, there must be an underlying process. If you are able to make the same mistake every time you go to a job interview, you must be applying that mistake consistently, and consistency requires process.

If the process works, in that it delivers a consistent result, then there are two possible reasons why the desired outcome is not achieved. Firstly, there is nothing wrong with the process itself, it just works best in a particular time and place. It needs the right context.

Secondly, there is a phrase used in computer programming; "Garbage In, Garbage Out". If you put fruit into a perfectly good sausage machine, don't complain when you get fruit sausages.

Actually, there is one more reason that people don't get the result they want. It's when they get exactly the result they want, it's just not what they say they want. Imagine a salesman who is not making sales calls. Secretly, he wants to open a restaurant by the sea. Although he says he wants to make sales calls, he is in fact achieving precisely his outcome – to get fired so that he has the push he needs to get out of his comfort zone and set up his restaurant. If someone's behaviour isn't getting them the result they say they want, but the result is consistent, first check their outcome.

Clients often present problems which are working perfectly, therefore they can be modelled as a strategy for achieving consistent results. This is a very powerful and useful technique for understanding a situation prior to using any NLP techniques or interventions. By treating the current situation as a working strategy, a lot of useful information can be gained and certainly the results will be different than if you approach the situation as a problem to be solved. In most cases, you can find that the situation separates into useful strategies and unwanted outcomes.

You will often find that the problem changes simply as a result of modelling it, and it's useful to understand why that is.

People do not, in general, enjoy frustration and stress. After they have changed everything they are aware of, they no longer know what to do. Therefore, the barriers that really stop people from performing at their best are not the ones they can see. The most obstructive barriers are the invisible, unconscious ones, so it doesn't matter how many options you ask the client to come up with, they cannot step over a barrier that they don't know is there.

The NLP modelling process is specifically designed to model unconscious behaviours. I think you can see where this is going.

By modelling the problem, you raise the barriers into your client's conscious awareness, and once the barriers are visible, your client will know exactly what to do about them.

Success stories

It's important to be able to describe successful coaching outcomes in a way that is compelling and informative for your prospective clients. As a sales tool, the ability to describe successful case studies is very important. As a change tool, the ability to tell a client a story that they can relate to is equally important.

For example, I was once approached by someone to run a NLP workshop at their annual company conference. I felt that there was some hidden need behind this which I didn't explore until one day, the person said that he was hoping to pick up a few tips from my presentation that would help him with his own fear of presenting. "Ahh! There's the real reason!" I thought to myself.

He said that he had been afraid of public speaking for 25 years, so I suggested that instead of him hoping to pick up a few tips that might help, why not meet up a couple of weeks before the conference, do some specific work on it and then he could introduce me at the conference?

He said, "Well, over the years I've tried a lot of things and nothing's helped, but you sound confident so I'll give it a go!"

We met up and it was all sorted in 30 minutes.

Coaching environment

I learnt something very important from that encounter, which came very early on in my coaching career.

I had intended for us to meet, mid morning, at a quiet country hotel in plush surroundings where we could work quietly and privately. When we arrived at the hotel, the plush, quiet main bar was closed and we were directed to the leisure bar where the ladies' aqua-aerobics session had just finished. The bar was packed full of very energetic woman, all radiating energy and exuberance.

A lot of coaches complain that they can't do many coaching sessions in a day because they feel drained after each one. Aside from the usual point that, as a coach, you should be getting the client to do all the hard work, the environment plays a much bigger role in the client's outcome than you might realise.

If you're in a quiet, empty room with just the client for company, you have to put a lot of energy into the room itself to keep the conversation moving. When you're surrounded by happy people, you draw energy from them and it definitely helps the process along.

So, in choosing a location to work with a client, pick an environment that supports the outcome. I usually find that people are happy to talk about confidential matters in a public place, as if their words get lost in the crowd.

As Michael Beale says, if you're going to get into rapport with people, get into rapport with rich, successful, happily married people.

Appraisals and performance management

When working within a company, it's important to understand how coaching fits into any existing HR management framework. Existing performance review, targets and appraisals may not always be accurate from the client's point of view, yet they do provide a useful means of externally benchmarking development.

For coaches working within organisations, linking coaching programs to business processes will likely be a necessity. Does this limit the role or scope of the coach?

The results of an appraisal can be a good starting point for coaching, as they give you some specific benchmarks to start from. Perhaps even more useful is the opportunity to explore the client's reaction to their appraisal. For example, if they were marked down in a particular point that they feel they excelled in, that gives you an opportunity to explore their perceptions, relationships and visibility in the organisation.

Their next appraisal also gives you the opportunity to have your coaching work externally assessed – a rare opportunity that not all coaches might want!

Many companies use 360° feedback systems, where someone is appraised by their manager, their staff, external observers or customers and also themselves.

The delivery and facilitation of this kind of feedback is critical, and a coach can play a very important role. I worked with two managers in an organisation that used a 360° feedback appraisal process. One of them (Fred) scored very highly in most areas and on most of the reports apart from one which scored him poorly. The other (Joe) scored highly in all the reports from other people, yet poorly in his own report.

When I first gave them the reports, their reactions were as follows:

Fred wanted to know who had rated him poorly. He started guessing and decided he knew who it was and why they had rated him poorly. After some initial anger, he dismissed their opinion as unimportant.

Joe took the reports as confirmation of his self image. He decided that everyone else was, for some reason, being kind in order to hide the reality that he was ineffective as a manager.

You can see why it is vital to facilitate these kinds of appraisal systems! You simply cannot give people the results of 360° appraisals and expect them to find the results useful.

At the end of our review session, these were the managers' views:

Fred recognised that, in most situations, he is a supportive, motivating manager who builds good relationships. In one situation, he jumped in at the deep end and focused on the task rather than the people, and damaged the relationship as a result. Even though that situation required immediate action, he could have still spent half an hour doing what he does best – building relationships that empower staff to take action.

Joe learned that his self image may not be realistic, and he is a much better manager than he had thought. He had compared himself to Fred and concluded that he was an inferior manager. In fact, his style was totally different, yet he still achieved the same results.

Coaching systems

Coaching a team is very different to coaching an individual. The coach will have a unique point of view of relationships within the team and it can often be difficult to resolve this with the opinions and beliefs of the individuals involved. The team seems to be an entity in itself, separate to the individuals who create it.

Group dynamics play an important role in team performance and this is another factor that a team coach needs to consider.

In reality, every client is part of a system - a team, organisation or family. That system plays a vital role in helping the client to achieve their coaching objectives. For someone aspiring to a goal, a supportive team or family can make the difference between success and failure.

If you are coaching someone with regard to a particular relationship, say with their manager, it can be difficult to make any lasting changes without also working with their manager. At best, you might only be able to help your client to develop ways of coping with their manager more easily. On the other hand, you also have an opportunity to meet their manager and sell more coaching.

Ethics

How do you handle a situation that tests your ethical boundaries? What do you do when a client tells you, in confidence, about something that is illegal or that will cause them physical harm? In a team or corporate situation, what happens when you are told information about employees in confidence and those same employees ask you to divulge that information? Who is the client in this case?

In a corporate coaching relationship, the person who pays the coach is not the person you are coaching. Where do your loyalties lie?

As a coach, it's important to first decide where your own ethical boundaries lie, so that you can quickly decide how to act decisively in any situation, for your client's benefit and to protect yourself.

Trust is an integral part of the coaching relationship, and this works both ways. Often, a client will tell you something because they trust you, even though that information might put you in a difficult position.

For example, if you're coaching in a company, you might find that someone tells you that they intend to leave the company. Do you have an obligation to tell the person who is paying you? On one hand, you could say that it's wrong for the company to pay the coaching bill in this instance. On the other hand, you could say that the best thing for both the client and their employer is for the client to make a decision as quickly as possible and take action. The most damaging situation, in my experience, is where the employee sits on the fence for a long time, being unproductive at work and dissatisfied personally.

The cost of a couple of coaching sessions is still small compared with even a month's additional salary bill.

Internal and external coaches

Coaches can operate both independently and within organisations. Although the tools and techniques may be the same, the environmental demands are different. The same differences apply between short term coaching that is focussed on a specific issue and long term, ongoing relationships where the client wants to explore many different issues over a period of time.

Benefits to an organisation of internal coaches

- Less risk
- They know the culture
- They know the systems
- The capability and experience of the coach is known
- The coach has realistic goals
- The coach can't walk away as easily
- Lower cost (depends on size of business)
- Ownership and control

Benefits to an organisation of external coaches

- Specialist experience or knowledge
- Lower cost (depends on size of business)
- Objective
- No legacy
- More focus on results
- Reputation
- External consultants perceived as being more effective
- Fresh approach
- Not bound by the culture
- Not bound by organisational expectations
- Confidentiality
- Experience of other business cultures
- Easy to hire and fire

Demonstrating value

All professionals need to be able to demonstrate that the client is getting good value for money. As a coach, your results may be harder to define than for a lawyer or accountant. How does a coach demonstrate value, both to existing clients and to prospective clients?

One traditional way is through case studies and testimonials. Often, these are very personal and you need to use them carefully. One of the most common things I see on websites and in brochures is the client list – a list of well known companies that the coach has apparently worked with. If you think your clients will be impressed by that then by all means have it on your website, but remember this. What we communicate to the outside world is often how we want to be seen rather than how we really are. Just bear in mind what that client list says about you.

What do you want from your clients?

As a coach, you are not your client's servant. It's important that you remain focussed on your own goals as a means to helping your clients achieve theirs so that you can remain in the most resourceful state at all times.

I meet many coaches, and people who have trained in disciplines such as NLP and counselling, who are on a mission to save the world. They want to help people to improve their lives. A wonderful sentiment, but as I often say, "sometimes, helping people doesn't help".

Think first about what you want, and then decide how the work you do fulfils that. By definition, whatever you choose to do for a living must have value to your clients, otherwise they would not pay you for it. So rather than trying to make your clients happy, focus on what you want and allow your clients to benefit from working with a happier, more successful coach.

As a coach, you are also a role model for your clients. Would you choose to be a client of a dentist with terrible teeth, a depressed counsellor or a penniless accountant?

Be what your clients aspire to – not to show them how wonderful you are, but to demonstrate that you live the values you advocate.

As a coach, you are a mirror for what your clients aspire to. Be sure to keep that mirror nice and clean.

Selling your services

Which would you rather have – amazing coaching skills but no clients, or competent coaching skills with many clients? How much time do you spend to developing each set of skills?

Professional services are often sold by giving the client an easy way to make a first commitment and then building the relationship by delivering the service being sold. International blue chip consultancies and local life coaches both sell in this way, but it's not really 'selling'. Why not?

- Sales people draw information from the client and match the client's needs to their product
- Buyers draw information from sales people and match it to their own needs

In an active sales situation, the sales person controls the process. This requires the sales person to have two key areas of knowledge; how to manage the sales process and what it is they are selling.

Selling a product seems easier – you know exactly what it is and what its benefits are. Is this less clear with a service, with no tangible product? Headhunters refers to the candidate as the product. They do not sell the recruitment service – they sell the candidate against the client's specific needs.

It's easy to learn a sales process – for many coaches it is much harder to define what they do. What is the product you are selling? What is the end result for the client? Are you selling a new, improved future version of the client?

What if you are selling through an intermediary such as a HR department? Organisations who have a channel sales model know how to sell to the sales channel as well as the end user. Consider the following examples:

- A car manufacturer
- A PC manufacturer
- An office furniture manufacturer

How do those examples help you to understand selling through HR departments?

Let's take the car manufacturer. For years, car manufacturers had showrooms to demonstrate cars to end users, and fleet sales people to sell to company fleet managers and leasing companies. Car manufacturers would sell the low cost of ownership to fleet managers, who would then dictate car policy to the company car driver. Then, some companies realised that cars are a huge motivator to people. Cars are not just transport tools – they are emotions on wheels.

When the company car policy became part of the employment package, manufacturers realised that they couldn't get away with producing dreadful cars that were cheap to service. They had to start making their cars more desirable to end users, who now had a choice. They realised that they had to make cars that had low servicing costs, and that were desirable to own.

Car manufacturers now sell to fleet managers and also to company car drivers. They have discovered that they need to 'sell to' and 'sell through' in order to be successful.

Taking this a stage further, they now also create desire in the driver so that he or she demands that the fleet manager makes a certain type of car available. This is a 'pull through' sales model.

So, apply this to a coach selling coaching services into a company. Many coaches don't know how to sell coaching, so they follow the advice of the life coaching schools, offer free trial sessions and hope for the best. It's hard to offer free coaching sessions to HR managers for a number of important reasons:

- They don't want coaching
- They get a hundred such offers every day
- The session is not free – it costs their time

So if you want to sell coaching into a company, you need to understand how the product meets the customer's need. This means that you have to understand what specific business and personal goals will be met by coaching, and how you demonstrate value to the person receiving the coaching as well as the person paying the bill.

When you are ready to sell your services, you need to be clear on these points:

- What the product is
- How that is necessary to the end user
- How that is necessary to the buyer

Remember – up until the point the client buys your service, they have no idea how good a coach you are. They only have experience of how good a sales person you are.

Ensuring referrals

Referrals are one of the most important methods of expanding your business. How do you ensure you get enough good quality referrals?

Think about the referrals you give yourself. If you find a good plumber, decorator, dentist, furniture shop or whatever, do you spontaneously tell all your friends?

An old sales adage is that we tell 7 people about a bad experience and 2 people about a good one. If your goal is publicity, it's better to give a client a bad experience than a good one!

The best way to guarantee business from referrals is to do it yourself. Firstly, you need to explicitly ask your clients to refer you. You might offer incentives or commission payments, but I have personally found that these make no difference. It seems that we pass on our good experiences for the pleasure of growing our networks, not for any financial gain.

Secondly, do not expect your clients to refer you to their colleagues and friends. Instead, ask them for the names and contact details of people who they would be happy to refer you to, and follow up on those referrals yourself. If you need your client to make an introduction, make your request specific and then follow up yourself.

As a rule of thumb, if you want referrals you need to actively manage the referral process instead of leaving it to chance.

Continually improving your skills

Using a coach yourself

Some people say that the most important thing to do, as a coach, is to get yourself a coach. Is this important? Is it helpful?

A cynical way of looking at this is that it's a good way for the coaching schools to guarantee work for their coaches. On the other hand, how can you say that coaching is important if you don't use the service yourself?

NLP Practitioner training is designed to give the course delegates a personal experience of change, so that they have a foundation for creating change in others.

Once you have completed your coach training, have you developed yourself enough? If coaching is designed to support a lifelong learning process, you are as much a part of that process as anyone else.

So, on balance, I am not necessarily in favour of you hiring a coach from the school you trained with. If you want to do that, find a coach who trained somewhere else. Maintain a network of colleagues who you can keep talking to, about your business strategy, your highs, your lows and your dreams.

Developing your support network

One of the most common problems described by self employed professionals is the lack of a support network. For anyone who has worked in an office, tea breaks, lunchtimes at the pub and gossip at the coffee machine are easy to take for granted. How do you get the support that you need? Who do you want in your network? Who will be most useful to you, remembering that the people who support you and agree with you most may not always have the most useful feedback for you.

The most common reason that I hear from coaches who give up and go back to their 'day job' is the loneliness. As usual, the problem contains the solution!

Making it work

The big coaching schools tell you that coaching is a wonderful, empowering occupation in which you can help your fellow human beings to lead happier lives. Whilst they may create coaches who are very helpful and kind, they do also give the impression that you can earn a good living from life coaching.

I have seen life coaches advertising in my local newspaper at £5 per hour. I don't really see how anyone can make a living at that hourly rate.

The coaches who I see as being successful focus on running a business. Coaching is their preferred product, but they have other interests and capabilities too.

Let's do some simple maths. If you want to turn over £40,000 per year (before tax), you will need to invoice about £800 per week, assuming you work every week of the year. Let's take out some time for you to have a holiday and be ill and we're left with a figure of around £900 per week.

The rest is simple. You either have to find one client a week who pays you £900 per session, or you have to find 18 clients who pay you £50 per session. 18 clients a week is about 3 or 4 per day.

The big coaching schools have a vested interest in telling you that you can make a living just delivering life coaching, whereas I do not. Therefore, I can tell you that in the past 5 years I have not met one single person who is making a living from coaching alone. Everyone I know who has been successful has delivered a range of services, including training and consultancy. I have, however, met quite a few people who make a living running life coaching training courses, and I wouldn't want to be stuck in a lift with any of them.

I believe that, in the future, coaching will become more widely recognised as a personal development tool and coaches will have practice rooms as hypnotherapists and dentists do today. With a steady stream of clients coming to you, it would be possible to make a living as a life coach. I think that business and executive coaching will always involve the coach visiting the client, although I suppose your accountant or lawyer doesn't come to visit you, so maybe this will change too. Regardless of what the future holds for coaching, the challenges that face you in building a coaching business are here today.

You had a life before coaching, and that life gave you a wealth of valuable experience that I suggest you do not turn your back on. This doesn't mean that if coaching doesn't work, you can always go back to sales, or running a shop, or whatever you did before. I strongly suggest you burn your bridges. As Clay Lowe says, never have a plan B. What I mean is that you have a wide range of professional capabilities to draw upon in building your business. Use them all to ensure your success.

Networking is becoming the business development tool of the 21st century, and it is one of the ways that the coaching schools tell you to find clients.

My experience is that you won't find clients at networking events, or at least it's not useful to expect that you will. There are a couple of reasons for this. Firstly, coaching is an 'on demand' development service, so the chances of finding a client at the exact moment they need a coach are slim. Instead, focus on building value and selling your product so that when the people you meet are ready, they call you. Secondly, an average networking event is like the ladies night disco on an oil rig, with about fifty coaches pursuing the one person who bears a passing resemblance to a real client

Many people who go to networking events say that they don't work, because they don't find any clients there. This is partly true, because finding clients is not what networking events are for. Networking events are for networking, not for selling.

Here is a really simple approach that you can use to make networking events – and any other opportunity to meet people – work for you.

- Take with you the tools of the trade – lots of business cards and a pen

- Have a very clear outcome in mind – think of the kind of people you want to meet

- At the networking event, focus on talking to the maximum number of people you can. Find out what each person does and who they know. Find out who they are interested in meeting.

- Give each person your card and tell them clearly what kind of contacts you're looking for. Get their card – do not rely on them to call you. Write a note on the back of their card to remind you about them.

- Do not aim to sell anything to the people you meet. This is so important I'll say it again. Do not go into your sales pitch – your objective is to grow your network as quickly as possible. Selling comes later.

- Do not do what the coaching schools tell you to do – do not start coaching the person you meet in the middle of the networking event!

- After the event, follow up. Call or email your new contacts to remind them about you, what you do and who you want to meet. Work in order of the most relevant people first, remembering that the people you think are not relevant could be the most important – there's just no way to tell.

- Use your contacts as a route to market. Ask for introductions, suggestions and ideas about how to grow your business. Think about partners, referral schemes and affiliate marketing. Use your network as a means of communicating indirectly with your potential clients.

And remember the most important thing of all. When a client decides to work with you, they have no idea how good a coach you are. They only know how good a sales person you are, so those are the skills you need to develop first in order to guarantee your success.

Recommended reading:

Six Questions	Peter Freeth
A theory of everything	Ken Wilber
Coaching	Richard R. Kilburg
Coaching in a week	Matt Somers
Executive coaching	Catherine Fitzgerald and Garvey Berger
Faster than the speed of change	Paul Lemberg
Get clients NOW!	C. J. Hayden
Powerful NET working	John Lockett
The NLP Coach	Ian McDermott and Wendy Jago
The handbook of coaching	Frederic M. Hudson
The inner game of work	W. Timothy Gallwey
The psychology of executive coaching	Bruce Peltier
The complete guide to coaching at work	Perry Zeus and Suzanne Skiffington
The coaching at work toolkit	Perry Zeus and Suzanne Skiffington

Presenting Impact

Public speaking is one of the most important skills in business today. In fact, Dale Carnegie's excellent book 'How to win friends and influence people' grew from his lectures on public speaking skills.

Almost everyone in a business has, at some point, the need to present – job information, project updates, at an interview or even at a friend's wedding. The difference between doing this easily and doing it with difficulty is immediate and obvious.

It's interesting that one of the most common problems presented by business coaching clients is a fear of public speaking. It seems that the ability to communicate with a group is simultaneously the most admired and most feared skill in business.

In this chapter and masterclass, we're starting from the same basic premise as in the others – that you can already do this well. If we break presenting down into its basic behavioural elements, we need two skills; the ability to speak, and the ability to stand up. If you can do both of those at the same time, you're already making a good start.

Of course, you can stand up and talk at the same time – you do it every day. The difference must be in doing it in front of an audience and the good news is that this affects your perception, not your behaviour, and perception is much easier for you to change.

What can people who are already confident and accomplished speakers learn from this masterclass? The first thing is group influence. When you present, you are using a highly specialised form of communication that allows you to communicate the same information to a number of people so that they then take specific action as a result. If you are using presentations to inform or update people then send them an email instead. A presentation is a very powerful group influence tool, so use it wisely.

As with everything, the key to success is planning. How do you plan a presentation? Do you start with what you want to say, or with what you want the audience to do? Do you start by designing slides or by designing states?

In this chapter, we're working both on your group influence skills and on your ability to present with impact. Group influence skills include your ability to communicate using multiple layers of information to multiple sensory preferences, intelligences and states and to get those different people to act in unison. Presenting with impact means tuning your physiology and attitude to enable you to achieve maximum congruence and effectiveness.

Storytelling is probably the most powerful group communication and influence tool that you can master. The good news is that you are already an accomplished and experienced storyteller, even if you didn't think you could describe yourself that way. When you tell a friend or partner about your day at work, or when you are telling a joke, you are using your natural storytelling skills to influence the state of another person. By refining and practicing those essential skills, you will be able to engage an audience and influence their state so that they act in the way you want them to – perhaps by making a decision or committing to a course of action.

So, let's get on with the show.

Modelling excellent presenters

A good place to start developing a skill with NLP is to find someone who has it and model it. Public speaking is such a commonplace activity that it is easy to find people who do it well and people who do it badly. Just turn on the TV or radio to find people giving speeches or press conferences, and notice what works well in terms of managing the audience's state towards a particular outcome.

Because we have seen so many public speakers, starting from when we first went to school, you already have all the information you need to be the most outstanding presenter right there between your ears. In your head is a model of excellence that we can draw upon for you to develop your skills. You already know what inspires you – the chances are that it will inspire other people too, because it will already be naturally congruent with your own style.

Think back to someone who you think of as being an exceptional presenter, trainer, teacher or performer. What do they do?

The answers that I typically get to this question include:

- Confident
- Relaxed
- Know a lot about the subject
- Are in control of the presentation

And, since we're talking about NLP, I have to ask, "How do you know they are confident, or relaxed, or that they know a lot?"

When we start to dig a little deeper, we find the specific behaviours that constitute 'good presenting':

- Smile and make eye contact with the whole audience
- Access many different states to reinforce the message
- Have a clear outcome
- Tell stories (that's how you know they are knowledgeable)
- Choose to answer or deflect questions
- Finish on time or early (tells you they're in control)

This information is not rocket science. For years, presentation skills courses have been trying to get people to emulate these behaviours. Unfortunately, they try to do this by getting course delegates to consciously copy those behaviours, giving them too much to think about and making them even more nervous than when they started!

The approach we're taking here is to develop the states and beliefs that underpin those behaviours, so you don't have to think about them – they just come naturally.

This also raises an idea that is absolutely critical to your performance as a powerful and persuasive presenter. When you think about someone you have seen who is a great presenter, that person is not in the same room as you – they are in your head. In fact, the model that you have in your head is not a complete model of that person, it is only a model of their performance 'on stage'. Therefore, no matter how good or bad a presenter you think you are, you already have a model of exceptional performance in your mind. All we need to do is unlock that and transfer it into your behaviour.

Setting the scene

What do audiences want to know? What meanings should all presentations convey regardless of topic or content?

What about:

- I'm telling the truth
- You can trust me
- This is really important to you
- I really believe in this
- You're going to love this!

It might be useful to think about the high level message that runs through you presentations, and to consider that first when you are planning a presentation. If you get that in place, everything else you do has a strong foundation to build on.

Your context

Take a moment to set your own personal context for presenting with impact – is it to clients, colleagues, shareholders or someone else? Are you selling, persuading, informing or something else?

It's also worth thinking about what the audience expect from you. Do they expect an expert, or just a different perspective? Do they expect a hero or a fall guy?

Planning outcomes

If you don't want your audience to do anything as a result of your presentation then you are wasting your time and theirs. An email could replace your presentation if all you want to do is transmit information. A presentation is a specialised communication tool, so use it to achieve the right outcome for you. Think carefully about what the presentation adds, over and above any other form of communication.

Even a decision or an opinion is an action because it requires the audience to process information and then do something. Forming an opinion is an active process, just as much as buying a product.

- What do I want?
- How will the people in this room help me to get it?
- What do I need them to do for me?
- What state do they need to be in to achieve that?

When you create a Well Formed Outcome for your presentation, you'll know it has to be under your control. If you want the audience to understand or agree, that's not under your control, so first you have to know what it is you want.

So many people in companies present to customers to 'inform' or 'educate'. That's not under your control!

If we work outwards in layers of control, the first thing that is under your control is your own state. When you're in rapport with the audience, your state will influence their state and their state will make it easier for them to achieve the outcome you want for them.

Planning states

What will be the starting state of the audience? Open minded? Curious? Impatient?

Many presenters just launch in and start talking at the audience instead of first tuning themselves into the audience's state. This is one of the most important things you can do as a professional communicator and it's called pacing.

Begin by thinking about the audience's starting state. Then, thinking about the desired outcome for the presentation, choose a useful end state for the audience. Finally, plan a route.

It is very important to be realistic about the audience's start state. You might want them to be curious, but if the reality is that they are tired and bored then you need to take that into account.

Start state

State 1

State 2

State 3

End state

You will probably recognise this as an extension of the concept of pacing and leading, and you'll remember that the first stage of pacing is to gain rapport. If the audience is feeling critical, there's no point pretending they are curious. First you need to pace their critical state in order to lead them out of it. How do you do that? Come on! Do you want me to come and do the presentation for you?

Get their attention

Tell them what to do

Give them the Information they need

Get them to do it

Presenters who don't have the advantage of this approach often start by planning what they want to say rather than how they want the audience to respond. This is why their presentations seem more like transmissions than interactions.

What about technical presentations? Surely they serve to inform or instruct the audience? Again, what do you want them to do with that information? Agree with it? Make a decision? Understand it? Use it?

The outcome for the audience is always your starting point for designing a presentation. Once you know this, the rest is easy.

Expectations

When do you think the trance induction begins for a stage hypnosis show? When the hypnotist first addresses the audience? In the music that is playing before the show starts? Upon entering the theatre, even? The answer is that it starts the moment you buy your ticket.

You will be communicating with your audience long before you stand up to speak to them, so it's very important that you start shaping their expectations to support your outcome.

For example, if your intention is to sell them something, don't tell them it's just an informative presentation because when you ask them to buy, the news will come as a surprise to them and they will react accordingly.

If your intention is to update them on a project, tell them that at the start and make it clear you do not need feedback or suggestions, otherwise people will pull your project apart, because that's what they think you want them to do.

Similarly, if you present them with detailed information and then ask them to make a decision, they will be unable to as they have not paid specific attention to what they need to understand in order to make a decision. If you tell the audience that, at the end of the presentation, you are asking them to make a decision, they will pay attention to whatever fits with their own decision strategy.

What communication do you have with the audience before the presentation that you can use to reinforce your presentation?

Environment

Bear in mind that the environment you're presenting in will greatly influence the audience and your outcomes, particularly if you plan the environment in conjunction with the audience's expectations.

You can think not only about the venue and room but also branding and signs which add to the expectations of the audience.

You can also think about things like refreshments, using a lectern and so on. If you stand behind a lectern, you will lose rapport with the audience because they can't see you. If you have water available, you can use it to give yourself time to think about questions.

The environment can support or hinder you in achieving your outcome, so it's worth taking some time to think about it.

Structuring the presentation

There are a number of formats that you can use to establish a powerful communication with the audience. Here are a few ideas for you to practice. Remember that success, in NLP terms, doesn't mean thinking about what will work and ruling out what you think won't – it means that you do everything and notice what really works!

Framing

By telling people what you want them to do, you are helping them to filter the information so that they pay attention to what is important for them. If you don't tell people what to do until the end, they will be completely unprepared for it and will not do what you ask. This process is called labelling or framing, and it's often used naturally by anyone who is a skilled communicator.

- I'm going to present some information after which I'd like you to give me your opinion.

- I'm going to present a project update after which I'd like you to give me feedback.

- I'm going to present a proposal to you after which I'd like you to make a decision.

Outcome focus

There's an old saying used by old presentation skills trainers: tell them what you're going to tell them, tell them, then tell them what you've told them. In other words, the audience have a limited attention span so you have to drum your message into them. Here's an updated version, for a more modern audience:

- Tell them what you want them to do
- Present the information they need in order to do it
- Tell them what you want them to do

Association (shifting referential index)

Begin talking about the wider context, people in general, then move to a more relevant section of the population, then to the people in the room, then to 'you' and finally to 'I'. Throughout the sequence, the referential index shifts as follows:

Everyone (everything) > them > us > you > I

Timeframe

Begin at some point in time before the present moment, listing all the shared experiences up until the present moment to elicit and agreement state, then continue forward in time to gain commitment to a course of action.

Frame/story/question

Frame the communication to direct the audience's attention, tell a short story and then ask a question to shift the audience's state and refocus their attention.

Pacing current experience

The first thing you need to achieve in your presentation is to get the audience's attention. You can ask questions, tell them about yourself, use an ice breaker, tell a joke, or do anything else that fits the context.

One very useful way to achieve this is to build your audience towards an 'agreement state' in which they are more likely to agree with you, consider your ideas favourably and make the decisions you want them to make.

So, right now, you're reading these words and you might think about your next presentation. Perhaps you've presented in the past, or experienced other people presenting to you. In either case, you may be the kind of person who really wants to achieve the best you can and refine the skills you're already developing. It's good that you're taking such an active interest in yourself because you know the results that it will bring you.

Was there anything in that last paragraph that you could disagree with? Was there anything to agree with?

In the first section we talked about pacing the audience's state. This is the same process, and this time you're pacing their experience. As you begin with very general facts that are true for the audience, you will see them nodding in agreement. As your presentation becomes more specific, or less factual, they will be more likely to agree with you than to disagree. For example, to say that you're reading about presentation skills is true. To say that you're reading the best way to develop your presentation skills is a belief. Your beliefs - product benefits, opinions or proposals - are more likely to be accepted if your audience is in an agreement state.

When practicing hypnosis, we use a simple script that rotates the client between their external experience and their internal focus:

Tell your partner three things that you know they can see/hear/feel

Tell your partner one thing that may be true - a suggestion

Ask your partner what they are aware of

Repeat 4 or 5 times

Why would we mention hypnosis in a chapter on presenting? Let's put it into the context of a presentation:

Tell the audience three things that are true now or are shared experience

Tell the audience one thing that may be true - a suggestion

Ask the audience for their agreement

And you might still be wondering what this has to do with presenting, so here are a couple of examples, starting with something that I hear at almost every sales conference.

> □ It's been a tough year
> □ Competition has been intense
> □ We've worked hard
> □ Your targets are doubling next year

> □ Leadership is key to business success
> □ Effective leaders inspire their staff
> □ Leaders can be both born and bred
> □ Peter Freeth can develop your leadership potential

It's always useful to have your audience in an agreeable state before you start transmitting information at them. This simple technique is a very powerful way to lead the audience into an agreeable state by telling them things that are true – either in their experience or in the present moment, for example:

□ You have all travelled to be here today

□ We are all together

□ You can hear me

□ You can take a moment to be comfortable

- We have some presentations before lunch
- Some of you might be curious
- Some of you may already know
- I know that you may be wondering
- You might be wondering, "what do I do with this?"

And of course, when the audience is in an agreeable state, they are more likely to agree with you.

Chunk size

You can start at a high level of detail and work down throughout your presentation, giving the audience the opportunity to 'tune in' when you reach their preferred level of detail.

Tell the audience the purpose of your presentation, what you want to achieve and what they need to do to help you.

Start with background, big picture, landscape, 'true' information. Talk about the wider context to your presentation, both what's good and what's missing from it.

Move onto the detail of your presentation, what you are presenting, what problems it solves, what it achieves, how that helps the audience, what it does for them.

Summarise the key points, information, benefits, outcomes. Tell the audience what you want to achieve and what they need to do to help you.

Timing

It's more important to stick to time than to say everything you want to say. The audience will be left with a far better impression if they feel the presentation is complete than if there is any sense of something being left out.

As a rule of thumb, when you plan your presentation content, create enough content to fill about three quarters of your allocated time. The rest of that time will most certainly be taken up by late starts, questions, conversations and all the other unexpected things that happen whenever you work with children, animals or audiences.

It is very easy to fill in time during a presentation, and by finishing early you give the impression of being very much in control - something that the audience will notice and appreciate.

If you have any activities or interactive sessions planned for your presentation, build in even more contingency, so that you create content for only half of the allocated time.

Many people take the approach that they have a lot to say about themselves and their companies, and it's very hard to pack all that into a short time. Certainly, if you believe that the function of a presentation is for you to tell the audience something, or give them information, then you will certainly find it difficult to pack in everything you have to say.

Let's take a different approach - one that takes a lot of pressure off you and makes the whole experience far more enjoyable. Simply ask yourself this question:

What one question can I ask that will get the audience to do what I want them to do?

After that, the only remaining question is what to do to pad out the remaining time!

Here are some examples:

- What one thing can I tell you about my company that will most help you make the right decision?
- What information will be most useful to you right now?
- What can we do in this next hour that will make this whole presentation worthwhile?

Starting from the point of cramming in everything there is to say is difficult. Starting from the point of what your audience needs to hear in order to take the next step is easy.

So, here is a useful idea for you. Always start your presentations with a question:

What would you most like to hear about that will be most helpful or useful for you right now?

By concentrating on the answer to that question, timing will never be a problem for you.

Language patterns

You can try out some different forms of language to find out the effect they have on the audience. Here are some examples.

Presuppositions

All language contains unspoken elements which must be accepted as true in order for the language to make grammatical sense. You can use this constructively, for example:

"When you buy a service like mine, what do you normally expect?"

The question is about customer expectation, but it makes no grammatical sense if the listener does not buy 'a service like mine'.

Questions

You can influence your audience's state and participation in a very simple and effective way. The more they participate, the more energetic and alert they will be. The more alert they are, the better they will respond to you and the more they will remember. The more they remember, the more effective you will be.

Reframes

Reframing can be used to change the meaning of information, for example, if the price of a product is high you can reframe that information to mean the price is an indication of exclusivity.

You can respond to even the most pointed objection or question with, "Excellent! What a great question", because it's important to recognise the value of the person even if their question may be inappropriate.

In coaching, you can use reframes to change the meaning of problems. I was recently asking a client to use their creativity to come up with options for a problem. One option was, "Move to a planet orbiting Mars" and my reply was, "Excellent! Your creative side is working really well!"

Whatever your audience does or says is good because it shows they are engaged. If they fall asleep, that's good too as they'll be easier to influence. You can't lose!

Embedded commands

These are instructions that sit within a language structure that is not itself a command. Often, analogue marking is used to draw unconscious attention to the command. The simplest embedded commands are questions:

When would you make a decision to <u>buy my product</u>?

What would you need to know in order to <u>hire me</u>?

But they can also be more complex:

I know that sometimes it seems difficult to <u>make a decision</u>, yet when you realise <u>you're looking at the best product</u> you just have to <u>go for it</u> and <u>trust yourself</u> to <u>do the right thing</u> for you.

Milton Model language

Milton Model language is a framework within which the listener can insert their own meaning. It is very powerful in situations where you have to address the needs of interests of many different people, for example:

You may have heard about this before or it may be new to you, in either case you might already be thinking about how to use this information and to learn even more before you make the right decision for you.

Stories

It's always useful to practice your storytelling skills. A good idea is to practice reading from children's story books as they are full of emotional content and even belief change, reframes, hypnotic language and embedded commands.

Stories are powerful communication tools as they bypass a listener's critical filters. Since a story isn't about you, there's no need to be defensive, is there? I once heard about someone who was reading a book and came across an idea so important that it immediately changed their lives. It's strange how words can affect a person in that way.

Nested loops

Hypnotic change stories can come in the form of a nested loop, where a suggestion is embedded within another story. A format using two nested stories looks like this:

Start story 1	Start story 2	Suggestion	End story 2	End story 1

Nested loops can be complex to set up and require rehearsal, yet can be very powerful when used well. It's certainly worth practising these ideas to find out what works best for you.

Sleight of Mouth - Conversational Belief Change

Reframing is an excellent way to handle questions and objections. A reframe is an intervention that changes the meaning someone has associated with a particular piece of information. For example, the price of a product or service is in itself meaningless – it is the audience's perception of it being cheap, expensive or good value that is important. Reframing allows you to change that subjective meaning in order to create the right outcome for your presentation.

'Sleigh of Mouth' patterns were identified by Robert Dilts from some of Richard Bandler's language patterns. However they are applicable to many famous natural communicators.

They are best used in combination rather than individual patterns, and they can be used to strengthen beliefs as well as change them. They are based on plausibility rather than 'proof'.

While there are 18 patterns they can divided into four basic types:

- Change meaning
- Change cause
- Comparisons
- Change logical level

Examples of Sleight of Mouth Patterns

Take an example belief:

"Business NLP is not appropriate for our company"

These responses are examples of the various patterns rather than the truth about business NLP!

Hierarchy of Criteria

To be effective the response must relate to the real values of the person you're talking to!

"Don't you think it's more important to concentrate on what your objectives are now, and how NLP could help you achieve them; rather than rely on past opinions?"

Consequence

"A consequence of that view is that some of your people won't get the best development opportunity that's available to them."

Another outcome

"The issue here is not whether it's appropriate for your whole company; which it isn't; the issue is whether it's very appropriate for some people in your company."

Metaphor / Analogy

"Would a football coach that studied how the best footballers scored goals not be appropriate for a football club? Business NLP is about how the best business people achieve results."

Redefine

"Business NLP is about producing best business results; are you really saying producing better business results is not appropriate for your company?"

Chunk Down

(Most of the Meta Model can be used)

"What particular parts of NLP are not appropriate for your company?"

"How specifically are they inappropriate?"

Chunk up / exaggerate

"So you mean that learning and improving performance will never be appropriate for your company?"

Counter example

Isn't it possible that one aspect of Business NLP will be appropriate for your company? There is at least one area of your company that could benefit from communication skills isn't there?

"What would be appropriate for your company?"

"Who would Business NLP be appropriate for?"

Intent

"My intention is not to sell you something inappropriate; it's to save you money and increase your effectiveness. Business NLP may be able to help you with both these."

Model of the world

"Whilst that may be true from the experience you've had so far; would you be interested in the experience of people from similar companies that have found it appropriate?"

Reality strategy

"What would you know if Business NLP was appropriate to your company?"

Apply to self

"That seems inappropriate; knowing how many other companies have benefited so much from it."

Change Frame size

"It may seem that now; however when you look at the potential benefit of how Business NLP can help you with the changes you face over the next five years; you'll see how necessary it is."

Meta Frame

"That may be because you don't know if you can handle the impact Business NLP will have. I can guide you through that to achieve the results you want."

Pattern interrupt

Whilst a pattern interrupt is not a sleight of mouth pattern, they're still a lot of fun to play with.

A pattern interrupt is where a mental routine is interrupted giving the speaker a brief opportunity to exert great influence. Derren Brown, a British TV mentalist, frequently uses pattern interrupts in his shows. One that just came to my mind that I am now keen to try out is:

"Business NLP is not appropriate for our company"

"I bet you a fiver it is!"

I'll let you know how I get on with it…

Presentation aids

Environment

How can you use the physical environment to help you achieve your outcome? You might think about the location of chairs, tables, refreshment, signs, posters – anything that will support you and make it easier for you to achieve your outcome.

In Derren Brown's Mind Control TV series, he gets some creative designers to come up with an idea for a brand. Of course, the branding, images and logos were very similar to what he had already drawn and sealed in an envelope, but how? He had carefully planned their journey from their office to his, with posters, stickers, logos on children's sweatshirts, items in shop windows and parcels carried by couriers to influence their thoughts. How could you do the same in your presentation?

Visual aids

You've probably seen a presentation where the presenter read out the words on the screen verbatim, and you probably thought, "I could read that myself…"

The more words you put on the screen, the less the audience will pay attention to you. When you put words on a slide, the first thing the audience will do is read the words. While they're doing that, they're not listening to you.

If you want to include a presentation script or detailed notes, put them into notes pages, not the main slides. Think of slides as signposts rather than guidebooks and you'll be on the right track.

What other presentation aids can you use to enhance the overall experience?

Computer projected slides

Easy and quick to create, easy to share a common layout or style, easy to change when you find out new information five minutes before your presentation!

Whiteboards

Good for keeping track of meetings or informal 'chalk and talk' sessions, not so good for presentations as you have to turn your back to the audience to use them, and you can't prepare your presentation beforehand.

Flipcharts

Good for presentations as you can write them beforehand, use different colours, draw pictures etc, and you can face the audience while using it. Not as easy to change or update as whiteboards.

Portfolios/desktop flipcharts

Good for product information but be wary of forcing your audience through your standard presentation pitch.

Music

Very effective for managing your audience's state. Don't underestimate its power.

Anything that's to hand!

You can use anything to highlight or add some extra dimension to your presentation. The obvious example is product samples or models, but you can use anything you want to give your presentation some extra impact.

Tuning in to the audience

Sensory preference

Whilst presenting, you can shift to different representational systems in order to engage the audience's senses fully.

Visual	See	Vision	Sharp
	Picture	Outlook	Background
	Look	Bright	Shine
	Watch	Clear	Reflect
	Perspective	Focus	Eye catching
Auditory	Listen	Quiet	Whistle
	Hear	Amplify	Whine
	Sound	Tell	Roar
	Noise	Resonate	Silent
	Loud	Hum	Tone
Kinaesthetic	Feel	Push	Down
	Touch	Embrace	Ache
	Grab	Warm	Gut reaction
	Hold	Cold	Queasy
	Contact	Sinking	Shaky

Motivation

Some people are motivated towards outcomes, others away from drawbacks. Towards people will be motivated by benefits and will tend to rush into decisions without weighing up the consequences. Away from people will be motivated by savings or avoidance and will tend hold back because of potential problems.

Reference

Some people make decisions based on internal information, others on external information. Internal people use their own experience and tend to think this applies to everyone. External people rely on other people or sources of information.

Choice

Some people need options, others need processes. Options people need alternatives and will create their own if they feel restricted. They often do things in a seemingly random order. Process people need step by step procedures and need to do things in the right order.

Everyone has a preference, and this can be influenced by context and state. Whilst you can quickly profile the people in your audience, the safest approach is to make sure you cover all preferences.

Make a decision because it achieves x and avoids y. You already know that you need to do this because everyone is doing it. By doing this the right way, you're giving yourself more choice in the future.

Personal tuning

Congruence

Congruence between your words, movements and words could be the most important aspect of presenting with impact. Similarly, incongruence can be a useful technique worth practicing.

Voice

You can have a much greater degree of control over your voice than you might have imagined – not just the volume but also the location in your body where your voice resonates. You can practice moving your voice around your body and listening to the difference it makes. When you are well balanced and breathing properly, your voice will be at its most resonant and compelling.

Balance

It's important to be well balanced, with your centre of gravity well centred. Not only does this mean you can move fluidly, it gives an impression of great presence.

Stage presence

What is stage presence? Presenting like you mean it, owning the space, voice, posture, gestures.

Stage presence is simply a state, and you already know many ways to access useful states. It's useful to set up anchors for useful states so that you can access them easily during your presentation.

Firstly, think of the specific state you want to access. 'Confident' is quite vague, and overconfidence can be as harmful as nervousness.

Remember a specific time when you were in this state. Remember what you saw, how bright the memory is, how sharp, how near, how big and how colourful. Next, remember what you heard, how loud, from where, what pitch, how clear. Finally, remember what you felt, where, how warm or cold, what movement, what sensation.

Now, make the picture bigger and brighter, the sounds louder and the feelings more intense as you double the feeling, and double it again. Say a word to yourself that represents this feeling and keep on repeating it as you concentrate on the feeling.

Finally, test the 'anchor' by saying the word and noticing how the feeling comes back. The more you practice this, the better it will work for you.

It's important that you are able to get into a resourceful state for presenting easily and quickly. Anchoring is an excellent technique to use for this, and it's a good idea to build a number of anchors for yourself so that you can access different states easily.

Here are some ideas for anchors you can use

- A big red mental 'On button' (build an off button too!)
- A word
- A physical movement
- A piece of music
- An item of clothing

Posture

Different postures will convey meaning to the audience. It's worth spending some time paying attention to your posture when you present and to develop a comfortably relaxed, open posture when that is helpful to you in your presentation.

Rhythm

Rhythm is one of the key factors in a hypnotic trance induction and is therefore a powerful aspect of any communication.

Delivering the presentation

State

If you ever worry or are nervous about a presentation, here are some very simple tools you can use to change that.

The first, and most important thing to remember is that the majority of people inadvertently make all kinds of everyday activities difficult, and these same people could make those same activities incredibly easy with just one simple, small adjustment.

Most people plan for the start of things, not the end

Public speaking, cold calling, going to the dentist and flying can be difficult, to say the least. How many times have you felt nervous about doing any of these? How many times have you felt nervous at the end? What many people experience is worry leading up to the event, nervousness at the start and relief at the end. Which of those three states would you like to feel, all the way through?

The processes of worry and excitement are the same, with just a tiny change in content:. Worry works like this:

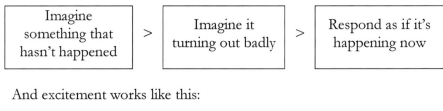

And excitement works like this:

| Imagine something that hasn't happened | > | Imagine it turning out well | > | Respond as if it's happening now |

So, here's the simple way that you can overcome doubt, worry, anxiety, nerves or fear:

Plan for the end!

So, when you imagine the presentation, imagine it from the point where you're saying thankyou, the audience is nodding approvingly and you feel good about having done a great job.

Anchoring for the audience

In the first few minutes of your presentation, you can set out spatial anchors that you will use later on.

You might want to set anchors for:

- Agreement
- Disagreement
- Reliable companies
- Your competitors

What else?

You can also set anchors with colours, sounds, music, gestures etc.

You can practice setting these anchors with the sequence of states you worked out at the beginning of the masterclass.

Getting attention

Good presenters are very good at getting and keeping the audience's attention. Aside from spatial anchoring, what other techniques can you use? Probably the most important is the pattern interrupt.

There's a simple technique you can use at the start of your presentation to reset expectations, which is very useful if you are presenting after your competitors, or if you want to reset the audience's expectations about your subject matter.

For this, you can use a flipchart, whiteboard or even a PC projector is you prepare carefully beforehand.

The technique is a version of the Swish pattern which is something covered on the NLP Practitioner course.

Begin by pacing the audience's expectations, honestly, on the flipchart, concentrating on those that are not useful and that you would like to change. When you have created rapport, tear off the sheet leaving the blank sheet underneath, screw the sheet into a ball and throw it into the corner of the room. Now begin writing what you want the audience's expectations to be.

Actually, there's a step before that: tear the edges of the flipchart sheet so that it tears smoothly across the perforation. If you're using a whiteboard, make sure you can wipe away quickly and easily. If you're using a PC, make sure your first slide has the audience's real expectations and make the slide after either blank or with the expectations you want.

The swish with the flipchart incorporates a pattern interrupt and therefore relies very much on your ability to pace the audience. A pattern interrupt can be as simple as you pacing the audience's state and then suddenly changing your state, or it can be as complex as the use of pyrotechnics and audio visual systems.

Pacing and leading

Using the state planning approach we covered earlier on, you can lead the audience through a smooth transition of states. The first step is to pace their current state and to then have a clear direction that you want to go in. Therefore, in order to pace and lead effectively, you must have a clear outcome.

Direction and misdirection

Directing the audience's attention can be as simple as saying, "pay attention, because this is very important" so you direct them to remember the parts of your presentation that you want them to.

Misdirection is harder and needs more practice, because you are focussing on what you want the audience to not focus on. Incongruence can be a difficult thing to master but once you have, you will find many ways to use it effectively in your presentations and other communications.

An easy way to misdirect the audience is to use a visual aid such as a PC projection. We can say that, in general, it is not a good idea to have a lot of text on slides because the audience will stop and read the slide before they carry on listening to you. Of course, while they are not listening, your words are still going in through their ears. You might be able to think of some interesting applications for this idea.

Questions and objections

Questions and objections are a wonderful source of feedback for you - they tell you that people are paying attention!

Questions demand a direct answer. Objections often provoke argument. Whilst they may be phrased differently, as the presenter it is not immediately obvious which is which.

Unfortunately, people ask questions for lots of different reasons, only one of which is to find out an answer, so it's not always useful for you to answer questions. Here are some possible reasons for asking a question:

- To demonstrate knowledge
- To demonstrate superiority over the presenter
- To disguise an objection
- To provoke a response from the presenter
- To provoke a response from another audience member
- To demonstrate attentiveness
- To waste time
- To set up for an attack
- To gain control of the presentation
- To learn something

If you want to learn more about the motivation behind questions, listen to the political interviews conducted on BBC Radio 4's Today program, every weekday morning (you can listen on the BBC website if you are outside the UK). For example, in this recent (paraphrased) exchange, the journalist wanted to know if a Conservative politician had been part of the plot to overthrow Iain Duncan Smith.

Journalist: Is it important for a government to be accountable?

Politician: Absolutely, yes

Journalist: So will you be accountable for demanding his resignation?

Politician: That's a private matter

The journalist's question was a blatant set-up, and the politician's answer is essentially, "yes I did". This wasn't a particularly elegant set-up, but it still trapped an unwary interview subject. I've seen many presenters trapped in exactly the same way.

The solution to this is very simple:

- Pause
- Repeat the question
- Check your understanding of the question
- Pause
- Answer the question

You can also turn an objection into a question, for example:

"But isn't this expensive"

"Are you asking for more information about the pricing structure?"

Feedback

How do you know you are on the right track? What signs do you pay attention to that let you know if your presentation is having the right effect on the audience, or if there is anything you need to change?

Could you suggest a feedback mechanism to the audience at the start of your presentation? Could you even build in an unconscious feedback mechanism?

How can you manage the audience's state in order to control feedback or interactivity?

Closing

It's very important that you give yourself time to close the presentation properly. Here are some points to bear in mind:

- Remind the audience of the purpose of your presentation
- Remind the audience of the key points
- Remind the audience of the questions that you answered
- Ask the audience to do whatever it is you want them to do
- Tell the audience what they need to do right now
- Make sure the audience knows how to get in touch with you
- And always remember to say thankyou!

It's a good idea in some situations to future pace at the end of your presentation, and summarising the presentation itself is the ideal foundation because you create a momentum by starting in the past and then moving forwards in time. By summarising what you have already covered in your presentation, the audience will shift into an agreement state that makes it easier for them to agree with your suggestions for future plans or next steps.

Your identity as a presenter

Logical levels is an excellent integration tool because it helps to create alignment between your identity (how you think of yourself), your behaviour and your environment. Traditional training, which only forces people to demonstrate their behaviour without creating behavioural alignment, creates presenters who say, "Well, I can present when I have to but it's not really me doing it, it's an act", just like sales people say, "I do sell, but I'm not a salesman".

An integration exercise like this gets the person to create a new identity which encompasses and embraces their new abilities and provides the foundation for creating new behaviour in new situations. By integrating skills in this way, the person will automatically become a more flexible, more effective presenter, even in situations you have never covered during the training course.

Set out 5 spaces on the floor to represent the 5 logical levels.

Step onto Environment. What is the environment for you as a presenter? The location, the audience, other factors.

Step onto Behaviour. What do you see yourself doing as a great presenter?

Step onto Capabilities. What skills have you developed?

Step onto Beliefs. What is now true for you as a presenter? What do you believe about yourself? What do you believe about your audiences?

Step onto Identity. What kind of presenter have you become?

Walk back though each level, taking with you what you have learned about yourself at each level.

Timeline

Where the Logical Levels exercise integrate through a person's mental hierarchy, a timeline creates instant experience and convinces the presenter that their new skills will continue to develop and grow over time.

A timeline is especially important for people who were nervous of presenting. A common concern is, "I feel good now, but I know that as soon as I go back to work and have to present for real, I'll be nervous again". By now, you'll recognise this as a worry program, where the person imagines something will happen in the future and then makes it happen through their state and behaviour.

Using a timeline is a more physical means of future pacing, so you can lead the presenter as far into the future as is necessary for them to really believe that they are a confident, comfortable presenter.

Imagine looking into the future and seeing a number of presentations that lie ahead of you, becoming more ambitious and important as time goes on. Take a step into that future, stepping into the next presentation you'll be doing. Be aware of the sense of satisfaction at presenting with impact, and see some of the new behaviours you exhibit. Take another step into the next presentation and see how you have developed again, noticing how that feels.

Continue to step forward through future presentations, being aware of how you grow and develop with each one. When you have arrived at a point in the future that you are comfortable with, stop and ask yourself, "what kind of presenter have I become?"

Now, turn and look back and see how much you have developed since you began. Walk back to the present moment, taking with you the new experiences and resources.

When you arrive back at the present, turn and face the future once more. Imagine the future looking bigger and brighter now and being much closer than you had imagined. Take a moment to enjoy the future that awaits you.

Bringing your ideas to life

As I said at the start of this chapter, I think that the ability to present well is probably the most important professional skill that you can master. Regardless of how good your ideas are, if you cannot communicate them to a large number of people in an inspiring and compelling way, they will never reach their full potential.

Every year, the number of new patents registered increases and yet this still represents the tip of the iceberg. Around 99% of new ideas just gather dust and never become reality. People will infer the importance of your idea, not from the content but from the way you communicate it.

I find that successful executives very quickly learn a survival mechanism which protects them from the overwhelming demands on their time – they say no to everything. They do not have the knowledge or experience necessary to evaluate every idea on its own merits, so they learn to judge the importance of an idea from the persistence and passion of the person presenting the idea.

Whether you are creating global businesses or inspiring children, the art of public speaking will always be key to the way we relate to each other as a species. After putting into practice the ideas in this chapter, you will have a much better chance of making your ideas, beliefs and desires a reality.

Appendices

Here's some additional information that didn't fit elsewhere in the book.

Interactive tools

More stories

NLP training

Useful quotes

Websites for further reading

The author

Interactive tools

This book has a unique interactive chapter which can be found at www.nlpinbusiness.com

At the website, you'll find a range of tools that demonstrate the applications of NLP in business, including swishes, language models and even a unique coaching tool called the Unsticker.

There are also links to other websites and online resources that will help you to apply NLP in business even more easily and effectively.

More stories

Here are a few more stories for you to enjoy learning from.

Go team

Once, there was a successful businessman who had a hobby that he was very passionate about. In his spare time, he loved motor racing. At first, he used to go along to as many races as he could and watch but as he became more successful, he could afford to take part. He was a very talented driver and quickly built himself a reputation as a serious competitor.

One day, he decided he would take the plunge and dedicate himself to his dream - to build his own racing team. He set aside some money of his own, gained commitment from sponsors and started to recruit his team.

At first, the recruitment didn't go very well. He couldn't afford to pay the same salaries as the top teams paid, so he was looking for talented but unknown drivers. He recruited some, but they didn't stay in the team long before they moved on. Like any manager, he knew that he needed to have a team that worked well together.

The other problem that he had was that he was himself a very accomplished driver. When he recruited a new driver he would try to teach them to drive better. Unfortunately, he didn't really know how he could drive so well as it was mostly intuitive. He would get angry with the drivers when they couldn't see for themselves how he was able to drive. He was on the brink of closing the team down, believing that the problem was one of recruitment.

He was watching a sports program on TV one day when he noticed something odd. When the interviewer was talking to a football manager, the manager kept referring to someone called a 'coach'. The same thing happened with some other sports too. He wondered what a coach could do that a manager couldn't. By chance, he then met someone who was a team coach, so he invited him down to the race track to see what would happen.

The coach watched the drivers practice, and he watched the team manager trying to tell the drivers how to drive. The drivers lacked confidence in their own talents and when they asked how the manager knew certain things, he said, "it just feels right", or, "you can tell by the way it sounds".

There were three drivers in the team, so the coach watched each one very carefully, and he also watched the manager very carefully. The first driver, Adam, was very good at accelerating. From the starting line, Adam was at least a car's length in front of anyone else at the first corner. He seemed to have an intuitive sense of when to change gear to maximise the car's performance. The second driver, Brian, could brake later than anyone else and so was much faster into the corners than any of the other drivers. He seemed to have an intuitive sense of knowing when to brake as he approached a bend. The third driver, Claire, could take corners faster than any of the other drivers on the circuit. She seemed to have an intuitive sense of the car's cornering ability and grip.

The downside of these talents was that Adam was always the first into the first corner, but the last out. Brian caught up with Adam at the bend but slowed down too much and was overtaken. Claire would overtake on the bend but lose her advantage on the straight.

The coach got the whole team together and pointed out to them their strengths. The drivers began to feel much better about this. Each driver, at a certain point on the track, was by far the fastest driver on the circuit but was let down by average performance in other areas. The coach began to ask some very special questions about how the drivers knew what they knew.

It turned out that Adam was listening for a certain tone from the engine, tyres and gearbox. He could hear when the car was at peak power output and he could change gear at the exact moment to take advantage. Consequently, he accelerated much faster than drivers who only changed gear at the 'red line' by watching the rev counter. With some help from the coach, he was able to teach the other drivers what to listen for.

Brian could brake much later because he was looking somewhere different to the other drivers. The other drivers were looking at the apex of the bend, whereas Brian was looking beyond the bend. He was able to judge the distance to the apex much more accurately, enabling him to brake late but still drive safely. With some help from the coach, he could easily teach the other drivers where to look.

Claire could actually feel the car's sideways motion. She could very accurately feel the movement of the suspension as the car leaned into the bend and she could feel how the motion changed as the tyres started to lose grip. She could actually feel the acceleration at different points in her body. With some help from the coach, she was able to teach the other drivers how to feel the movement of the car.

The team went from strength to strength, not because they were taught something new, but because they were able to share their talents and exploit them for the benefit of the whole team. Each driver still had their unique talent, they just helped each other achieve above average results across the range of skills needed to be successful. The coach didn't need to be an expert in driving, only an expert in learning.

What about the manager? Well, the coach had a special job for him. He had to go to every newspaper, sports journalist, sponsor, TV station and racing promoter and tell them that he had a new team. He had to tell them that this was the best team on the planet and they were going to re-write the motor racing rules. He had to prove to everyone that he believed in them. And so, the new team was reborn.

Working holidays

There was once a salesman for a company that made special metal alloys for weapons. He had travelled the world, selling his company's products to every developed nation. He loved his job and he couldn't help doing it, even on holiday. One year, he took his holiday in the Amazon Rainforest (it could happen!) and he came across a tribe of Indians who were hunters. He asked them what they used for their arrow heads and they said, "We hunt a wild cat that lives in the forest. We use its fur for clothing, its meat for food and it's teeth for arrow heads. They are very sharp and easily penetrate the skin of small animals." The salesman asked how many teeth could be used from each cat and they said, "Four". Then he asked how accurate their hunters' archery skills were. They said, "Every child serves a ten year apprenticeship to become a master archer. If they cannot shoot arrows straight, they run out of cat's teeth and the village people have no meat".

So the salesman immediately recognised a great opportunity, and he also realised that he needed to keep his best product until last so that he could build up his sale. He asked the leader of the village, "If I could show you a way to hunt more cats, and bigger animals, with a limitless supply of arrow heads and reduce your apprenticeship for archers to just one year, would you be interested?" The wise, yet strangely gullible village leader said, "Of course, can you do a presentation to my board tomorrow?"

So, the salesman showed the villagers arrow heads made from steel. They were heavier than cat's teeth but harder and sharper. They could buy a limitless supply of arrow heads (because they happened to have natural gold deposits in their village that they didn't understand the value of) so the hunters didn't have to be so accurate. With just some basic training in how to use a bow and arrow, anyone could hunt a cat. The villagers rejoiced.

After a few days, the salesman returned and showed the villagers his titanium alloy arrow heads. They were as sharp as steel yet as light as a cat's tooth. Now that everyone in the village was a hunter, he had more users to demonstrate the product to. Sure enough, the arrow flew further than the steel headed arrow. To the salesman's surprise, the villagers said, "yeah, very nice, but we're happy with our steel arrows". The salesman said, "But you'll use fewer arrows because these will fly further" and the villagers said, "So?"

The next day the salesman returned with tungsten carbide arrow heads, and had the same reaction as the day before. He was very confused – normally his customers would be getting more and more excited. He decided to go back to the village and show them his best product. "Look", he said, "I have here arrow heads made with tungsten carbide tips, titanium alloy bodies and with a depleted Uranium filling." He fired one at a tree and it went straight through, like a hot knife through butter. The villagers said, "Impressive, but we don't eat trees". Now the salesman was really upset. Couldn't these people see the applications of his marvellous arrow heads? Perhaps they were too stupid too understand. His wife had warned him about this when he left her by the poolside in Rio a week earlier.

The wise village leader said, "We can see your arrow heads are indeed marvellous, but remember we are a simple people with simple needs. Your steel arrow heads already represent a step change in technology for us, enabling greater exploitation of our natural habitat without disturbing our learning based culture." It turned out that a management consultant had been on holiday there just the week before. "Your top of the range arrow heads are too advanced for us. We have neither the skills nor needs to exploit their full potential, therefore we only require something that is one level better than what we have today. Besides, I'm going on a dream quest this afternoon and I'll be off my head on psycho-active herbs for a few days, so I can't make a decision until next week"

The salesman learned a very important lesson on that holiday - that he shouldn't leave his wife alone in Rio with only a book for company, but that's another story. Do you know what else he learned?

NLP Training

You can become a licensed Practitioner of NLP through many training companies now established in the UK and worldwide.

Personally, I have worked with PPI Business NLP since 1999 because they have a business background, whereas many of the other training companies in the UK have a therapeutic background and this is reflected in the way that they position and deliver their NLP training. PPI also work with small, interactive groups of professional people, which is a great environment to learn NLP in. Some companies run their courses in theatres with hundreds of people. Not surprisingly, these companies favour the, "you don't need to ask any questions because you're learning unconsciously" approach. You just need to choose which suits you.

Many NLP training companies are introducing new levels of NLP training, including diplomas, certificates, Business Practitioners and even MSc courses. The fact is that there are only three levels as far as licensing is concerned - Practitioner, Master Practitioner and Trainer. Diplomas and certificates are usually at a foundation level and do not result in licensed certification. The MSc courses typically comprise some HR or management modules wrapped around a Practitioner course. Decide what you want to do with it before you sign up.

The three levels of licensed training are quite distinct in terms of the aims of the training. At Practitioner level, the key aim is to give you a personal experience of change. Before you start learning how to change other people, it's very important that you have a personal reference for the way that people change and how the tools work. You will learn some basic change tools and by the end of the course you will have experienced some kind of personal change such as solving a problem or curing a phobia. At Master Practitioner level, you gain more insight into the structure and application of the tools so that you can create new tools yourself and refine the use of techniques such as hypnosis. At Trainer level, you will learn how to learn about NLP so that you can train others.

You don't need any training at all to use NLP, but you'll only get a license to practice if you complete the course. You need to decide for yourself if that's important to you but I would say that the experience of Practitioner training is far more useful to you than the certificate will be, and it is totally different to just reading a book - even as good a book as this!

Practitioner training is a very personal experience - even a journey - and therefore your relationship with the trainers and other delegates is the most important factor. You need to be working with people who you feel comfortable with to get the most out of the training.

Before signing up with any NLP training provider, first go to a free taster session or ask to attend a course for an hour before you make up your mind. Make sure you feel comfortable with the kind of people who attend that course, as this gives you a lot of information about where that trainer positions themselves in the market.

The personalities and capabilities of NLP trainers differ hugely, yet the real content of NLP Practitioner courses is much the same. All Practitioner course content is prescribed by the NLP licensing bodies, of which there are now several. The original licensing body is the Society of NLP - the one associated with Richard Bandler, co-creator of NLP. All of the other worldwide licensing bodies essentially derive their content and licensing criteria from the SNLP, with just minor differences on course length or additional content.

The SNLP favour shorter, more experiential courses – typically around 8 days, whilst the ANLP and other bodies favoured longer courses of around 20 days.

You can learn the basic tools and mechanics of NLP in a couple of days, but that doesn't mean that you can use them elegantly and effectively. I've been learning and applying NLP for about 10 years, and I still learn something new from every course I run and every client I work with. To think that anyone could learn everything there is to know in either 8 or 20 days is interesting – it's far more important that you practice constantly and remember that the training course is only the start of the learning process.

The reality is that the certificate does not coach your clients for you, nor get you a job. Treat it as evidence of your continuing personal and professional development.

The important thing in choosing NLP training is picking a trainer who you are comfortable with, in an environment that suits you. The Practitioner course is very much about personal change, so choose a trainer and environment that will help you to explore this fully - anything less means you're just not getting the full value from the training.

Finally and most importantly, the training courses are neither the beginning nor the end. The beginning must be an immense curiosity about people and about self improvement. There is no end, because you can always learn something new from each person you meet.

Useful quotes

If there is any one secret of success, it lies in the ability to get the other persons point of view and see things from that person's angle as well as your own. *Henry Ford*

Let him that would move the world first move himself *Socrates*

The important thing is not to stop questioning *Albert Einstein*

The greatest discovery of our age has been that we, by changing the inner aspects of our thinking, can change the outer aspects of our lives *William James*

Believe you can't, believe you can. Either way you're right! *Henry Ford*

When you put a limit on what you will do, you put a limit on what you can do. *Charles Schwab*

Obstacles are things a person sees when he takes his eyes off his goal. The greatest power is often simple patience. *E. Joseph Crossman*

Chance favours the prepared mind. *Louis Pasteur*

I like nonsense, it wakes up the brain cells *Dr Seuss*

You cannot depend on your eyes when your imagination is out of focus *Mark Twain*

As long as you're going to think anyway, think big. *Donald Trump*

When you get to the edge, step off...you'll always land somewhere *If you know which pop star sang this, let me know!*

Trying is the first step towards failure. *Homer Simpson*

It is common sense to take a method and try it. If it fails admit it frankly and try another. But above all, try something. *Franklin D. Roosevelt*

Nurture your mind with great thoughts, for you will never go higher than you think. *Benjamin Disraeli*

Remember, happiness doesn't depend upon who you are or what you have; it depends solely upon what you think. *Dale Carnegie*

Ideas won't keep, something must be done about them *Alfred North Whitehead*

It's the possibility of our dreams coming true that makes life worth living *The Alchemist*

Imagination is more important than knowledge *Albert Einstein*

You should never, never doubt what nobody is sure about *Willy Wonka*

Those are my principles, if you don't like them I have others *Groucho Marx*

Be who you are and say what you want, because those who mind don't matter and those who matter don't mind *Dr Seuss*

Life is not the way it's supposed to be. It's the way it is. The way you cope with it is what makes the difference *Virginia Satir*

You must be the change you wish to see in the world *Mahatma Gandhi*

And my personal favourite….

We are the music makers, we are the dreamers of dreams. *Willy Wonka*

Websites for further reading

NLP In Business is a knowledge base of research and information on the applications and business benefits of NLP.

www.nlpinbusiness.com

PPI Business Coaching is the author's business coaching consultancy, based in the UK with clients all over the world.

www.ppibc.com

Communications In Action is a specialist publisher of personal and professional development books and CDs.

www.ciauk.com

Change Magic is a complete toolkit for change engineering and organisational problem solving featuring the Brain Fairies and the world famous Unsticker.

www.changemagic.com

Executive and Business Coaching Network is a community of executive coaches, featuring profiles and coaching information.

www.execcoach.net

PPI Business NLP is the training company that I work with to deliver NLP Practitioner and Master Practitioner courses.

www.ppimk.com

Ascent is the adventure coaching experience that can change your life, combining transformational coaching with outdoor activities that help you achieve your wildest dreams.

www.ascent-experience.com

The Author

Peter Freeth is a leading business coach, trainer, author and consultant with a rare mix of communication, technical and business skills and an interest in learning and developing new tools and techniques that help others get the results they want, more easily and more often.

Peter has been learning about and developing NLP business applications since 1993 and is recognised as being an innovative and inspirational leader in the field of personal and professional development.

"Peter provides a highly polished mirror through which one sees a deeper, calmer and more confident self - and then provides the keys to help unlock this potential. A great coach - particularly for those operating at a high level."

Michael Roberts, Scott Roberts & Associates

"Peter Freeth shares his light, intelligence and love of people with skilfully articulated enthusiasm."

Paul Hunting, Natural Leadership Centre

"Peter, you are a very talented performance coach who inspires me by empowering me to dare to see beyond my own boundaries.

You have a unique way of making it fun and often come up with classic one liners that are so spot on you make me laugh uncontrollably as I am enlightened! You seem to encapsulate my vision by tapping into my world as if you're seeing and experiencing it too.

Peter, you help me to discover the path towards my dreams and re-connect me with my inner desires. Sincere thanks..."

Jenny Tranfield, England International Squash Player